Other Titles in the Fawcett Premier

LITERATURE AND IDEAS SERIES

IRVING HOWE, General Editor

THE AMERICAN
NOVEL
SINCE WORLD WAR II

Edited with an Introduction by

MARCUS KLEIN

ESEA 74

'13461

A FAWCETT PREMIER BOOK
Fawcett Publications, Inc., Greenwich, Conn.
Member of American Book Publishers Council, Inc.

CONTENTS

THE AMERICAN
NOVEL
SINCE WORLD WAR II

Introduction

EVERYTHING depends, of course, on the kind of one's sample, and any general characterization might be sustained. In the years since the end of World War II the novel in America has been: nihilistic, existential, apocalyptic, psychological; it has asserted the romantic self; it has recorded the loss of the self; it has explored the possibilities of social accommodation; it has withdrawn from social considerations; it has been radical and conservative. In form it has been loosely picaresque, it has returned to its beginnings in myth, it has been contrived with a cunningness of technique virtually decadent, it has been purely self-reflexive and respondent to its own development. And the novel has died.

All of these things and more have been said credibly, some of them in the following pages. It might be said therefore, given so many contradictory convictions, that as a whole and as a category of cultural enterprise, the novel in these years has been essentially aimless and at best frenetic. No definition is valid when everything can be maintained. Moreover, any fair sample would have to include individual novels and modes of imaginative endeavor apparently almost totally discordant. The years since the War comprise a generation, by arithmetical definition. What could be the palpable shape of a generation which includes—to name merely a few indisputable prominences—*The Naked and the Dead,* Truman Capote's *Other Voices, Other Rooms,* Bernard Malamud's *The Assistant,* and *The Catcher in the Rye, The Sot-Weed Factor, Invisible Man, Lolita, Lie Down in Darkness, The Adventures of Augie March,* and *Naked Lunch*? Which includes as its most discernible conjunctions of sensibility such evidently minor events as that of the Beats (not to be more archaic than the subject demands) and that of Black Humor? These novels and events would seem to be related by nothing more urgent than the accident of their contemporaneity.

Indeed, it must be concluded that this literary generation

has not worked to make of itself a school, a discipline, a partisan movement.

That fact in itself might well point toward a definition, but not such a one as is likely to satisfy usual expectations. We anticipate that the types of literature of a period and place will be broadly definable by their action in history, whether public history or that of their own literary form. So, for instance, in the mid-eighteenth century in England "the novel" had for its purpose comment on the rise of the new bourgeoisie, and also the initial exploration of its own formal possibilities. The "Victorian novel" speculated on the problem of belief, perhaps, or the idea of progress, or the necessity of humane value in an industrial society. Obviously no such generalization is more than approximately right, but in all such instances there is enough evidence so that a sense of common endeavor might be perceived. Or, where there is not, we are apt to find a period of transition and consolidation.

It happens that in the earlier years of this century, this sense of a common endeavor in literature was explicit and imperative. That was the meaning of the "little renaissance" and the "resurgence," the period in this country extending from about 1912 to the early 1930s, when the field was suddenly filled with banners and manifestoes. The leadership of the renaissance was diverse in temperament, talent, and specific ambition—as different as was Ezra Pound from Van Wyck Brooks—but it was united in the belief that literature was a cause and that it had a job to do, a job which referred both inside and outside of itself. ("Has literature a function in the state . . . ?" asked Pound. "It has. . . . It has to do with the clarity and vigour of 'any and every' thought and opinion."—"A new age has begun," said Brooks, ". . . and it is the creative life that the nation calls for now.")

In the brief new age there was, on one side, a continuous effort at technical innovation, and the effort bore the implication that experiment in literary form was in itself an assertion. Especially with the abrupt effusion of the little magazines, "experimentalism" was in effect institutionalized. And if as early as 1923 T. S. Eliot reported the death of the novel [1]—to

[1] In "Ulysses, Order, and Myth," Eliot wrote: "The novel ended with Flaubert and with James." Like so many of Eliot's casual and occasional overstatements, this one has been crystallized into majestic pronouncement. Eliot himself some thirty years later commented: "To say that the novel ended with Flaubert and James was possibly an echo of Ezra Pound and is certainly absurd."

stay with the one form—his obvious intention was to record progress, not failure. The "mythical method" of Joyce, he said, was to replace conventional narrative method. To some extent that did happen, as in Faulkner, for instance, but more important was the general idea in which Eliot participated, that literature depended on a progress for its life. Pound declared repeatedly, in the accents of a Yankee tinker, that the history of literature was a history of inventions, and that idea took. It was the clear duty of the writer to be an inventor. All the best writers of fiction were enlisted by the idea—Gertrude Stein, who made it her whole career, Hemingway, Faulkner, Dos Passos—and even solid, essentially conservative novelists like Willa Cather and James Branch Cabell.

At the same time it was the duty of the writer to save civilization, particularly by exposing the hypocritical and valueless pieties of modern civilization. The mass of men was conceived to be murmurously half asleep. The writer was to be dissident, alarming, antagonistic, malcontented, and conspicuously alienated. (The alienation of the writers of the Lost Generation, Ralph Ellison has commented, "had something of the character of putting on a mask in Macy's window at high noon and pretending that no one knows who you are.") The posture of dissidence, moreover, was substantiated in almost every conceivable instance by clear need, and no insult was unfair. H. L. Mencken's arrogance or Randolph Bourne's deliberate fractiousness or Sinclair Lewis' comic imitations were as relevant as the episode of postwar disillusion, the celebrations of flaming youth, the battles for freedom in language, the rebellions conducted in the names of Freud and Nietzsche, and the uses of varieties of traditionalism (as in Eliot, Fitzgerald, Hemingway, Faulkner) as a way of scourging the present. It was a happy situation for literature, in which moralities were outworn and constrictive, and public beliefs were out of touch with realities. The enemies high and low were really there, altogether constituting an Enemy of the Spirit, and literature high and low was therefore altogether a coherent cultural action. The writers and artists of *The Masses*, for instance, who promoted an annual "Anti-Obscenity Ball" by publishing risqué advertisements, were quite conceivably engaged in the same broad work as the most subtle of the modernists. *Fun*, too, was a polemic, just as literary iconoclasm was a moral act.

In the 1930s some of these opportunities for literature were rescinded, of course, but there were also new opportuni-

ties, and the new made still more explicit the idea that literature, generally, played a role. Art was a weapon. In fact the
influence of the idea of a "proletarian literature" as it was
sponsored by the American Communist Party is not very discernible, even among those who sponsored it. The outlines of
the idea remained ambiguous—the question of the actual content of proletarian writing was never settled—and the Communist Party's interest in the idea was both casual and brief.
The impulses that went into the new writing of the 1930s
were, certainly, more multifarious. They would include not
only the blunt facts of the Depression, communism, and fascism, but also the fact of the ethnic and social origins of the
new writers, and the fact that the movement of modernism in
which they had learned literature contained some presump-
tions about the nature of reality which were not theirs, and
the fact that the modern movement was no longer the news it
had been. Some of its soiled dilettantism was showing. But all
of these impulses were intricate with a sense that some classes
of men had been overlooked and they were to be overlooked
no longer. And once again the enemy was really there. "Prole-
tarianism" was not in itself very much the program of the
1930s, but it was a rallying point. It solicited a new advance
guard, which was dissident on the sure basis of class and
which also, at the least, was willing to consider a connection
between strict political ideology and literature. The advance
guard wrote novels with titles like: *Jews Without Money, The
Disinherited, The Unpossessed, Marching! Marching!*

It also, we should recall, looked for advances in technique,
though now in the direction of the common rhetoric. It ex-
perimented with spectacle (as in the "living newspaper"),
"reportage," documentaries, photography, and common language. And such innovation, once again, was an assertion of
a cause. A scene in Albert Halper's *Union Square* (published
in 1933) presents the matter succinctly. The protagonists of
the novel attend a Communist Party rally at which the chief
speakers are some writers who have recently been down
South to investigate a coal strike, presumably in Harlan
County, Kentucky. The audience is bored to tears when the
writers speak. Then a real miner, untutored and awkward,
takes the stage, and when he talks, the audience is electrified.

This is to say that, in a good many years of the recent
past, literature—or, still more generally, art—had the presence of an independent political force. But of all the arts fic-

tion was the most political because its subject is most likely
to be social fact.

Now in the years since World War II this political presence of fiction has become something quite uncertain. On the
one side, fiction has not made emphatic the need of a previous generation for—in the words of T. E. Hulme—"a new
technique, a new convention, to turn ourselves loose in."
There have been new inventions, obviously. In the evident
and purest sense every novel is a new invention, and there
have been also discernible trends in—and nodules of enthusiasm for—kinds of invention. There have been a great many
such kinds, some documented in the following essays. But
quite as obviously such incidence has not created a period of
fiction vivid for its urge to experiment or for its exploration
of a new novel. (In the late 1940s the editors of the *Partisan
Review*, fabricating a symposium on the state of American
writing, could lay it down as "the general opinion" that "unlike the twenties, this is not a period of experiment in language and form." In the recent 1960s the critic Susan Sontag,
speaking with equal authority, complained that today in
America "the sense of what might be done with *form* in fiction" is "rudimentary, uninspired, and stagnant.") And on
the other side, the enemy is not so clearly and simply present
as once he was.

American fiction since World War II might indeed be defined in terms of the lack of cultural material it has had to
work with. As Henry James might have said, there has been:
no puritanism, no Babbitry, no Booboisie, no Comstockery.
No tyranny of ideology, no ideology at all in the proper
sense, no hollow patriotism, no evangelical Christianity. No
Prohibition, and scarcely any prohibitions, no prudery, no social complacency, no somnolent insularity. Worse still, it is
conceivable that the energies of fiction in the earlier years of
the century have dissipated into their own success. In a recent
essay Lionel Trilling speaks of "the adversary intention, the
actually subversive intention" that characterizes "the literature of the modern age," and then he goes on with some despair to observe that this "adversary culture" which has been
constituted by modern literature has, if not won the day
against the middle class, at least "captivated the allegiance"
of a considerable part of it. The people who will accept the
idea of an adversary culture have increased in numbers and
coherence. It is now possible, says Mr. Trilling, to think that
they themselves create a "class," and it follows that they have

less to be adversary to. And Mr. Trilling's response to this situation is instructive: as a professor of literature he chucks the whole business, and resolves not to teach the moderns.

But there is no necessity for *literature,* which is a most abstract conception in the first place, to be what is implied by this description, an elite revolutionary cadre. The particular revolution proposed by the moderns, as Mr. Trilling sees the matter, was in behalf of the private, instinctual, autonomous human actualities. At this time, he says, what is to be seen is "sex, violence, madness, and art itself" raised to an "ideational and ideological status." That is a probable fact, and probably an awful one. It indicates for *literature,* however, only that a time of a certain tacit agreement on principles among writers, made in response to a certain cultural condition, is now finished. And it indicates that social facts, upon which fiction depends, are a great deal more ambiguous than they used to be. The possibility of the easy assumption of a "we" and a "they" has disappeared. In its stead is a situation in which the principle of the instinctive human actualities—to stay with the one category of social fact—has been cast into considerable doubt, and not only by the success of modern literature. After Auschwitz who would care to be D. H. Lawrence? This modernist revolution leads on the one hand to middle-class bohemianism and on the other hand to horrors.

There, in that uncertainty, is the likely social fact. And as with it, so with virtually every other fact that goes to make up the culture. The Lost Generation made a portion of its career, for instance, by exposing the anachronism and the betrayal of late Victorian values. It was a thing to do. In his essay in the following pages John Aldridge argues to the effect that in these years the country has failed to provide any alternative values to which the novelist can subscribe. William Barrett, in his essay "American Fiction and American Values," says that "the apparent absence of values is in fact an immense groping" for affirmative values. In any case, the action of the disappearance of values has itself long ago disappeared, and what is left is uncertainty. In the same way— to look at some other obvious instances—war is no longer the direct invitation to disillusion that it used to be. (Or, the bitter disillusion of a book like Dos Passos' *Three Soldiers* has retreated into a kind of distraught whimsy, as in Joseph Heller's *Catch-22.*) And class consciousness is no longer a sure consciousness of the general social reality, yet there is no other large awareness to take its place. Perhaps, as William

Phillips has suggested, in recent years we have had numbers of what might be called novels of manners, but if so the areas of manners staked out from writer to writer have been widely disparate. And even if so, as Phillips has also said, more recently the tide has been toward the denial that there are "any social or moral institutions, any psychological norms, by which people measure themselves and against which they rebel." The sense of a civilization, against which or within which a fiction might act, has in these years been entirely precarious.

The country has indeed had its "problems," and after all it might be wondered why there has not been more serious fiction about, say, crime, or poverty in an affluent society, or the disasters of foreign affairs, or race, or that insistency that still underlies everything, the Bomb. Books have been written, of course, especially about the situations of minorities, Jews and Negroes, but any generalization about those books would be likely to argue the unavailability of the subject—the problem part of the subject—for serious fiction. On the one hand, there is a literature of documentary exposé, of the kind of Laura Z. Hobson's *Gentleman's Agreement* or Lillian Smith's *Strange Fruit*. These particular examples (published in 1947 and 1944 respectively) are already distant anachronisms, but they are therefore the more exemplary. The trouble encountered by such literature is that the action, the unraveling of the plot, is likely to be elsewhere, in the streets or the courts or in political events or public catastrophes. Moreover, there is not much margin in such a subject for a novelist to exploit. At a given moment what is available to be exposed is likely already to be very familiar, at least to the readers of serious fiction. On the other hand we might construe a literature about minorities that would include such novels as Saul Bellow's *The Victim,* Bernard Malamud's *The Assistant,* James Baldwin's *Go Tell It on the Mountain,* and Ralph Ellison's *Invisible Man.* But those novels, about Jews and Negroes, clearly have little to do with minorities as an issue. Their object is to universalize. And so it is with the Bomb. An exposé literature exists—such novels as *The Descent* by Gina Berriault, *A Canticle for Leibowitz* by Walter M. Miller, *Level 7* by Mordecai Roshwald. Despite their decency, competence, and passionate commitment, those particular novels, all published about 1960, tug but weakly at memory. Even in the moment of their appearance they suffered from redundancy, because within the given

subject their only possible function was to vivify the danger.
But the danger is already very vivid. What can be said about
the Bomb that is not fully inherent in the fact of its existence?
On the other hand, when the Bomb has figured in our contemporary fiction it has usually had a function, as R. W. B.
Lewis has remarked, comparable to that of the Turkish
hordes for the Reformation: it has been taken for a symptom
and an instrument, "the inevitable product of the diseased energies of mankind, and the physical force that can bring
about that grand conflagration which, morally speaking, mankind has long been striving to deserve." Its uses generally,
that is to say, have had nothing to do with the "problem."

The state of the culture since World War II, as it affects
fiction, might be described entirely in terms of negatives and
losses. Or the time might be described not even as a period of
the breakup of things, a condition that would clearly invite
new energies, but as one of dissolution and dubiety. Such a
sense of the culture is to be discovered in the essays in the
first section of this book. The areas of reference in those essays are class, values, and ideology, which are perceived in
their growing dimness.

But that dubiety in itself might be a definition, and it
would be a probable one to account for the fiction that we
have actually had and that—so it might be perceived—has
performed an action in contemporary history. The range of
our fiction in the past quarter of a century has been enormous by any measure. Without great arbitrariness, however,
certain prevalences of subject and mood might be noticed, and
certain kinds of achievements.

It has been observed by some numbers of writers and critics, for one thing, that the peculiar subject for our time has
been the self, the individual personality. The observation has
been made in despair, for the littleness and timidity of contemporary fiction. (In this volume see the essays by Alfred
Kazin and Philip Roth.) And the observation has been made
as an invitation to an overlooked necessity. (See Saul Bellow's
"Some Notes on Recent American Fiction.") Others have observed that the subject has been the felt disjunction between
self and society. (See Marcus Klein, *After Alienation: American Novels in Mid-Century*.)

For another thing, there has been an underground, a very
public one, the more undeniable because it has been unusually subject to publicity—the publicity made by journalists
who no doubt like to think that literature is a sinfully glamor-

ous underground. Nonetheless, and allowing for serial muta-
tions (Beat-to-Hip-to-Head), it has had a distinct character.
Its direction has been not rebellion against so much as escape
into . . . into some variety of conceptions, which tend to be
abstract and which propose not individual freedoms but *Freedom*. Freedom is to be discovered in the feckless democracy
of the early Beats, in drugs, in homosexuality, in the dan-
dyism of "camp," in Negritude, in religiosity and mythicism.

For still another thing, there has been in our contemporary
fiction a great deal of talk about love, of the modest and impossible domestic variety. And at least one prevalence in
form might be noticed: the open-ended picaresque.

The listing might be extended, but this number of tendencies will account for many serious works in contemporary fiction, and these tendencies do have some things in common. As
they look for the excitement of a subject, they turn away
from social facts. Discrete social facts are regarded at
best—in the best part, probably, of contemporary fiction—as
an overbearing confusion, and at worst they are dismissed. It
is a common aim within these various modes, nevertheless, to
search for the possibility of an assertion. It is a common aim,
that is to say, to make existence manifest where, precisely, no
institutions are to be taken for granted. And that aim provides a comment, however oblique, on contemporary history.
When no supporting social presence is articulated, it may well
be that personal identity becomes a necessary speculation. Or
the same awareness works the other way around: the strange
"I" and the indistinct "they" are both to be discovered, and
the terms of a common humanity worked out. The distance
between the two is to be tested and, if possible, diminished.
Then the rudiments of a society will exist. Or where external
factuality is sensed to be simply egregious, then a passionate
simplicity calls for a response equally without particulari-
zation—as is the general case with our underground—but
also equally assertive. Moreover, in this underground whatever else freedom may mean, it does not mean strict individu-
ality. The dropouts are joiners, with each other; this underground is especially given to a yearning for deep, subrational
communion, which is to say a sense of basic social presence.
And if, as some of the essayists in this volume point out, in
contemporary fiction there has been much falling back on
love, that action too is evidently a first endeavor toward establishing a firm social institution. Finally, where all values
and endeavors are uncertain, the picaresque is a salient for-

mal maneuver. It is a way of throwing an assertion into the void.

Achievements vary, obviously, but this general action, the making manifest a token of existence where no institutions are to be taken for granted, occurs in contemporary novelists so absolutely diverse otherwise—to make a random test of the case—as Truman Capote, Saul Bellow, John Barth, Ken Kesey, and Richard Fariña.

In Truman Capote's *Other Voices, Other Rooms* (1948), the action found its occasion in gothic Southern decadence confronted by youthful melancholy. The orphaned innocent, Joel Knox, is settled into the isolated, decrepit Southern mansion called, conveniently, "The Skulls," and then mementos of canceled possibilities are made to breed thickly around him. First of all, his mother has just died, and therefore that normalcy has departed. His father's house, in which he finds himself, is a corpse, which is slowly sinking into the earth. The father is a paralyzed mute. The stepmother is an ancient belle out of her time, turned witless and alcoholic. The Negro servants, Jesus Fever and Zoo Fever, suggest ancient passions which are now decrepit or brutalized: religion and animal sexuality. Joel is offered a girl friend, who is an incipient lesbian. All around there are suggestions of an ancient (and ambiguous) evil by which the viability of the South was destroyed, and all the adults around Joel are engaged in looking backward to a dream of the past, the other voices and other rooms. Quite evidently, in this symbolization there is not any thrust of criticism of the facts of life of Southern society. The closest Capote permitted himself in this book to come to historical actuality is the episode in which a mule named John Brown is accidentally hanged. All events, names, and symbols tend to be arbitrary and bizarre, to the effect precisely of creating an ambient indefiniteness, within which it then becomes the boy's necessary ambition to find a certainty that will guarantee his existence. And he accepts a liaison with the pederast Cousin Randolph, who seems to stand for salvaging inversions, ideal beauty, and stasis.

Saul Bellow's fiction is different in almost every respect—in tone and mood, in the landscape that is confronted, and in the area of knowledge comprehended—but the central action is significantly similar. To take widely separated instances: In *Dangling Man* (1944) the occasion for the fiction was a young man, Joseph, having to wait a number of months between his call to the draft and his induction into the Army.

Because of the unusual situation, first of all, Joseph's normal sustaining routine is taken from him, and he has no place in the human community. Then the suspended time gives him opportunity to reflect at large on the possibility of accommodating oneself to the human community in any contemporary circumstances. One after another his hopeful speculations are destroyed by facts. In the past he has entertained the notion of a perfectly rational, enlightened organization of men, and he thinks of the possibility of living one's life according to what he calls an "ideal construction," an ideology, and he has some ambitions to establish what he calls a "colony of the spirit," which would be a group of like-minded people agreed to be against spite, bloodiness, and cruelty. But men are not rational, and ideologies tend to get divorced from the real world, and his domestic experiences during the months of his dangling teach Joseph that spite, bloodiness, and cruelty are within, within him too. What is left, after all these attempts at creating the idea of a society, is freedom, which has the effect of making this exemplary man sluggish and irritable, his personality diminished to randomness. It becomes Joseph's desperate ambition, given such freedom, to discover any relevance for himself to the world-at-large. In his last moments in the novel, he joins the Army, crying out in his exhaustion: "Hurray for regular hours! And for the supervision of the spirit! Long live regimentation!" Say what one will about the United States Army, it is a way of life.

And twenty years later, in *Herzog,* Bellow's protagonist moves through an entirely similar action, though the particular certifications of existence that he loses are different ones. Herzog begins as a man who has just been through his second divorce, implying conspicuous failure in human relationship. He has been estranged from his children. He has been betrayed by his best friend. He is no longer young. He has trouble with women. His hair is falling out. He says of himself that he has risen from humble origins to complete disaster. In the moment of the novel he has taken time off from his professorial duties in order to recover, and therefore, like Joseph, he has nothing to do. He devotes a considerable amount of this suspended time to writing letters, by which device he is made to speculate on involvements ranging from his earliest family life to national politics to vastnesses of humane learning. He thus picks his way through his memoirs. Their general meaning seems to be that he himself is divorced from virtually everything, in a time when dissolution and the sense of loss are accepted generally as being not only normal but also normative. And once again the given perceptions breed the necessity for an assertion of the possibility of an existence, with others. With little more hope than Joseph had he takes up life in the country and he takes a girl friend who is also willing to try.

That terminal note of desperate, probably vain assertion is the sign of the times and of our contemporary fiction. It occurs in unlikely places, as even in John Barth's *Giles Goat-Boy* (1966), which moves otherwise toward elaborate allegory and broad farce and broad impersonality. Barth's novel is worked out with such lofty, ranging control that it should allow no seepage of desperation. The novel establishes huge, indeed metaphysical, contradictions; it ends by unraveling none of them but rather in a muted, passive, mystical acceptance of all of them, which is to say, in an arbitrary assertion of pure faith in existence. Barth's story is about a boy who wants to be a Hero, in every literal way. He is therefore set forth into the universe, which by the terms of the allegory is converted into a University. The correspondences then extend multitudinously through some seven hundred intricate pages: The protagonist becomes Oedipus and Jesus Christ, and along the way he recapitulates fragments of Socrates, St. George, Dante, Aeneas, St. Giles, Giles of Rome, and the living Buddha. The University is, appropriately, a confusion of polarities—as between East and West, Male and Female, Passion and Intellect, Science and Humanism, Time and Eternity, Life and Death, and so forth infinitely—containing the intimation that at the end of the course the hero will find himself either "passed" or "failed." And, in brief, all the radical opposites—all the *facts* in an exemplary boy's career—are further confused to the point where the place of the hero's testing is an enveloping uncertainty, without distinctions. Finally the exhausted boy settles for anticlimax: he proposes a metaphysics based on a notion of the circular interpenetration of all phenomena, including passage and failure.

In Barth's novel the system of perceptions is extensive and energetically intellectual. Ken Kesey's *One Flew over the Cuckoo's Nest* (1962) is personal, restricted, and fiercely naïve. But the central action in the two books is, again, significantly similar. Kesey's locale is an insane asylum. The protagonists are a high-spirited rogue and his pal, Chief Broom Bromden, who is a catatonic Indian. They are made to suffer the arbitrariness and crazy authoritarianism of the

hospital. In this situation there is a directness of correspondence that would be difficult to evade—the madhouse is society; the protagonists and all the inmates are free spirits who
have been entrapped. In fact, however, the indictment is
much less circumstantial than might be expected, to the point
that what is revealed is Kesey's lack of discriminating knowledge of or interest in the enemy, Society. The hospital works
some of its will by the use of diabolical machines, which
might constitute a comment on contemporary technology.
The group therapy sessions in the hospital become actually a
system conceived to frighten the patients and impose guilt,
which might constitute a comment on the motives of organ-
ized social service. And the authorities in the hospital are for
the most part ignorant, brutal, and—inevitable paradox—insane, all of which might constitute a comment on one or another kind of public authority. What is put under attack here,
however, is the thing repeatedly referred to as "The Combine," which is to say something like The Establishment or
The Whole System. Indeed the thing attacked is seen even the
less clearly because, in a trope repeated by the novel, it controls a Fog Machine, by which it cunningly obscures perception. The huge generalization is something more and less than
social comment. It becomes a document of lyrical feeling.
The central trouble with The Combine is that it overbears, it
tries to "adjust" everyone, it attempts to rob everyone of his
pure and essential life. So the plot works to the point where
Chief Bromden, become ambulatory, will just manage to escape back to the mythic free life of his Indian forebears,
which is an item of faith.

Finally, in a certain way the most exemplifying of these
few novels is the late Richard Fariña's *Been Down So Long
It Looks Like Up to Me,* published in 1966. Fariña—to an
extent unwittingly, certainly—made blatant the loss of clear
social fact in these times and one's consequent desperate motion to assert an existence. On the one side, the version of
social fact is, symptomatically, both ingenuous and porten-
tous. Once again, in Fariña's novel, the scene of the hero's
striving is a college campus, but here the small model of society is characterized by such materials as: an exceedingly
prissy and ineffectual dean of students, a prevalence of college
fraternities, and an issue, the university's banning of coeds
from the men's dormitories. Within this society are revolu-
tionaries, necessarily. The hero is not one of them. He seems
to be taught by the plot of the fiction that revolution is a

kind of complicity. He, on his side, stands for a purity of un-corrupted being. He is one of today's young dropouts, a non-student whose field of non-study is astronomy. The *being* for which he stands is made manifest, symptomatically, in the relative exoticism of his tastes and knowledge and manners, which are shared by a tiny, arcane community. The true friends are connoisseurs of marijuana and narcotic mush-rooms (*not* hard drugs). They like ragas, they are extremely fond of children, they prefer "organic" foodstuffs, and so forth. It happens that within this scene and situation one may find the rudiments of a revelation which at one time excited people toward a real insurrection in culture; that time was 1920, when the disaffected college student F. Scott Fitzger-ald, in *This Side of Paradise,* announced the romantic pres-ence of flaming youth at Princeton. The comparison is infor-mative. The area for conflict remaining to Fariña is utterly di-minished. This college boy no longer speculates on the free-dom of the passional life. The sequence of exotic, fairly arbi-trary mannerisms which he demonstrates are actually very re-strictive, and they are much more definite than the large social entity which is the presumed enemy. That would seem to be their value. They constitute a regimen, which in turn implies a life.

This is to say about these various novels nothing more than that there is a similarity in the direction of their energies. Achievements vary tremendously, probably in part according to the sheer amount of any writer's awareness of the difficul-ties of any assertion. The general theme invites abstraction and arbitrariness. But within a general public situation in which nothing can be taken for granted, within which a pri-mary metaphysical assertion is an urgent necessity, there is also the sustaining opportunity of a terrible state of nerves. That is where the excitement is likely to be, in the effort made against the manifest uncertainties, rather than in any assertion in itself.

That state of nerves is what we have had in American fic-tion in the past quarter of a century, rather than a school, or a discipline, or a partisan movement. Our fiction is not there-fore lacking in perspicuous identity, nor does it fail to per-form an action in our history. It is inevitably born of that his-tory and it reflects upon it. In a general situation that does not permit much or even ask for much in the way of organ-ized partisanship, it clarifies the bad news. That too is a polit-ical activity. No doubt the state of nerves from which this fiction derives converts public and private lives into a continuous adjustment of hysterias. It has, in fact, caused an immensity of energies in the novel.

In this anthology it has been my intention to bring together a number of discussions bearing on the general character of American fiction since 1945. These essays seem to broach four broad categories of speculation, as indicated by the table of Contents. Obviously these essays are not written from the point of view of a common retrospect. Within contemporary fiction and its criticism there is a history that goes year by year. By arranging these essays chronologically within the various categories, I have tried to indicate that history.

MARCUS KLEIN

March 1969
Kenmore, N.Y.

PART ONE

||||||||||||||||||||||

Class, values,

and ideologies

Notes on the decline of naturalism

PHILIP RAHV

QUITE a few protests have been aired in recent years against the sway of the naturalist method in fiction. It is charged that this method treats material in a manner so flat and external as to inhibit the search for value and meaning, and that in any case, whatever its past record, it is now exhausted. Dissimilar as they are, both the work of Franz Kafka and the works of the surrealist school are frequently cited as examples of release from the routines of naturalist realism, from its endless bookkeeping of existence. Supporting this indictment are mostly those writers of the younger group who are devoted to experimentation and who look to symbolism, the fable, and the myth.

The younger writers are stirred by the ambition to create a new type of imaginative prose into which the recognizably real enters as one component rather than as the total substance. They want to break the novel of its objective habits; some want to introduce into it philosophical ideas; others are not so much drawn to expressing ideas as to expressing the motley strivings of the inner self—dreams, visions, and fantasies. Manifestly the failure of the political movement in the literature of the past decade has resulted in a revival of religio-aesthetic attitudes. The young men of letters are once again watching their own image in the mirror and listening to inner promptings. Theirs is a program calling for the adoption of techniques of planned derangement as a means of cracking open the certified structure of reality and turning

loose its latent energies. And surely one cannot dispose of
such a program merely by uncovering the element of mystifi-
cation in it. For the truth is that the artist of the avant-garde
has never hesitated to lay hold of the instruments of mystifi-
cation when it suited his purpose, especially in an age such as
ours, when the life about him belies more and more the rational ideals of the cultural tradition.

It has been remarked that in the long run the issue between naturalism and its opponents resolves itself into a philosophical dispute concerning the nature of reality. Obviously
those who reject naturalism in philosophy will also object to
its namesake in literature. But it seems to me that when faced
with a problem such as that of naturalist fiction, the critic
will do well not to mix in ontological maneuvers. From the
standpoint of critical method it is impermissible to replace a
concrete literary analysis with arguments derived from some
general theory of the real. For it is plainly a case of the critic
not being able to afford metaphysical commitments if he is to
apply himself without preconceived ideas to the works of art
that constitute his material. The art-object is from first to last
the one certain datum at his disposal; and in succumbing to
metaphysical leanings—either of the spiritualist or materialist
variety—he runs the risk of freezing his insights in some kind
of ideational schema the relevance of which to the task in
hand is hardly more than speculative. The act of critical eval-
uation is best performed in a state of *ideal aloofness* from abstract systems. Its practitioner is not concerned with making
up his mind about the ultimate character of reality but with
observing and measuring its actual proportions and combinations within a given form. The presence of the real affects
him directly, with an immediate force contingent upon the
degree of interest, concreteness, and intensity in the impression of life conveyed by the literary artist. The philosopher
can take such impressions or leave them, but luckily the critic
has no such choice.

Imaginative writing cannot include fixed and systematic
definitions of reality without violating its own existential
character. Yet in any imaginative effort that which we mean
by the real remains the basic criterion of viability, the crucial
test of relevance, even if its specific features can hardly be
determined in advance but must be *felt anew* in each given
instance. And so far as the medium of fiction is concerned,
one cannot but agree with Henry James that it gains its "air
of reality"—which he considers to be its "supreme

virtue"—through "its immense and exquisite correspondence with life." Note that James's formulation allows both for analogical and realistic techniques of representation. He speaks not of copies or reports or transcripts of life but of relations of equivalence, of a "correspondence" which he identifies with the "illusion of life." The ability to produce this illusion he regards as the storyteller's inalienable gift, "the merit on which all other merits . . . helplessly and submissively depend." This insight is of an elementary nature and scarcely peculiar to James alone, but it seems that its truth has been lost on some of our recent catch-as-catch-can innovators in the writing of fiction.

It is intrinsically from this point of view that one can criticize the imitations of Kafka that have been turning up of late as being one-sided and even inept. Perhaps Kafka is too idiosyncratic a genius to serve as a model for others, but still it is easy to see where his imitators go wrong. It is necessary to say to them: To know how to take apart the recognizable world is not enough, is in fact merely a way of letting oneself go and of striving for originality at all costs. But originality of this sort is nothing more than a professional mannerism of the avant-garde. The genuine innovator is always trying to make us actually experience his creative contradictions. He therefore employs means that are subtler and more complex: *at the very same time that he takes the world apart he puts it together again.* For to proceed otherwise is to dissipate rather than alter our sense of reality, to weaken and compromise rather than change in any significant fashion our feeling of relatedness to the world. After all, what impressed us most in Kafka is precisely this power of his to achieve a simultaneity of contrary effects, to fit the known into the unknown, the actual into the mythic and vice versa, to combine within one framework a conscientiously empirical account of the visibly real with a dreamlike and magical dissolution of it. In this paradox lies the pathos of his approach to human existence.

A modern poetess has written that the power of the visible derives from the invisible; but the reverse of this formula is also true. Thus the visible and the invisible might be said to stand to each other in an ironic relation of inner dependence and of mutual skepticism mixed with solicitude. It is a superb form of double-talk; and if we are accustomed to its exclusion from naturalistic writing, it is all the more disappointing to find that the newly evolved "fantastic" style of the experimentalists likewise excludes it. But there is another consideration, of a more formal nature. It seems to me a profound error to conceive of reality as merely a species of material that the fiction writer can either use or dispense with as he sees fit. It is a species of material, of course, and something else besides: it also functions as the *discipline of fiction,* much in the same sense that syllabic structure functions as the discipline of verse. This seeming identity of the formal and substantial means of narrative-prose is due, I think, to the altogether free and open character of the medium, which prevents it from developing such distinctly technical controls as poetry has acquired. Hence even the dream, when told in a story, must partake of some of the qualities of the real.

Whereas the surrealist represents man as immured in dreams, the naturalist represents him in a continuous waking state of prosaic daily living, in effect as never dreaming. But both the surrealist and the naturalist go to extremes in simplifying the human condition. J. M. Synge once said that the artist displays at once the difficulty and the triumph of his art when picturing the dreamer leaning out to reality or the man of real life lifted out of it. "In all the poets," he wrote, and this test is by no means limited to poetry alone, "the greatest have both these elements, that is they are supremely engrossed with life, and yet with the wildness of their fancy they are always passing out of what is simple and plain."

The old egocentric formula, "Man's fate is his character," has been altered by the novelists of the naturalist school to read, "Man's fate is his environment." (Zola, the organizer and champion of the school, drew his ideas from physiology and medicine, but in later years his disciples cast the natural sciences aside in favor of the social sciences.) To the naturalist, human behavior is a function of its social environment; the individual is the live register of its qualities; he exists in it as animals exist in nature.[1] Due to this emphasis the naturalist

---

[1] Balzac, to whom naturalism is enormously indebted, explains in his preface to the *Comédie Humaine* that the idea of that work came to him in consequence of a "comparison between the human and animal kingdoms." "Does not society," he asks, "make of man, in accordance with the environment in which he lives and moves, as many different kinds of man as there are different zoological species? . . . There have, therefore, existed and always will exist social species, just as there are zoological species."

Zola argues along the same lines: "All things hang together: it is necessary to start from the determination of inanimate bodies in order to

mode has evolved historically in two main directions. On the one hand it has tended toward passive documentation (milieu-panoramas, local-color stories, reportorial studies of a given region or industry, etc.), and on the other toward the exposure of socioeconomic conditions (muckraking). American fiction of the past decade teems with examples of both tendencies, usually in combination. The work of James T. Farrell, for instance, is mostly a genre-record, the material of which is in its very nature operative in producing social feeling, while such novels as *The Grapes of Wrath* and *Native Son* are exposure-literature, as is the greater part of the fiction of social protest. Dos Passos' trilogy, *U. S. A.,* is thoroughly political in intention but has the tone and gloss of the methodical genre-painter in the page by page texture of its prose.

I know of no hard and fast rules that can be used to distinguish the naturalist method from the methods of realism generally. It is certainly incorrect to say that the difference is marked by the relative density of detail. Henry James observes in his essay *The Art of Fiction* that it is above all "solidity of specification" that makes for the illusion of life—the air of reality—in a novel; and the truth of this dictum is borne out by the practice of the foremost modern innovators in this medium, such as Proust, Joyce, and Kafka. It is not, then, primarily the means employed to establish verisimilitude that fix the naturalist imprint upon a work of fiction. A more conclusive test, to my mind, is its treatment of the relation of character to background. I would classify as naturalistic that type of realism in which the individual is portrayed not merely as subordinate to his background but as wholly determined by it—that type of realism, in other words, in which the environment displaces its inhabitants in the role of the hero. Theodore Dreiser, for example, comes as close as any American writer to plotting the careers of his characters strictly within a determinative process. The financier Frank Cowperwood masters his world and emerges as its hero, while the "little man" Clyde Griffiths is the victim whom it

---

arrive at the determination of living beings; and since savants like Claude Bernard demonstrate now that fixed laws govern the human body, we can easily proclaim . . . the hour in which the laws of thought and passion will be formulated in their turn. A like determination will govern the stones of the roadway and the brain of man. . . . We have experimental chemistry and medicine and physiology, and later on an experimental novel. It is an inevitable evolution." (*The Experimental Novel.*)

grinds to pieces; yet hero and victim alike are essentially implements of environmental force, the carriers of its contradictions upon whom it stamps success or failure—not entirely at will, to be sure, for people are marked biologically from birth —but with sufficient autonomy to shape their fate.

In such a closed world there is patently no room for the singular, the unique, for anything in fact which cannot be represented plausibly as the product of a particular social and historical complex. Of necessity the naturalist must deal with experience almost exclusively in terms of the broadly typical. He analyzes characters in such a way as to reduce them to standard types. His method of construction is that of accretion and enumeration rather than of analysis or storytelling; and this is so because the quantitative development of themes, the massing of detail and specification, serves his purpose best. He builds his structures out of literal fact and precisely documented circumstance, thus severely limiting the variety of creative means at the disposal of the artist.

This quasiscientific approach not only permits but, in theory at least, actually prescribes a neutral attitude in the sphere of values. In practice, however, most naturalists are not sufficiently detached or logical to stay put in such an ultraobjective position. Their detractors are wrong in denying them a moral content; the most that can be said is that theirs is strictly functional morality, bare of any elements of gratuity or transcendence and devoid of the sense of personal freedom.[2] Clearly such a perspective allows for very little self-awareness on the part of characters. It also removes the possibility of a tragic resolution of experience. The world of naturalist fiction is much too big, too inert, too hardened by social habit and material necessity to allow for that tenacious self-assertion of the human by means of which tragedy justifies and ennobles its protagonists. The only grandeur naturalism knows is the grandeur of its own methodological achievement in making available a vast inventory of minutely described phenomena, in assembling an enormous quantity of data and arranging them in a rough figuration of reality. *Les Rougon-Macquart* stands to this day as the most imposing monument to this achievement.

[2] Chekhov remarks in one of his stories that "the sense of personal freedom is the chief constituent of creative genius."

* * *

But in the main it is the pure naturalist—that monstrous
offspring of the logic of a method—that I have been describing here. Actually no such literary animal exists. Life always
triumphs over methods, over formulas and theories. There is
scarcely a single novelist of any importance wearing the
badge of naturalism who is all of a piece, who fails to compensate in some way for what we miss in his fundamental
conception. Let us call the roll of the leading names among
the French and American naturalists and see wherein each is
saved.

The Goncourts, it is true, come off rather badly, but even
so, to quote a French critic, they manage "to escape from the
crude painting of the naked truth by their impressionistic
mobility" and, one might add, by their mobile intelligence.
Zola's case does not rest solely on our judgment of his naturalist dogmas. There are entire volumes by him—the best, I
think, is *Germinal*—and parts of volumes besides, in which
his naturalism, fed by an epic imagination, takes on a mythic
cast. Thomas Mann associates him with Wagner in a common drive toward an epic mythicism:

> They belong together. The kinship of spirit, method, and
> aims is most striking. This lies not only in the ambition to
> achieve size, the propensity to the grandiose and the lavish;
> nor is it the Homeric leitmotiv alone that is common to
> them; it is first and foremost a special kind of naturalism,
> which develops into the mythical. . . . In Zola's epic . . .
> the characters themselves are raised up to a plane above
> that of every day. And is that Astarte of the Second Em-
> pire, called Nana, not symbol and myth? [*The Sufferings
> and Greatness of Richard Wagner*.]

Zola's prose, though not controlled by an artistic conscience,
overcomes our resistance through sheer positiveness and
expressive energy—qualities engendered by his novelistic
ardor and avidity for re-creating life in all its multiple
forms.[3] As for Huysmans, even in his naturalist period he
was more concerned with style than with subject matter.
Maupassant is a naturalist mainly by alliance, *i.e.* by virtue of
his official membership in the School of Médan; actually he

---

[3] Moreover, it should be evident that Zola's many faults are not
rectified but merely inverted in much of the writing—so languidly allusive
and decorative—of the literary generation that turned their backs on him.

follows a line of his own, which takes off from naturalism
never to return to it. There are few militant naturalists
among latter-day French writers. Jules Romains is sometimes
spoken of as one, but the truth is that he is an epigone of all
literary doctrines, including his own. Dreiser is still unsur-
passed so far as American naturalism goes, though just at
present he may well be the least readable. He has traits that
make for survival—a Balzacian grip on the machinery of
money and power; a prosiness so primary in texture that if
taken in bulk it affects us as a kind of poetry of the commonplace and ill-favored; and an emphatic eroticism which is the
real climate of existence in his fictions—Eros hovering over
the shambles. Sinclair Lewis was never a novelist in the
proper sense that Zola and Dreiser are novelists, and, given
his gift for exhaustive reporting, naturalism did him more
good than harm by providing him with a ready literary technique. In Farrell's chronicles there is an underlying moral
code which, despite his explicit rejection of the Church,
seems to me indisputably orthodox and Catholic; and his
Studs Lonigan—a product of those unsightly urban neighbor-
hoods where youth prowls and fights to live up to the folk-
ideal of the "regular guy"—is no mere character but an archetype, an eponymous hero of the street-myths that prevail in
our big cities. The naturalism of Dos Passos is most completely manifested in *U.S.A.*, tagged by the critics as a "col-
lective" novel recording the "decline of our business civilization." But what distinguishes Dos Passos from other novelists
of the same political animus is a sense of justice so pure as to
be almost instinctive, as well as a deeply elegiac feeling for
the intimate features of American life and for its precipitant
moments. Also, *U.S.A.* is one of the very few naturalist
novels in which there is a controlled use of language,
in which a major effect is produced by the interplay
between story and style. It is necessary to add, however,
that the faults of Dos Passos' work have been obscured
by its vivid contemporaneity and vital political appeal. In the
future, I think, it will be seen more clearly than now that it
dramatizes social symptoms rather than lives and that it fails
to preserve the integrity of personal experience. As for
Faulkner, Hemingway, and Caldwell, I do not quite see on
what grounds some critics and literary historians include

them in the naturalist school. I should think that Faulkner is exempted by his prodigious inventiveness and fantastic humor. Hemingway is a realist on one level, in his attempts to catch the "real thing, the sequence of motion and fact which made the emotion"; but he is also subjective, given to self-portraiture and to playing games with his ego; there is very little study of background in his work, a minimum of documentation. In his best novels Caldwell is a writer of rural abandon—and comedy. His Tobacco Road is a socio-logical area only in patches; most of it is exotic landscape.

It is not hard to demonstrate the weakness of the natural-ist method by abstracting it, first, from the uses to which in-dividual authors put it and, second, from its function in the history of modern literature. The traditionalist critics judge it much too one-sidedly in professing to see in its rise nothing but spiritual loss—an invasion of the arcanum of art by arid scientific ideas. The point is that this scientific bias of natural-ism was historically productive of contradictory results. Its effect was certainly depressive insofar as it brought mechanis-tic notions and procedures into writing. But it should be kept in mind that it also enlivened and, in fact, revolutionized writ-ing by liquidating the last assets of "romance" in fiction and by purging it once and for all of the idealism of the "beauti-ful lie"—of the long-standing inhibitions against dealing with the underside of life, with those inescapable day-by-day actu-alities traditionally regarded as too "sordid" and "ugly" for inclusion within an aesthetic framework. If it were not for the service thus rendered in vastly increasing the store of lit-erary material, it is doubtful whether such works as Ulysses and even Remembrance of Things Past could have been writ-ten. This is not clearly understood in the English-speaking countries, where naturalism, never quite forming itself into a "movement," was at most only an extreme emphasis in the general onset of realistic fiction and drama. One must study, rather, the Continental writers of the last quarter of the nine-teenth century in order to grasp its historical role. In discuss-ing the German naturalist school of the 1880's, the historian Hans Naumann has this to say, for instance:

Generally it can be said that to its early exponents the doctrine of naturalism held quite as many diverse and con-fusing meanings as the doctrine of expressionism seemed

to hold in the period just past. Imaginative writers who
at bottom were pure idealists united with the dry-as-dust
advocates of a philistine natural-scientific program on the
one hand and with the shameless exploiters of erotic
themes on the other. All met under the banner of naturalism—friends today and enemies tomorrow. . . . But
there was an element of historical necessity in all this.
The fact is that the time had come for an assault, executed with glowing enthusiasm, against the epigones . . .
that it was finally possible to fling aside with disdain and
anger the pretty falsehoods of life and art. [*Die Deutsche
Dichtung der Gegenwart,* Stuttgart, 1930, p. 144.]

And he adds that the naturalism of certain writers consisted
simply in their "speaking honestly of things that had hereto-
fore been suppressed."

But to establish the historical credit of naturalism is not to
refute the charges that have been brought against it in recent
years. For whatever its past accomplishments, it cannot be
denied that its present condition is one of utter debility. What
was once a means of treating material truthfully has been
turned, through a long process of depreciation, into a mere
convention of truthfulness, devoid of any significant or even
clearly definable literary purpose or design. The spirit of discovery has withdrawn from naturalism; it has now become
the common denominator of realism, available in like measure to the producers of literature and to the producers of
kitsch. One might sum up the objections to it simply by saying that it is no longer possible to use this method *without
taking reality for granted.* This means that it has lost the
power to cope with the ever-growing element of the problematical in modern life, which is precisely the element that is
magnetizing the imagination of the true artists of our epoch.
Such artists are no longer content merely to question particular habits or situations or even institutions; it is reality itself
which they bring into question. Reality to them is like that
"open wound" of which Kierkegaard speaks in his *Journals:*
"A healthy open wound; sometimes it is healthier to keep a
wound open; sometimes it is worse when it closes."

There are also certain long-range factors that make for the
decline of naturalism. One such factor is the growth of psy-

chological science and, particularly, of psychoanalysis. Through the influence of psychology literature recovers its inwardness, devising such forms as the interior monologue, which combines the naturalistic in its minute description of the mental process with the antinaturalistic in its disclosure of the subjective and the irrational. Still another factor is the tendency of naturalism, as Thomas Mann observes in his remarks on Zola, to turn into the mythic through sheer immersion in the typical. This dialectical negation of the typical is apparent in a work like *Ulysses,* where "the myth of the *Odyssey,*" to quote from Harry Levin's study of Joyce, "is superimposed upon the map of Dublin" because only a myth could "lend shape or meaning to a slice of life so broad and banal." And from a social-historical point of view this much can be said, that naturalism cannot hope to survive the world of nineteenth-century science and industry of which it is the product. For what is the crisis of reality in contemporary art if not at bottom the crisis of the dissolution of this familiar world? Naturalism, which exhausted itself in taking an inventory of this world while it was still relatively stable, cannot possibly do justice to the phenomena of its disruption.

One must protest, however, against the easy assumption of some avant-garde writers that to finish with naturalism is the same as finishing with the principle of realism generally. It is one thing to dissect the real, to penetrate beneath its faceless surface and transpose it into terms of symbol and image; but the attempt to be done with it altogether is sheer regression or escape. Of the principle of realism it can be said that it is the most valuable acquisition of the modern mind. It has taught literature how to take in, how to grasp and encompass, the ordinary facts of human existence; and I mean this in the simplest sense conceivable. Least of all can the novelist dispense with it, as his medium knows of no other principle of coherence. In Gide's *Les Faux-Monnayeurs* there is a famous passage in which the novelist Edouard enumerates the faults of the naturalist school. "The great defect of that school is that it always cuts a slice of life in the same direction: in time, lengthwise. Why not in breadth? Or in depth? As for me, I should like not to cut at all. Please understand: I should like to put everything into my novel." "But I thought," his interlocutor remarks, "that you want to abandon reality." "Yes," replies Edouard, "my novelist wants to abandon it; but I shall continually bring him back to it. In fact that will be the subject; the struggle between the facts presented by reality and the ideal reality."

1949

The search for values

JOHN ALDRIDGE

THE quality and intensity of a literary work will depend, to a very large extent, upon the success with which the writer can find and communicate his private truth in the public truth of his age. If we take the subject of a work to be the writer himself and his subject matter to be the fund of values, attitudes, customs, and beliefs which he shares with his audience and in terms of which he discovers what he has to say —his private truth—then it becomes clear that the events of the last fifty years, particularly the breakdown by science of public truth into countless isolated individual truths, have dangerously narrowed the area of subject matter available to writers and, consequently, crippled their means of discovering themselves and their age.

In their attempts to compensate for this, modern writers have been forced generally into one of two avenues of escape. Either they have tried to exploit their isolation from the life of their time and to buttress their paralysis before the failure of public truth with a private symbolism based on a concern for themselves alone, or they have turned away from the reality of the present and sought to find, in the worship of old gods or a simple primitivism, some substitute for all that they have lost. A third course not involving escape depends for its success on the marriage of talent and a propitious moment of history. In the modern age it has been possible for a short time under peculiarly fortunate circumstances

From *After the Lost Generation* by John W. Aldridge, pp. 85-106. Reprinted by permission.

for writers to discover dramatic material in the process and residue of the value breakdown itself; and it is this possibility which a few of them have until recently exploited admirably.

Most of the writers who came to maturity in the twenties found relief in all three courses at various stages of their careers. Stein and Joyce developed a private language and to a large extent avoided the problem of direct communication. Their preoccupation with pure technique was a substitute for the community of values to which their writings might otherwise have referred. The later Joyce, however, went back to classical literature—as the later Eliot went back to ancient myth and finally to religious orthodoxy—in his search for a structure that would give his symbols meaningful reference outside themselves. The cult of the primitive obsessed Hemingway, Fitzgerald, and Dos Passos from time to time—as it did Lawrence, Conrad, and Huxley as well as Eliot and Stein —but it is as followers of the third course that they are important here.

All three of these writers—Hemingway, Dos Passos, and Fitzgerald—were able to turn the failure of traditional values into a value of art and to exploit a subject matter which was discoverable for the first time in the midst of that failure. Hemingway's code—that cloak of chivalric morality and nerve with which his characters covered their inner nakedness —is a concrete, dramatic expression of the distrust of all values outside those which the individual invents for his own survival. In his first novels and stories it served him as a frame of artistic comprehension. Violence set against the code of loss was his formula, his instrument for discovering the truth of his age. Within that formula he was able to function as the superb writer he is. But the moment he tried to transcend it, to affirm rather than deny, he gave way to those curious excesses which made partial failures of his last two novels. His major themes, furthermore, derive much of their power from their great capacity to shock: the importance of sex, violence, war, and death in his work is indistinguishable from their importance in an age just emerging from the dogmatic position of refusing to recognize their existence. In Dos Passos an almost identical pattern can be traced. The order of his art is formed directly out of the chaos of the society which it depicts, and its success, when it does succeed, is founded on the ironic spectacle of the individual going down under the shocking injustices of his time. Fitzgerald, the barometer of his generation's extremes, cannot be separated in

either his life or his work from the time which formed him
—its magic glamour, its poverty of faith, and, at the end, its
sickness and ruin. In his vision of Paradise he too found a
correlative of art. It was a dramatic symbol for a belief which
was being destroyed—the belief, that is, in the possibility of
happiness through material success—and it was effective not
only as Fitzgerald's means of entry into the life of his time
but as the means by which his time discovered him. What is
important about Fitzgerald's Paradise is that both he and his
generation sought it and that the failure to find it led to an
identical disintegration in both. There was also on Fitzgerald's side, as on Hemingway's, the freshness and shock value
of his material. When one considers how many of his early
books were interesting almost solely as records of the rebellion of the young against the old and of the postwar moral
decline, one realizes that he could not have been the writer
he was in any other time.

But in the years since Hemingway, Dos Passos, and Fitzgerald began to write, the forces that gave impetus to their
development—particularly the forces of disillusionment and
denial released by the broken promises of the first war—have
declined. The young novelists of the present generation are
consequently deprived of that impetus at the same time that
their own age and experience offer them nothing comparable.
They have come through a war even more profoundly dis-
turbing than the first; but the illusions and causes of war,
having once been lost, cannot be relost. Their world, ironically enough, is almost the same world their predecessors discovered; but the fundamental discoveries of modern life can
be made but once. America is more than ever a machine-
dominated, gadget-minded country. There are more Babbitts
now than when Sinclair Lewis invented the term and the expatriates shouted it in their battle cry for freedom, art, and
exile. But who cares today to take up that cry, to denounce
again with the same fury, or to escape forever into artistic
exile?

One aspect of the problem is reflected in the technical
differences between the writings of the two wars. Where
Hemingway, Dos Passos, and E. E. Cummings (in *The Enormous Room*) were from the beginning innovators of new
methods—even of a whole new literary language—with
which to present the new experience of war, the new war
novelists seem, for the most part, incapable of technical discoveries and resigned to working within the tradition handed

down to them from the twenties. One explanation is that the experience of war is no longer new and, consequently, does not require a new method of presentation. Another is that the Lost Generation writers were engaged in a revolution designed to purge language of the old restraints of the previous century and to fit it to the demands of a younger, more realistic time. Idiosyncrasy and defiance were part of their work because the things that had happened to them had happened to no generation before them, and because they were aware of their uniqueness and determined to communicate it to the world.

Today that revolution is over. The innovations of Hemingway, as he himself remarked, were "a certain clarification of the language" and are now "in the public domain." The unique has become the ordinary; young writers using the effects of their predecessors are often not even aware that those effects did not belong to our literature until years after many of them were born. The assimilation into the public domain has, in fact, been so complete that what we have now seems a technical conservatism. Certainly the styles of Vance Bourjaily, Norman Mailer, John Horne Burns, Irwin Shaw, Robert Lowry, Alfred Hayes, Merle Miller, Gore Vidal, Truman Capote, Paul Bowles, and Federick Buechner—while they contain overtones of practically everyone from Dos Passos and Hemingway to James T. Farrell and Henry James—show little evidence of new developments and, with the exception of Capote's, Burns's, and Buechner's, do little to flavor the material they present.

But there has been this change: the single perspective and narrow scope of the World War I novels have given way to huge comprehensiveness in which whole armies and social masses are encompassed. From the individual, neoromantic hero we have progressed to the multiple-hero or, more correctly, to the subordination of all heroes to the group. Mailer carries an entire army division—from general down to private—through a complex military engagement and then goes back to the beginnings of his characters and sketches them against the background of peace. Burns and Shaw take even more characters through action on three or four continents and months of closely packed experience; and all three manage to pay careful attention to detail and to give the actual texture of the background or event described.

This would be achievement indeed if it did not come so often at the expense of insight, form, and power. Taken as a group or singly, the novels of this war simply do not have the impact that those of the first war had—nor, for that matter, do the novels that have been written so far about the aftermath. They are incomparably better written, to be sure. Almost any one of them will show fewer lapses and roughnesses than can be found in the best of the earlier group—*A Farewell to Arms, Three Soldiers, The Enormous Room*. But it is as if they had been written too easily and their authors had had too painless an apprenticeship. Their finish is more often that of a machine-made, prefabricated product than of a finely wrought piece of craftsmanship, the sort that can be obtained if more problems are avoided than are met and overcome.

But it is in the material itself with which their novels must be concerned that the new writers face their greatest difficulty. Although they have arrived at the end of the tradition of loss, negation, and revolt, and have known none of its benefits, they have inherited the conditions out of which that tradition emerged. They are finding that modern life is still basically purposeless, that the typical condition of modern man is still doubt, confusion, and fear. But because they have never known life otherwise and were not exposed, as their predecessors were, to the process by which it became as it now is, they can write of it from neither the perspective of protest nor that of disillusionment and loss. They are faced with the same material from which Hemingway and Fitzgerald drew their artistic impetus, but they are denied the dramatic values which those men found in it. Loss is no longer the spiritual climate of the age, but the chaos of loss is still its typical material.

To compensate for the lack of that climate and the symbols which made it demonstrable in art as well as for the failure of a new climate and new symbols to appear, these writers have up to now shown signs of developing in at least four directions, all of them overlapping and interwoven. If, first of all, they have insight into values that seem worthy of affirmation and point the way out of the chaos of loss, they can superimpose them upon the old material which is still available. They can, in other words, assert the need for belief even though it is upon a background in which belief is impossible and in which the symbols are lacking for a genuine affirmation in dramatic terms. Second, they can escape into journalism, exploit facts and events for their own sake, and thus conceal for the moment their lack of an attitude toward their material. Third, they can seek new subject matter in what little material remains which has not been fully exploited in the past and which, therefore, still has emotive power. They have so far made two important discoveries in this area—homosexuality and racial conflict. Fourth, they can conceal their failure to find something significant to say by elaborating their manner of saying. Pure technique—technique, that is, which has been detached from its proper base in subject matter—has become for some of them not a means of expressing new material or insights but of revitalizing old and worn-out material and insights; and it has helped to give their writing a veneer of idiosyncrasy and life. Nearly all the novels the new writers have produced show one or more of these tendencies; but none, unfortunately, has offered more than temporary relief from the dilemma which made it necessary.

The false note of courage in literature, like the uneasy grin on the face of a boy lost at midnight, is a compensation for the lack of a suitable attitude toward feelings of confusion and fear. It most often takes the form, in the new novels, of an insipid reminder made by the author to his characters that all will at last be well, that even as they are engaged in futile and mechanical lovemaking, compulsive drinking, and considerations of suicide, he has great plans for them and they should not despair. The empty young man without talent will nonetheless write his novel and be very famous; the Jew beset on every side by prejudice will nonetheless escape and find peace and understanding among his own people; the career girl with the uncontrollable passion for taking strange young men into her bed will nonetheless make the happiest of marriages. By the end of the novel only the suicide who did not wait to consult the author will miss the delights that are in store for him.

The defect of such writing is that the solutions or conclusions presented are incompatible with the presented material: the young men act and speak in a milieu of futility and grow daily more morose, the young women are motivated by a lust which can arise only from a sense of the utter hopelessness of all higher action. Yet even as the narrative sets the scene for suicide, nervous collapse, and the triumph of that lust, the author is preparing a destiny which is affirmative and, therefore, contrary to the facts as they appear.

One explanation is that the author is trying to squeeze fresh meaning out of old material. If he remains true to his insight, he cannot avoid describing the situations of his time as they predominantly are, that is, as meaningless, valueless, and futile. His world is crowded with young men and women who do not know what they are or were meant to be and who express, or escape, their confusion in incessant drinking and automatic sex. But at the same time that he perceives this world and is bound by his perception to portray it as it is, the author is also aware of the need to discover some hope and value for it, some assurance that all is not as bad as it seems. His attempt to dramatize this need, however, usually requires him to invent some other outcome for his characters than their situations make logically possible, and he is at once committed to forcing them against their natures in the direction he wishes them to go. The result, of course, is that instead of dramatizing the need, making it grow organically out of the substance of the novel, he has succeeded merely in converting it to an empty optimism which has about the same relation to the plight of his characters as a patriotic speech to a demoralized army.

The young writer is faced, from the moment he begins his first novel, with the unavoidable fact that the only hope for a successful dramatic effect lies today in the depiction of the grotesque and abnormal; for it is there and there only that the tragic situation of modern life exists. The mediocre and the undaring, the businessman who goes unswervingly to business, the family man who lives out his days in domestic mediocrity, are unpresentable in dramatic terms. Their adjustment to life is made at the expense of no conflict. Their happiness has no consequences. The most that can be said for them is that they have managed to arrive at a state of life in which nothing of importance is ever likely to happen. If the writer sets out to depict them, he finds himself poverty-stricken in events and symbols. They may represent a *condition* of positive value, of hope and virtue, but they take no *action* in the name of virtue, and it is upon action that literary art depends.

Suppose, however, that the businessman can be made to throw up his business or the family man to desert his family, crises so admirably described in the books (and the life) of Sherwood Anderson. At once the situation becomes dramatic and suited to the writer's purpose. But it has ceased to be the typical situation. The typical has been sacrificed to the more desirable intrusion of the spectacular, the chance deviation from the dull, and with it are sacrificed the affirmative values which existed only in the typical or inactive state and which cannot exist, as long as the mass of society is what it is, outside that state. If at some future time it should become necessary for people to exert a little daring to become good citizens or to fight as hard to achieve virtue as they do now to avoid thinking about it, our writers might be able to produce a literature of goodness equal in quality to a literature of evil. But as long as goodness is synonymous with conventionality and conventionality with inaction, they never will.

A careful distinction should at once be made, however, between the writers who are sincere and the writers who are palpably fake, between those who are trying to find an honest basis in experience for the values they wish to affirm and those who are willing at every moment to serve up synthetic values drawn from synthetic experience. The second- and third-rate writers of any time will endeavor to write not as they must but as their public wishes them to write. In a time like the present they will attempt to allay the prevailing confusion and fear by offering clichés in place of truth, a prefabricated Heaven for every natural Hell. They will gain entrance into the minds of the uncritical by appealing to their little wishful dreams and the myths which they currently hold sacred.

The great danger of such writers is the danger of any charlatan in any profession; and it is proportionate to the extent to which their work is not literature but a willful misrepresentation of the facts. If we think of literature as the meaningful arrangement of truth, then we can have no patience with an attempt made under the masquerade of literature to falsify or distort the truth. If we think of the effect of literature as a heightening of awareness, then we cannot accept an effect which involves a decrease of awareness and a substitution of baseless fantasy for thought. The picture of American life which some of these writers give in their novels has no more relation to American life than the fairy-tale America manufactured in Hollywood. It is founded not on things as they are but on things as the writers and their readers wish them to be; and things as they are wished to be are almost never in this country either attainable or worthy of being attained.

It is true that today people everywhere are asking to be reassured and comforted. It is also true that in the last several years no work of fiction of genuine quality has been able to do either. That fact may indicate not only that a successful affirmative writing cannot be produced without affirmative experience but that the values which most people wish to see affirmed are really false and unworthy. It seems to me that the best literature in America will continue to be negative so long as the country's values are such that no writer of honesty or insight can possibly take them seriously.

Reading through some of the new novels is rather like going through a well-furnished house in which every chair, table, and picture has been arranged with the skill of a professional decorator but which manages, nevertheless, to give an effect of utter lifelessness and sterility. Their perfection of style seems to have been achieved, in far too many cases, at the expense of subtlety and symbolic richness. The very ease with which they are executed seems to indicate that the basic problems of art have been avoided rather than solved and that genuine insight has found too convenient a substitute in mere facility. Many of them are not novels at all but pseudo novels, works of skilled journalism contrived to pass as fiction but lacking the one ingredient which all good fiction must possess—the power to make meaningful and orderly the chaotic processes of life.

Journalism is a helpful crutch for a writer of slight or immature talent in a time of doubt and confusion. Through journalism he is able to present material without taking an attitude toward it or judging its significance. As long as he concentrates on facts, the way things *seem,* and on events, the things that happen, he is relieved of the task of determining what things *are* and what happenings *mean.* He is, of course, desperately dependent on the strength of his facts and events to stand by themselves without support from him, and his entire success will depend on the power they have of evoking a strong emotion in the reader. If for one moment the events chosen cease to be important or the reader, having been exposed to too many events, ceases to react to them, then the writer is thrown into a dilemma from which only greater talent than he possesses can possibly free him.

There is reason to believe that that moment is now at hand. For years writers have exploited the devices of journalism to keep alive in a period during which events have occurred so rapidly that all but their surface implications have been lost and they themselves have been in great doubt as to what to say and how to say it. But the ironic dilemma of journalism has at last begun to claim them: just as they have been unable to judge the significance of events, so events are losing their significance to the public. The sex incident, the brutality of war, the grotesque contents of the insane mind are ceasing to be satisfactory substitutes for artistic talent and insight.

It might be said that journalism was the special province of the writers of the twenties. It was usable to them because the events they exploited were still sensational and could still be counted on to arouse in the reader the kind of response which, if he did not discriminate too finely, could be taken for the sort traditionally aroused by the great literature of the past. The intrusion of sex into a novel, if it was intruded skillfully enough, could be made to seem as important as, if not identical with, a portrayal of complete love. Sex was still a function startling enough in itself to need no support beyond itself. The depiction of the violence of war was effective so long as violence and war were new and the emotion aroused by them could still obscure the writer's failure to show in precisely what way they were meaningful or dramatic within the terms of his work. Sensationalism thus became in much of the writing of the twenties a substitute for insight; journalism was able to appropriate some of the effects of literary art; and the mere event was made to stand for the meaningful interpretation of event.

But as literature has evolved beyond sensationalism to a point where its most standard materials are no longer shocking by themselves, it has become clear that journalism is a decadent form and that the new writers have already carried it beyond the limits of exhaustion. That they have not been motivated by any intent to compromise is obvious when one realizes that they have had no other means of presenting the chaotic experience of recent years and no such convenient attitude toward that experience as their predecessors had toward theirs. If the age of transition and loss is past, its passing has shown how dependent upon the sensational values of transition and loss its writers were; and it has left the new writers without those values at a time when they have been unable to find new ones.

One of the last successful uses of journalism can be found in some of the novels that have come out of the second war; and it is a reinforcement of the argument to observe that now that the events of the war have begun to fade in memory the dramatic value of most of these novels has faded with them. But at the time of their appearance such novels as *The*

Naked and the Dead and *The Young Lions* were greatly en-
hanced by the sheer power of the events they described and
almost entirely because those events were at once too
immediate in time to be overly familiar and too involved in
the destinies of all of us to be unexciting. The achievement of
Mailer and Shaw, as of most of the other war novelists, consisted mainly of an exceedingly workmanlike job of recording
in minute detail the progression of event after event, violence
after violence, in a war situation which was by itself perfectly
suited to their purposes. Wars have a beginning, a middle, and
an end and are, therefore, vastly more adaptable to fiction
than the normal human situation which, lacking innate form,
must be artificially arranged. Events occur in wars with such
intensity that they need not signify or connote. Characters
may react to them in any way they will. They may collapse
inwardly, be destroyed outwardly, or they may feel nothing.
In any case, the events and the reactions do not need to be
meaningfully related to one another. The events are significant enough simply because they have happened. The reactions can take care of themselves because they will be incon-
sequential next to the impact of the events.

A young writer who has produced one war novel has thus
actually revealed relatively little about his true or potential
stature as a writer. The war relieves him of the necessity to
invent a dramatic situation and to discover a precise motivation for the feelings and actions of his characters. He is able
merely to present the war, and his presentation will be effective if it is true to the facts and for as long as the facts retain
their freshness. To prove himself as a writer he must, therefore, write a second novel outside the frame of the war and
take up characters and situations that will demand some
imaginative support from him. That many of the novelists of
both wars have failed to fulfill the promise of their early war
writing is an indication of the extent to which their best
achievements have depended on the ready-made dramatic
structure which only war provides.

It is in some of the second novels which the new writers
have produced that the weaknesses of journalism show
through most clearly. Merle Miller's *That Winter,* for example, represents an attempt to vitalize a thin substance through
the devices of journalism, and it is a failure to the extent that
those devices are no longer capable of arousing the intended
emotion or of replacing invention and insight. Sex in *That
Winter* is the nearest any of the characters come to dramatic

action but it shows itself to be mere shadow action as soon as one perceives that it is a disguise to cover the lack of all real motivation within them. When Miller can think of nothing else for his people to do, he puts them to bed together or he gets them drunk or he has them commit suicide. At any other time these incidents might have passed for drama; but they have been so thoroughly exploited and we have become so thoroughly weary of them that they seem merely pointless and dull.

The fault of such books is that as soon as these incidents cease to be exciting or pseudodramatic and the facts they report cease to be topical, the basic failure of the writer to find something important to say and to say it significantly begins to show through. Deprived of sex, drinking, and suicide, *That Winter* is deprived not only of the elements which might have allowed it to pass as a novel but of the elements which might have made it good journalism. A novel expands symbolically the world it presents; good journalism makes good copy of the world it presents. *That Winter* does neither: its characters and situations have not been expanded beyond themselves and they have not been made interesting enough for even cursory mention in tomorrow's headlines.

Homosexuality and racial conflict seem to be the only discoveries which the new writers have been able to make so far in the area of unexploited subject matter; and they are promising discoveries to the extent that they have served to replace the old subjects as sources of potential melodrama. If the vein of public response to novels of ordinary lust and violence has about run dry, it has been possible for the novels of homosexuality and racial conflict to set it coursing again, this time on a slightly different level and through different channels.

Both subjects are excellently suited to a time when writers have lost almost all contact with their audiences and been unable to find dramatic material in the normal situations of life. Homosexuality, like ordinary sex in the twenties, carries with it such vast potentialities for shock, strikes so deeply into the obscure hatreds and secret yearnings of the human mind, that the writer is assured that at least on that level he will be able to reach an audience. Besides, his subject is likely to be dramatic in itself. The homosexual, like the Negro and the Jew to a lesser degree, is a man in conflict with his environment, a tragic figure fighting for life against overwhelming odds. As an outcast, he affords the writer a perspective from which the evils of society can be observed and condemned. He is thus an ideal subject, one that is practically guaranteed not only to reach an audience but to attain the widest possible significance as a symbol.

Unfortunately, most of the novels of homosexuality have not been successful as novels. Too many of them come through simply as social tracts, and their authors have been too content to let the sensational values of their material replace the literary values which, under other circumstances, they might have struggled to achieve. Gore Vidal's *The City and the Pillar,* for example, was purely a social document that was read because it had all the qualities of lurid journalism and not because it showed the craft and insight of an artist. Ward Thomas's *Stranger in the Land*, a very similar book, had almost nothing to recommend it except the homosexuality with which it dealt. Yet up until recently it too was being read, and Thomas may well achieve a stature in the popular mind that will be wholly incommensurate with his talents as he has so far demonstrated them.

The main defect of both these novels, as of most of the others of their kind, is that their characters quickly recede into types rather than expand into symbols. The young homosexual is always and only the homosexual: the other qualities which he might be expected to have and which might have made him human have been sacrificed to the one quality which the author wishes him to represent. In the case of Vidal's Jim Willard in *The City and the Pillar* we know only one real fact about him, and he is presented as having only one real motive—the desire to renew an adolescent homosexual love affair. He is forced into such an infernal consistency that from the first chapter of his story to the last we are aware, in every detail of the narrative, of the exact outcome. Nothing can possibly change that outcome, for Willard is a static figure, a lifeless puppet manipulated by Vidal only at such times and in such ways as will best emphasize the product he has been created to sell.

A strong preoccupation with homosexuality as a literary theme runs through nearly all the novels the young writers have produced, and it has become one of their most distinguishing characteristics as well as the most curious. When it is not part of the central theme of their books—as it is in *The City and the Pillar, Stranger in the Land, A Long Day's Dying,* and *Other Voices, Other Rooms*—a novel of pure homosexual fantasy—it appears as a subsidiary theme. *The End of My Life* contains one character who is destroyed by homosexual tendencies. A distinct but submerged homosexual tension exists between Lieutenant Hearn and General Cummings in *The Naked and the Dead;* and both of John Horne Burns's novels, *The Gallery* and *Lucifer with a Book*, are often obsessively concerned with homosexual types and situations. When one considers that the authors of these books make up almost the entire younger literary group, such a preoccupation becomes interesting indeed.

One explanation is, as I have already shown, that the homosexual is one of the last remaining tragic types. His dilemma, like that of the Negro and the Jew, provides a conflict which is easily presentable in fiction and which can be made to symbolize the larger conflicts of modern man. But this hardly seems adequate to explain the recurrence of the theme in the novels of Gore Vidal, the intense narcissism and sexual symbolism in all of Truman Capote's work, or the coy posturing and giggliness just behind so much of what John Horne Burns writes. Their preoccupation with the theme is such that it seems to preclude their coming to grips with whole areas of normal emotion. Vidal has not yet created a single convincing female character. His women are either mother types, sister types, or men dressed up as women. Capote's Idabel is more grotesquely masculine than she is feminine. Burns's women are often feminine enough, but they are usually simply lust objects for men, and they are seldom introduced at all unless they are intended to fulfill some sexual function.

The importance of homosexuality in the development of a writer is always difficult to determine. At its best it is probably no more crippling than a strong taste for women or dry martinis. It may even be beneficial insofar as it frees the writer from the dangers of premature domesticity and enables him to go on having fresh emotional experience long after his more normal contemporaries have settled into a comfortable emotional fog. But the homosexual experience is of one special kind, it can develop in only one direction, and it can never take the place of the whole range of human experience which the writer must know intimately if he is to be great. Sooner or later it forces him away from the center to the outer edges of the common life of his society where he is almost sure to become a mere grotesque, a parasite, or a clown. The homosexual talent is nearly always a precocious talent, but it must necessarily be a narrow one, subject to all the ills of chronic excitation and threatened always with an end too often bitter and tragic.

Since the end of the war there has been scarcely a serious novel produced which has not at least touched on the dilemma of the Negro or the Jew in modern society, whether in the fascist circumstances of war or the mistrustful atmosphere of dubious peace. Yet of all the novels that have attempted to deal with the problem of race not one has been completely successful as dramatic literature nor fully escaped the weaknesses which have inhered in the novel of homosexuality.

Like all special social problems, the Negro and the Jew will be plausible in fiction only so long as they are conceived and portrayed within the limits of their specialness. They may have great capacity to symbolize the entire human dilemma, but they cannot be effective if, in terms of action, they are made to usurp or replace that dilemma. Within a novel their problem must occupy the subsidiary position it occupies in life, and it must not be detached from the other problems with which the novelist must be concerned if he wishes to give a balanced interpretation of life. This is another way of saying that the Negro or the Jew, like the homosexual, is usable to the novelist in so far as he is allowed to preserve his humanity: his uniqueness as an individual must not be sacrificed to his universality as a type.

Yet the Jewish character in three of the new novels of the war and the aftermath—*The Naked and the Dead, The Young Lions,* and *That Winter*—is distinguished by his Jewishness only; and in the last two novels, that one quality so distorts the authors' perspective that it forces the character to act in a way that is inconsistent with reality and with human nature.

Shaw in *The Young Lions* was apparently able to see Noah Ackerman as simply a symbol of Jewish fortitude and loyalty. He was required, therefore, to endow him with only those virtues and to place him in only such situations as would demonstrate them effectively. But after surviving the first of his ordeals—a series of brutal beatings given him by the most powerful members of his army unit—Ackerman emerges as a creature of such incredible fortitude that one can no longer believe him possible. He has, in fact, ceased to exist as human in the midst of that ordeal and become the

godlike champion of his race. And when, toward the end of
the book, he is made to act at considerable personal risk out
of great loyalty to a friend, and the friendship, as it has been
portrayed, does not warrant such action, one is finally convinced that Shaw's Ackerman, like Vidal's Jim Willard, is
simply a puppet figure designed to function solely as an allegorical device.

Lew in *That Winter* is seen entirely in terms of his conflict
with the forces of racial prejudice. He is rushed on the stage
only when those forces are in play and he is rushed off into
the wings the moment the scene shifts. His sole purpose is to
belabor the point that racial discrimination is a bad thing, a
point Miller might have made more convincingly if he had
written an essay about it. But the real trouble with Lew is
that in making his point he makes no other. The man he
might possibly be is perpetually obscured by the type he is.
His quarrel with his fiancée, his attempt to change his name,
his final decision to face his problem and return to his father's business are all stereotypes in the history of the cardboard Jew. And as he struggles through them, as an actor
struggles through a part he hates, it is as if he were growing
increasingly bored with his own triteness.

It is probable that racial conflict and homosexuality will be
imperfectly presented in fiction so long as writers go on attempting, through journalistic rather than symbolic means, to
make them something more than they are. The truth is that
at the moment and on the purely factual level they remain
simply minor issues. They cannot, therefore, be other than
minor subjects for a kind of writing which operates only on
that level; and they will cease to be usable altogether as soon
as the public tires of them or ceases to find them shocking.
The new writers have not yet discovered subjects which are
as central to the meaning of this age as despair and the sense
of loss were to the twenties. Until they do, it cannot be said
that they have really discovered this age at all.

By technique we ordinarily mean the writer's instrument for
discovering his subject matter. The best technique will be the
one which discovers a given subject matter the most thoroughly, which illuminates and makes meaningful the greatest
area of raw material through which the writer moves in his
search for meaning. Raw material cannot be subject matter
until it is illuminated by technique, just as crude ore is not

gold until it is illuminated by the miner's lamp. But it is possible for writers gifted with an acute sense of language to exploit the devices of technique without illumination or discovery and to make technique serve as a compensation for the lack of subject matter at a time when they are in doubt as to what their true subject matter is.

At least three of the new writers—Truman Capote, John Horne Burns, and Frederick Buechner—have elaborated their techniques to a degree that is in excess of the demands of their raw material. It is as if, in their confusion before the exact implications of that material, they had tried to create a false reality of words alone that would give it an appearance of life and truth which it did not by itself possess. They have dealt with a thin substance and managed to make it rich by perfecting their manner of presenting it; and in the process they have made the obvious obscure and the familiar overly strange.

The real world behind the nightmare which Capote gives us has been refined almost completely out of existence. Where in successful ironic fiction—such as Kafka's—and in successful caricature—such as Abner Dean's—the real qualities of the thing commented upon are constantly heightened and enriched by the outlandish manner in which the artist presents them, in Capote the outlandish and grotesque stand alone. They do not refer back to models in the reality we know, nor does their validity depend upon an innate satiric or ironic comment. Joel, the central figure in *Other Voices, Other Rooms,* is neither a boy nor a caricature of a boy. He is a creation entirely of Capote's talent for the grotesque, and is what he is entirely because Capote invented him in a burst of pure technique and not because Capote perceived his original in life and evolved the technique that would best express him. Cousin Randolph, Joel's father, Idabel, and Miss Wisteria are similarly creatures who have meaning only within the context which Capote invented for them. They die the moment the eye is lifted from the page. They haunt some secret horror chamber of Capote's mind where their distortion is sufficient unto itself but not to us.

In John Horne Burns's second novel, *Lucifer with a Book,* pure technique is made to cover the vacancy left by the disappearance of the kind of subject matter which Burns discovered through *The Gallery.* In that book he evolved a technique suitable to the immense store of material at his command, but in the second the technique alone has been inherited, and one can watch it being cast frantically about in search for something important enough for it to say.

The result of the failure of this search is that the world of *Lucifer with a Book* is a world of invented significance. It is puffed up to size by the strength of Burns's passion and anger and not by the strength of the conditions it presents to evoke passion and anger. We are faced throughout with the brilliant spectacle of Burns in the act of being bitter, but it is part of the failure that we are not sufficiently aroused to join him. This is mostly because his characters have been exaggerated to a point where their humanity becomes grotesqueness and their every act an hallucination and not a burlesque of life.

Mr. Pilkey, his son Herman, the son's wife—Nydia, Philbrick Grimes, Guy Madison, Betty Blanchard, and Mrs. Launcelot Miller, the woman with the corncob pipe, are all monstrous abstractions who have lost their real-life counterparts. What they say and do is justified only because Burns tells us it is. Herman openly fondles Nydia's breasts at a public gathering, and the act, instead of illuminating Herman's character, merely impresses us with his implausibility. Mrs. Launcelot Miller's pipe is significant only because she smokes it. What Mrs. Miller is to the pipe or the pipe to Mrs. Miller we do not know, any more than we know what Guy Madison and Betty Blanchard are to each other. Ostensibly they enjoy being together in bed, but the situation is at once complicated by the fact that up to the introduction of Betty we have been subjected to a number of Hudson's reminiscences on past love partners whose sex is left in considerable doubt.

The work of both Capote and Burns suffers from their effort to give it freshness through idiosyncrasy and from their tendency to confuse idiosyncrasy and life. They have strained every nerve to keep from being trite and, in the process, they have committed the opposite crime of excessive uniqueness. With a suitable and discoverable subject matter, a set of values which they could make the basis of their work, they would not need to strain so hard. But it is part of their dilemma that, lacking those values, they must continually seek a substitute in sheer technical display. The way of attempted affirmation, the way of journalism, and the way of homosexuality and race are also part of that dilemma. They are ways of compensation and not of solution. They serve for a little while as frames through which the chaos may be ordered, and, as such, they afford the new writers one last chance to have their say in a time when all writers, both young and old, are working under an immense compulsion to be silent.

1951

NOTE: Aldridge responded to critics and further developed the terms discussed in this essay in: "Manners and Values" (*Partisan Review*, May–June 1952), and "The Heresy of Literary Manners" in his book *In Search of Heresy*. [M. K.]

American fiction and american values

WILLIAM BARRETT

SUPPOSE we approach the literary production in America during the last decade in a thoroughly American spirit. As Americans we know that the problem of production involves such factors as labor, capital investment, energy, brains, and the mastery of technique, and that success in production is nothing but the product of all these quantities together. If we carry through this kind of calculation for our literary enterprise, we should be startled to think that America is not now producing the greatest body of literature in the history of the human race. Certainly, there are now more typewriters tapping, more paper soiled by expectant writers, more brains cudgeled and sweat poured; more writing courses, writing conferences, writing fellowships, critical symposia, critical schools, and critical organs; more money made, spent, or lost from writing or matter that resembles writing than at any time in the past. Reflect on all these varied details in our pursuit, aid, and abetment of literature; realize thus that we Americans expend more energy in the production of literary works than did Periclean Greece, Elizabethan England, or nineteenth-century Russia; and then reflect that within these past ten years America has not produced an *Oedipus*, a *Hamlet*, or a *Brothers Karamazov*. This must be a very painful and embarrassing situation to all Americans whose patriotism is not self-deception, and it calls for a serious effort at explanation.

There are probably many reasons for this literary failure.

Some of these we have been discussing for a long time, almost *ad nauseam:* the position of the writer in American society, the newness of our culture and its lack of tradition, the morass of mass culture, and all the other sad and true things that [readers] must be tired of hearing by this time. It is time we moved on to something deeper. No doubt, one fact to balance our literary bookkeeping above is that not all this prodigious quantity of energy currently expended in America is directed toward the real thing. Our mass media consume millions of words daily, which nobody but a few misguided hacks would think of preserving in books. This distinction between writing and literature, however, becomes somewhat obscured in some of the more pretentious efforts where the writer has been able to create a new and ambiguous literary façade: thus a novel a few years back, *The Young Lions* by Irwin Shaw, covers a great sweep of canvas and professes to deal with some major themes in modern life, but in substance is so slick and spurious that we have in it an example of something new in literary history, a kind of make-believe of serious literature. Since America places such a premium upon "know-how" and technique, much energy and real accomplishment goes into producing the efficient surface of good writing, and a great number of agile brains are consumed in this kind of thing, in journalism and books, without having the time to worry whether the substance behind the surface even exists, so that we call the thing literature only for lack of another name. But facts like these only partially explain our ultimate literary shortcomings. However new our circumstances, writers in the past were often alienated, at odds with their society or seduced by it, suffered from debts, poverty and publishers. Life, when urgent and quick in the writer, finds a way of getting over material hindrances. The facts compel us to recognize a deeper cause: that American life itself in this period tends away from the emotional and organic depths out of which the greatest literature has sprung. This generalization bites off a great deal, I am aware; and the rest of what I have to say here must be by way of documenting and qualifying it.

If in his *After the Lost Generation,* Mr. John W. Aldridge had begun with some such line of reasoning as the above, his book would have made much better sense, since the unspoken emotional premise behind his whole argument is a rage of disappointment that a large, vital, and industrious country

like the United States is not now producing the great literature that, from all purely rational considerations, we should
expect of it. The book attempts to define the present post-war
literary generation by a roundup of some of its novelists:
Norman Mailer, Irwin Shaw (for his war novel, *The Young
Lions*), Burns, Hayes, Merle Miller, Capote, Vidal, Paul
Bowles. Frederick Buechner, and others. It may be that Aldridge has moved a little too fast in trying to sum up a generation before it has really got under weigh, but in America
these days we travel at great speed, and in intellectual matters
too. The American, so far as he is conscious, is engaged everywhere in asking himself who he is; and one sign of our
extraordinary self-consciousness as a nation is that we have
produced so many books of literary introspection like this
one during the past few years. Such books can be useful, and
most of them have been genuine in that they have come of a
deep-felt sense that we Americans do not yet have enough
past to be definite to ourselves; and if they have sometimes
been spurious in surrendering to the illusion that this past
could be conjured up at will and in a hurry, by talk rather
than the arduous processes of life itself, we have on the other
hand to remember that no tradition is ever built without all
the talk and thought and introspection necessary to define
it. . . .

Aldridge's thesis is that the fiction of the present literary
generation suffers from an essential nihilism: since the writer
no longer shares with his readers the assumption of a stable
set of values, he has come, out of this state of spiritual deprivation, to portray the life around him as futile and meaningless. This current nihilism has its roots in the revolt of the
original Lost Generation after the First World War, whose
theme and prayer might very well have been that beautiful
invocation of Nothingness by the waiter in Hemingway's
story "A Clean Well-Lighted Place"; and, accordingly, Aldridge sets the stage by a critical account of the three novelists
of the first Lost Generation—Hemingway, Fitzgerald, and
Dos Passos—who were the literary fathers of the present. But
the despair of the twenties was considerably different from
what we have now, for their revolt was a passion to the Lost
Generation, while that of the present (if we judge from their
fiction) is so tame, dispirited, or disorganized that it too has
lost its meaning. Here and there Aldridge writes as if he were
berating a group of delinquent writers, . . . but on the whole
he makes no bones about the fact that his accusation incrimi-

nates the whole nation: *"The best literature in America will continue to be negative so long as the country's values are such that no writer of honesty or insight can possibly take them seriously."*

Now, a lack of values in a writer may be an entirely superfluous diagnosis in a case of plain artistic incompetence, and some of Aldridge's diatribe might have been more accurately directed against downright bad writing. Before grappling, then, with the thorny question of what values did or did not corrupt the past decade, we ought to be sure about its proper literary rating. If we are to weigh the forties by the twenties, the forties will certainly be found wanting—nobody dissents from this judgment, and so nobody seems to raise the necessary qualifications that complicate this comparison. The three most memorable novels to emerge from the last war seem to be: *The Naked and the Dead,* Burns's *The Gallery,* and James Jones's *From Here to Eternity* (which is rightly considered a war book since its subject matter is military and it closes with the bombing of Pearl Harbor). This may look like a pretty thin showing for a whole generation of writers, but one or two things have to be said in its favor in relation to the older decade. Is it altogether certain, for example, that *The Naked and the Dead* is inferior to Dos Passos' *Three Soldiers*? In the twenties Hemingway brought to the language of the novel a style whose originality no contemporary can match; yet we should not forget that Hemingway's deliberate stylization is also a sterilization of experience, a refinement away from the complexity of emotion. *The Sun Also Rises* is a tight formal work of art, while John Horne Burns's *The Gallery* is uneven and in many ways a failure; yet Burns is attempting to react to a far more complex experience of Europe, and of the American confrontation of Europe during the war, than Hemingway ever permitted himself to deal with. Beside Hemingway's mastery of a style, *From Here to Eternity* is a great loose sprawl of stenography; yet Jones has the remarkable virtues of the primitive and naive, so that through all his diffuseness and immaturity there break certain types of American character and vitality that never enter Hemingway's stylized world.

But with all such qualifications made, the fact remains that the present generation has produced a literature below the level of the twenties and far below what should be expected of 150 million people living in the most prosperous country in the history of the world. No doubt, a more adequate selec-

tion of writers by Aldridge would have made the period look
better, but our dissatisfaction with its artistic output would
remain. Indeed, some of the books he deals with hardly seem
worth being remembered by any lengthy critical comment,
except by a critic hell-bent to produce a lengthy critical comment on any available material.

All of which brings us back to our initial question: Why
are Americans not writing better books? At this point Aldridge introduces the word "values" in token of explanation.
To be sure, he remains very vague about the values he intends, but this vagueness is typical of most literary and philosophical discussion of the subject: "values" are an easy halt-
ing place, sometimes a camouflage, for what lies beyond
them. The highest values may be held in a lifeless and stifling
way (as the values of religion by T. S. Eliot); on the other
hand, some great artistic periods have been decadent in their
morality, and nihilism itself, passionately held, has produced
some great fruits. Beyond values there lies the depth of the
human commitment and choice from which the values come.
The trouble with a novel like Shaw's *The Young Lions,* to
revert to our previous example, is that it has, not none, but
too many and too obvious values: those of a facile liberalism
held from the top of the head and thoroughly false to life.
What matters in the end, both for values and for art, is the
depth of life as a felt thing; and it is this, and not some intellectual explanation, that is lost whenever we say that the
meaning of life has been lost. And if our young writers now
experience the life around them as meaningless, it is this
meaning they have lost.

Nowadays in America we have new ways of going at this
age-old problem of the meaning of life. Some time last year
the *Daily News* published in its column "The Inquiring Pho-
tographer" an interview in which six people encountered on
the streets of New York City were asked, "What are you living for?" This interview was more instructive about modern
life and the question of values than any academic article
published in the philosophical journals for that year. The
confusion of the answers was to be expected; more remarkable was the willingness of these Americans to live in open
confrontation of the question and their confusion about it;
and perhaps most remarkable of all that the question itself
should be asked with such open-air and democratic directness
in the pages of the *Daily News.* A hundred or a few hundred
years ago nobody could have been stopped on the streets for

this purpose: ordinary people did not worry in public about the meaning of life so long as they knew the answer handed to them by acknowledged authority; but today in America, if the *Daily News* is evidence, we have become so radically committed to democracy that each individual is expected to live through this question for himself. This is the key to our situation in America: the apparent absence of values is in fact an immense groping, often confused and at odds with itself and even antihumanistic in its actual directions, but in its intentions real and positive nevertheless.

Obviously, then, it is grappling with Proteus to try to sum up American values in any simple formula. The question divides and subdivides again, and has almost to be examined separately at each level of our society.

Beginning from the bottom, what we find persistently remarkable about our current fiction is that the affirmative values are usually found in the characters of the lower classes. The roots of this lie deep in the American past, but here we need not go back beyond Faulkner, in whom the dumb and the inarticulate and the primitive are almost always the characters with the deepest and most positive adherence to life. James Jones's enlisted men are *lumpen* characters, but they are also bursting with a positive energy of life, in comparison with which the officers and their middle-class wives appear decadent and corrupt. Mailer's G.I.'s, however coarsened and degraded by their experience, are vital and real human beings; but when Mailer wants to create a character of some intellectual awareness, in whom values would be held in conscience and self-consciousness, he can only give us his Lieutenant Hearn, a futile and drifting nursling of the middle class with a vacuum at his heart. In American fiction the values seem to become uncertain when they are to be held consciously; and therefore the educated middle classes appear as the social stratum where nihilism has made its chief inroads.

Our middle class has become such a fluid and uncertain thing that we have, significantly, to go back beyond the present generation, for an accurate novelist of the social manners of this class: J. P. Marquand is the nearest thing we have to such a social novelist, and his novels make up a prolonged and ambiguous lament over the death of the heart of our older middle class. The Marquand bourgeoisie, while still attached to them, finds the old ideals of its class harder to justify amid the scramble of modern life: against the amoral,

hard-driving, and cosmopolitan life of New York the code of
old New England looks very paradoxical indeed. Within the
limits of his talent and material, Marquand is one of the best
observers we have, and the historical fact implicit in his novels is confirmed by such recent social analyses as those of
David Riesman. From old Boston to New York (substitute
any other high-strung urban area, like Washington and Hollywood)—such is the spiritual journey of the American middle
class, in the course of which this class may have become
more clever and sophisticated, but also more brittle, violent,
hard-drinking, neurotic, and nihilistic.

New York, of course, is the nightmare from which we are
all trying to awaken. But New York is also only America become thoroughly urban, high-strung, and nakedly honest
about the most powerful drives in American life. Here the
middle class as a moral entity disappears into the middle-in-
come bracket, there being nothing left to characterize a class
but its money, and the only value universally discernible is
that of being desperately on the make. New York as a whole
has yet to be done in fiction, it is too many worlds at once;
and possibly the emptiest novel during the last decade was
Merle Miller's *That Winter,* which dealt with the drinking,
fornication, and petty despair of the young careerists in midtown Manhattan. There would be no point at all in remembering Miller's novel except that it illustrates its period and
place, and Aldridge so memorializes it as one of the plainest
statements of general futility. But the real message of the
book is something quite different from this: Miller's values
are really the values of making a career in midtown, but he
lies about them because, when he sits down to write, he re-
members serious literature with its older human norms and so
must condemn the lives in his novel as futile. For the thousands of Americans who come every year to New York to
take their chances in Miller's world, success, sociability, and
drinking are the values that American life, stripped of all hypocrisy, provides; and these are no moral monsters, but people we all know, quite typical Americans who take life very
much as they find it, and unless any of them crack up, most of them
survive without ever needing any other values; as America itself, unless it cracks, may yet succeed in doing.

In the midst of this strange but very representative island
of American civilization we come upon *The New Yorker,* a
magazine of many paradoxes, whose fiction Aldridge scores
as one of the most deleterious literary influences of our time.

However that may be, this fiction does tell its own truth about American life. One of the paradoxes of *The New Yorker* is that it has very little relation to the city from which it takes its name: fifty-two weeks a year this magazine, struggling bravely to affirm its gentle values of urbanity, good manners, and civilized good humor against the roaring life of New York, resembles a man in a Brooks Brothers suit walking into the teeth of a gale. And every week, alongside the brave editorial affirmations, in the hard little cameos of stories we meet the faceless and nameless people who are earning more than ten thousand dollars a year and dying of emotional anemia: snapshots of the nihilism of a middle class bored with itself, tepid in its emotions, fighting the uncertain battle of cocktail parties, divorces, and fragile family memories. One is tempted to say that the stories in *The New Yorker* show what the values of *The New Yorker* become when exposed to the rough edges of American life.

Thus wherever they crop up in recent literature, as in Marquand and *The New Yorker*, the traditional norms appear to be at bay. This appearance, is, I believe, a reality, our fiction is social fact, and for the very simple reason that the real values of America, whether or not Americans themselves always know it, represent a radical break with tradition. America may not yet be an entirely new civilization, but it contains in itself the seeds of such, a fact which most of us recognize only intermittently and usually when we are in conflict with the new life of this continent because of some more traditional background. It is only natural then that Americans are confused about their values and that our writers stammer in trying to express this confusion. Though this situation is new, something like it has occurred in the past, and a relevant comparison can be made with the position of the Russian writers of the last century: they too were unsure of themselves in a culture that they felt as raw and unformed in relation to the developed cultures of Western Europe, and they too groped for an identity, in dreadful haste to assimilate Western Europe and in even more dreadful conflict about the assimilation. And they produced Tolstoy and Dostoevsky. We can hardly expect a Tolstoy or Dostoevsky in America when the deepest experience of these writers is not an organic and recognized part of American life: our extrovert civilization has developed other means of adjusting to life without their spiritual struggles. We have the crack-up and the breakdown, neurosis and maladjustment, but we do not have the tragic sense of life. Of course, a society does not exist in order to produce a literature, and the American sense of life may yet succeed in founding a civilization superior in many ways to anything in the past: I do not argue these matters, but only that from what we have so far been able to see the literature of such a new civilization is not likely to be able to compete in interest with that of the past. The American sense of life, however, being new, may very well develop into something quite different from what we know; it may not even survive: remember that America in this respect merely continues along the path on which Europe itself was headed until the upheavals of recent history brought it face to face with the abysses of human existence that a facile rationalism had let itself forget.

Something like this, I imagine, was what Aldridge was trying to get at in his book, and his failure to get it right may be in good part due to the fact that he makes so much of his case turn about the bad little boys of our literature—Capote, Vidal, Bowles, Merle Miller—whose adolescent and neurotic material never provides the slightest inkling of all the good and solid American lives being lived all over the nation. Now, it is just these decent and solid American lives that I wish to place in question here, so far as the purposes of literature are concerned; and if I were to choose a single book to support my thesis, it would be a novel like James Gould Cozzens' *Guard of Honor* . . . , a work "positive" enough in its values to win the acclaim of even so staunch a guardian of the public virtues as Bernard De Voto. Cozzens shows an amazingly competent grasp of the machinery of fiction, his story runs ahead smoothly on very little fuel, and his characters are recognizably real Americans that we have all met one time or another in our lives. But the book will have no permanent place in our literature: it lacks depth, its characters are the kind of decent and struggling Americans whose perplexities about life are only practical problems to be solved, while the ultimate or primitive things, never articulated and faced, are hardly more than faint shadows in the background.

Sex may be the deepest (it is certainly the most sensational) subject in our novels that has to do with values. In its sexual codes the America of 1950 is certainly a different civilization from the America of 1900. Our novels now deal with sex frankly as a matter of course; and such frankness is hardly a matter of mere literary convention, but a part of the changed *mores,* a consequence of the deeper fact that sexual freedom itself is now taken for granted and therefore cannot be for us the thrill that it was, in its newness, for the original Lost Generation of the twenties. This may be why sex in some quarters has lost its value, so that we encounter the interesting phenomenon of *nihilism in the bedroom*: a novel like *Anna Karenina,* for example, could hardly be written nowadays; if we were to have a tragedy of sex at all, it could not be in this form, for all the rules of the game have changed. One profound sign of this devaluation of sex is the figure of the homosexual, as the sexual grotesque, looming very large in our recent literature. But one need not go to homosexual fiction to discover that the relation between man and woman does not play the same part in life it once did: *From Here to Eternity* is in this respect a perfectly indicative book; if Jones is an adolescent about women, his adolescence is nevertheless very American, and there is more than private meaning in the fact that the significant human relations in his novel are between man and man, those between man and woman being in the long run much less important for either party concerned. But here again we are grappling with Proteus when we try to sum up American values, for part of our sexual unrest is that we have higher human ambitions for sex than Europe ever realized; and amid all the desperate experimentation, here and there one discerns signs of something positive. The trouble, for ourselves and our novelists, is that the rules have been so radically changed that nobody seems to know what they are, and most of us have to discover our own only after considerable anguish and instability.

With all these changes going on, we should not be surprised that the voice of traditionalism has become so loud in the last decade. Perhaps there is no clearer sign of the possibilities of a radical break with the past inherent in our civilization: when change seems too threatening, some people have to protect themselves from becoming giddy by clinging to the ready-made structures of the past. Hence the coteries of traditionalist intellectuals now proliferate all over the country, and the shadow of T. S. Eliot is long upon the land. The traditionalists have been valuable against some of the shallower aspects of American life, but they would be more valuable still if their devotion to tradition were not always a one-sided adherence to tradition already made rather than one in the process of making itself. Since they cut themselves off thus from the possibilities of American development, their writings show progressively less relation to the realities of life in this country. American civilization, in some of its tendencies, may exist in total error; that is the conviction held here too; but we have to temper this judgment by the memory that every civilization in the past existed in its own form of falsehood. To sum up: what has happened in America is that democracy has become, more than a mere political form, a positive *ethos* permeating the whole society, from the bottom up, and therefore has also come to involve a bold experimentation with life itself and with the traditional human norms in which the life of the past sought to contain itself. To avoid historical short-sightedness, we have to remember that the breakdown in traditional norms we are currently living through was something brewing for a very long time within European civilization itself, to become acute in the period 1870 to 1939. All this suggests that the word *breakdown*, though it has such menacing overtones, may also denote the clearing away of a rigid structure that was doomed to death anyway. As a civilization, we are in midpassage; and what we Americans will be like when we have lived through our tragedy, nobody can predict now.

1951

The argument reinvigorated

NORMAN MAILER

ASSUME I am a lecturer in the fields of Fellowship surrounding Literature (American) and am trying to draw some grand design in twenty minutes on a talk devoted to "The Dynamic of American Letters." Knowing attention is iron for the blood of a Fellow, I will not be so foolish as to perish without a look at the topical and the interesting. No, I will use "The Dynamic of American Letters" as preparation for a lightning discussion of Herzog and Terry Southern, with a coda on the art of the absurd. Let me then have my first sentence as lecturer: "There has been a war at the center of American letters for a long time." That is not so poor. The look of absolute comprehension on the face of the audience encourages the lecturer to go on.

The war began as a class war; an upper-middle class looked for a development of its taste, a definition of its manners, a refinement of itself to prepare a shift to the aristocratic; that was its private demand upon culture. That demand is still being made by a magazine called *The New Yorker*. This upper-class development of literature was invaded a long time ago, however, back at the cusp of the century, by a counterliterature whose roots were found in poverty, industrial society, and the emergence of new class. It was a literature which grappled with a peculiarly American phenomenon—a tendency of American society to alter more rapidly than the ability of its artists to record that change. Now, of course, one might go back two thousand years into

China to find a society which did not alter more rapidly than its culture, but the American phenomenon had to do with the very rate of acceleration. The order of magnitude in this rate had shifted. It was as if everything changed ten times as fast in America, and this made for extraordinary difficulty in creating a literature. The sound, sensible, morally stout delineation of society which one found in Tolstoy and Balzac and Zola, in Thackeray and in Trollope, had become impossible. The American novelist of manners had to content himself with manners—he could not put a convincing servant into his work, and certainly not a workingman, because they were moving themselves in one generation out from the pantry into the morning dress of the lady in the parlor and up from the foundry to the master of the factory. The novelist of manners could not go near these matters—they promised to take over all of his book. So the job was left to Howells, Stephen Crane, to Dreiser, and in lesser degree to such writers as Norris, Jack London, Upton Sinclair—let us say it was left to Dreiser. A fundamental irony of American letters had now presented itself. For in opposition to Dreiser was the imperfectly developed countertradition of the genteel. The class which wielded the power which ran America, and the class which most admired that class, banded instinctively together to approve a genteel literature which had little to do with power or the secrets of power. They encouraged a literature about courtship and marriage and love and play and devotion and piety and style, a literature which had to do finally with the excellence of belonging to their own genteel tradition. Thus it was a literature which borrowed the forms of its conduct from European models. The people who were most American by birth, and who had the most to do with managing America, gave themselves a literature which had the least to say about the real phenomena of American life, most particularly the accelerated rate, the awful rate, of growth and anomaly through all of society. That sort of literature and that kind of attempt to explain America was left to the sons of immigrants who, if they were vigorous enough, and fortunate enough to be educated, now had the opportunity to see that America was a phenomenon never before described, indeed never before visible in the record of history. There was something going on in American life which was either grand or horrible or both, but it was going on—at a dizzy rate— and the future glory or doom of the world was not necessarily divorced from it. Dreiser labored like a titan to capture the phenomenon; he became a titan; Thomas Wolfe, his only peer as giant (as the novelist-as-giant), labored also like a titan, but for half as long and died in terror of the gargantuan proportions of the task. Yet each failed in one part of the job. They were able to describe society—Wolfe like the greatest five-year-old who ever lived,[1] an invaluable achievement, and Dreiser like some heroic tragic entrepreneur who has reasoned out through his own fatigue and travail very much how everything works in the iron mills of life, but is damned because he cannot pass on the knowledge to his children. Dreiser and Wolfe were up from the people, and Dreiser particularly came closer to understanding the social machine than any American writer who ever lived, but he paid an unendurable price—he was forced to alienate himself from manner in order to learn the vast amount he learned. Manner insists one learn at a modest rate, that one learn each step with grace before going on to the next. Dreiser was in a huge hurry, he had to learn everything—that was the way he must have felt his mission, so there is nothing of manner in his work; which is to say, nothing of tactics.

If the upper class quite naturally likes a literature which is good for them, a literature at the surface perhaps trivial, but underneath amusing, elucidative, *fortifying,* it is because this kind of literature elaborates and clarifies the details of their life, and thus adjusts their sense of power, their upper-class sense of power, which is invariably lubricated by a sense of detail. So too does that other class of readers in American literature, that huge, loose, all but unassociated congregation of readers—immigrant, proletarian, entrepreneur—wish in turn for a literature which is equally good for them. That is where Dreiser had to fail. He was only half-good for such readers. He taught them strategy as Americans had never gotten it before in a novel. If they were adventurers, he was almost as useful to them as Stendhal was exceptionally useful to a century of French intellectuals who had come to Paris from the provinces. But not quite. Dreiser, finally, is not quite as useful, and the difference is crucial. Because a young adventurer reads a great novel in the unvoiced hope it is a

---

[1] This Argument was delivered, originally, as a talk to The American Studies Association and the M.L.A. This remark brought laughter from the audience. Since I did not wish to insult the memory of Wolfe, it would have been happier and perhaps more accurate to have said: like the greatest fifteen-year-old alive.

grindstone which sharpens his axe sufficiently to smash down doors now locked to him. Dreiser merely located the doors and gave warnings about the secret padlocks and the traps. But he had no grindstone, no manner, no eye for the deadly important manners of the rich, he was obliged to call a rich girl "charming"; he could not make her charming when she spoke, as Fitzgerald could, and so he did not really prepare the army of his readers for what was ahead. His task was doubly difficult—it was required of him to give every upstart fresh strategy and tactics. No less than the secret sociology of society is what is needed by the upstart and that strategy Dreiser gave him. But tactics—the manners of the drawing room, the deaths and lifes of the drawing room, the cocktail party, the glorious tactics of the individual kill—that was all beyond him. Dreiser went blind climbing the mountains of society, so he could not help anyone to see what was directly before him—only what had happened and what was likely to come next.

That was the initial shape of the war, Naturalism versus the Genteel Tradition it has been called, and one might pose Henry James against Dreiser, but James is sufficiently great a writer to violate the generalizations one must make about the novel of manners which must always—precisely because it deals with manners—eschew the overambitious, plus extremes of plot—which James of course did not. So let us say the war was between Dreiser and Edith Wharton, Dreiser all strategy, no tactics; and Wharton all tactics. Marvelous tactics they were—a jewel of a writer and stingy as a parson—she needed no strategy. The upper-class writer had all strategy provided him by the logic of his class. Maybe that is why the war never came to decision, or even to conclusion. No upper-class writer went down into the pits to bring back the manner alive of the change going on *down there,* certainly not Edith Wharton, not James Branch Cabell, of course not, nor Hergesheimer nor even Cather or Glasgow, not Elinor Wylie, no, nor Carl Van Vechten, and no diamond in the rough was ever reshaped by the cutters of Newport. The gap in American letters continued. Upper-class writers like John Dos Passos made brave efforts to go down and get the stuff and never quite got it, mainly in Dos Passos' case because they lacked strategy for the depths—manners may be sufficient to delineate the rich but one needs a vision of society to comprehend the poor, and Dos Passos had only revulsion at injustice, which is ultimately a manner. Some upper-class writers like Fitzgerald turned delicately upon the suppositions of their class, lost all borrowed strategy and were rudderless, were forced therefore to become superb in tactics, but for this reason perhaps a kind of hysteria lived at the center of their work; lower-class writers like Farrell and Steinbeck described whole seas of the uncharted ocean but their characters did not push from one milieu into another, and so the results were more taxonomic than apocalyptic.

Since then the war has shifted. No writer succeeded in doing the single great work which would clarify a nation's vision of itself as Tolstoy had done perhaps with *War and Peace* or *Anna Karenina,* and Stendhal with *The Red and the Black,* no one novel came along which was grand and daring and comprehensive and detailed, able to give sustenance to the adventurer and merriment to the rich, leave compassion in the ice chambers of the upper class and energy as alms for the poor. (Not unless it was *Tropic of Cancer.*) Dreiser came as close as any, and never got close at all, for he could not capture the moment, and no country in history has lived perhaps so much for the moment as America. After his heroic failure American literature was isolated—it was necessary to give courses in American literature to Americans, either because they would not otherwise read it, or because reading it, they could not understand it. It was not quite vital to them, it did not save their lives, make them more ambitious, more moral, more tormented, more audacious, more ready for love, more ready for war, for charity and for invention. No, it tended to puzzle them. The realistic literature had never caught up with the rate of change in American life, indeed it had fallen further and further behind, and the novel gave up any desire to be a creation equal to the phenomenon of the country itself; it settled for being a metaphor. Which is to say that each separate author made a separate peace. He would no longer try to capture America, he would merely try to give life to some microcosm in American life, some metaphor —in the sense that a drop of water is a metaphor of the seas, or a hair of the beast is for some a metaphor of the beast— and in that metaphor he might—if he were very lucky—have it all, rich and poor, strategy and tactics, insight and manner, detail, authority, the works. He would have it all for a particular few. It was just that he was no longer writing about the beast but, as in the case of Hemingway (if we are to take the best of this), about the paw of the beast, or in Faulkner about the dreams of the beast. What a paw and what dreams!

Perhaps they are the two greatest writers America ever had, but they had given up on trying to do it all. Their vision was partial, determinedly so, they saw that as the first condition for trying to be great—that one must not try to save. Not souls, and not the nation. The desire for majesty was the bitch which licked at the literary loins of Hemingway and Faulkner: the country could be damned. Let it take care of itself.

And of course the country did. Just that. It grew by itself. Like a weed and a monster and a beauty and a pig. And the task of explaining America was taken over by Luce magazines. Those few aristocratic novelistic sensibilities which had never seen the task of defining the country as one for them —it was finally most unamusing as a task—grew smaller and smaller and more and more superb. Edith Wharton reappeared as Truman Capote, even more of a jewel, even stingier. Of writers up from the bottom there were numbers: Dreiser's nephews were as far apart as Saul Bellow and James Jones. But the difference between the two kinds of writers had shifted. It had begun to shift somewhere after the Second World War, and the shift had gone a distance. One could not speak at all now of aristocratic writers and novelists whose work was itself the protagonist to carry the writer and his readers through the locks of society; no, the work had long since retreated, the great ambition was gone, and then it was worse, even the metaphor was gone, the paw of the beast and the dreams of the beast, no, literature was down to the earnest novel and the perfect novel, to moral seriousness and Camp. Herzog and Candy had become the protagonists.

Frank Cowperwood once amassed an empire. Herzog, his bastard great-nephew, diddled in the ruins of an intellectual warehouse. Where once the realistic novel cut a swath across the face of society, now its reality was concentrated into moral seriousness. Where the original heroes of naturalism had been active, bold, self-centered, close to tragic, and up to their nostrils in their exertions to advance their own life and force the webs of society, so the hero of moral earnestness, the hero Herzog and the hero Levin in Malamud's *A New Life*, are men who represent the contrary—passive, timid, other-directed, pathetic, up to the nostrils in anguish: the world is stronger than they are; suicide calls.

Malamud's hero is more active than Herzog, he is also more likeable, but these positive qualities keep the case from being so pure. There is a mystery about the reception of *Her-*

zog. For beneath its richness of texture and its wealth of detail, the fact remains: never has a novel been so successful when its hero was so dim. Not one of the critics who adored the book would ever have permitted Herzog to remain an hour in his house. For Herzog was defeated, Herzog was an unoriginal man, Herzog was a fool—not an attractive God-anointed fool like Gimpel the Fool, his direct progenitor, but a sodden fool, overeducated and inept, unable to fight, able to love only when love presented itself as a gift. Herzog was intellectual but not bright, his ideas not original, his style as it appeared in his letters unendurable—it had exactly the leaden-footed sense of phrase which men laden with anxiety and near to going mad put into their communications. Herzog was hopeless. We learned nothing about society from him, not even anything about his life. And he is the only figure in the book. His wives, his mistress, his family, his children, his friends, even the man who cuckolds him are seen on the periphery of a dimming vision. Like all men near to being mad, his attention is within, but the inner attention is without genius. Herzog is dull, he is unendurably dull—he is like all those bright pedagogical types who have a cavity at the center of their brain.

Yet the novel succeeds. There is its mystery. One reads it with compassion. With rare compassion. Bored by Herzog, still there is a secret burning of the heart. One's heart turns over and produces a sorrow. Hardly any books are left to do that.

Of course, Herzog is alive on sufferance. He is a beggar, an extraordinary beggar who fixes you with his eye, his breath, his clothing, his dank near-corrupt presence; he haunts. Something goes on in Herzog's eye. It says: I am debased, I am failed, I am near to rotten, and yet something just as good and loving resides in me as the tenderest part of your childhood. If the prophet Elijah sent me, it is not to make you feel guilt but to weep. Suddenly, Herzog inspires sorrow—touch of alchemy to the book—Herzog is at the center of the modern dilemma. If we do not feel compassion for him, a forceful compassion which sends blood to warm the limbs and the heart, then we are going to be forced to shoot him. Because if Herzog does not arouse your compassion there is no other choice—he is too intolerable a luxury to keep alive in his mediocrity unless he arouses your love. The literary world chose to love him. We were not ready to shoot Herzog. It all seemed too final if we did. Because

then there would be nothing left but Camp, and Camp is the
art of the cannibal, Camp is the art which evolved out of the
bankruptcy of the novel of manners. It is the partial thesis of
these twenty minutes that the pure novel of manners had watered down from *The House of Mirth* to the maudlin middle
reaches of *The Rector of Justin;* had in fact gone all the way
down the pike from *The Ambassadors* to *By Love Possessed.*
So, one does not speak of the novel of manners any longer
—one is obliged to look at the documentary, *In Cold Blood*
—or one is obliged to look at satire. The aristocratic impulse
turned upon itself produced one classic—Terry Southern's
The Magic Christian. Never had distaste for the habits of a
mass mob reached such precision, never did wit falter in its
natural assumption that the idiocies of the mass were attached breath and kiss to the hypocrisies, the weltering gran-
deurs, and the low stupidities of the rich, the American rich.
The aristocratic impulse to define society by evocations of
manner now survived only in the grace of any cannibal sufficiently aristocratic to sup upon his own family. *The Magic
Christian* was a classic of Camp.

Note then: The two impulses in American letters had
failed, the realistic impulse never delivered the novel which
would ignite a nation's consciousness of itself, and the aristocratic impulse clawed at the remaining fabric of a wealthy society it despised and no longer wished to sustain. Like a
Tinguely machine which destroys itself, Camp amused by the
very act of its destruction. Since it was also sentimental, the
artifacts were necrophiliac.

Literature then had failed. The work was done by the movies, by television. The consciousness of the masses and the
culture of the land trudged through endless mud.

The American consciousness in the absence of a great tradition in the novel ended by being developed by the boot-
licking pieties of small-town newspaper editors and small-
town educators, by the worst of organized religion, a formless
force filled with the terrors of all the Christians left to fill the
spaces left by the initial bravery of the frontiersman, and
these latterday Christians were simply not as brave. That was
one component of the mud. The other was the sons of the
immigrants. Many of them hated America, hated it for what
it offered and did not provide, what it revealed of opportunity and what it excluded from real opportunity. The sons of
these immigrants and the sons' sons took over the cities and
began to run them, high up in the air and right down into the

ground, they plucked and they plundered and there was not an American city which did not grow more hideous in the last fifty years. Then they spread out—they put suburbs like blight on the land—and piped mass communications into every home. They were cannibals selling Christianity to Christians, and because they despised the message and mocked at it in their own heart, they succeeded in selling something else, a virus perhaps, and electronic nihilism went through the mass media of America and entered the Christians and they were like to being cannibals, they were a tense and livid people, swallowing their own hate with the tranquilizers and the sex in the commercials, whereas all the early cannibals at the knobs of the mass media made the mistake of passing on their bleak disease and were left now too gentle, too liberal, too programmatic, filled with plans for social welfare, and they looked and talked in Show Biz styles which possessed no style and were generally as unhealthy as Christians who lived in cellars and caves.

Yes, the cannibal sons of the immigrants had become Christians, and the formless form they had evolved for their mass media, the hypocritical empty and tasteless taste of the television arts they beamed across the land encountered the formless form and the all but tasteless taste of the small-town tit-eating cannibal mind at its worst, and the collision produced schizophrenia in the land. Half of America went insane with head colds and medicaments and asthmas and allergies, hospitals and famous surgeons with knives to cut into the plague, welfares and plans and committees and cooperations and boredom, boredom plague deep upon the land; and the other part of America went ape, and the motorcycles began to roar like lions across the land and all the beasts of all the buried history of America turned in their circuit and prepared to slink toward the market place, there to burn the mother's hair and bite the baby to the heart. One thought of America and one thought of aspirin, kitchen commercials, and blood. One thought of Vietnam. And the important art in America became the art of the absurd.

1966

PART TWO

||||||||||||||||||||||||||||||

Society and self

Art and fortune

LIONEL TRILLING

IT is impossible to talk about the novel nowadays without having in our minds the question of whether or not the novel is still a living form. Twenty-five years ago T. S. Eliot said that the novel came to an end with Flaubert and James, and at about the same time Señor Ortega said much the same thing. This opinion is now heard on all sides. It is heard in conversation rather than read in formal discourse, for to insist on the death or moribundity of a great genre is an unhappy task which the critic will naturally avoid if he can, yet the opinion is now an established one and has a very considerable authority. Do we not see its influence in, for example, V. S. Pritchett's recent book, *The Living Novel*? Although Mr. Pritchett is himself a novelist and writes about the novel with the perception that comes of love, and even by the name he gives his book disputes the fact of the novel's death, yet still, despite these tokens of his faith, he deals with the subject under a kind of constraint, as if he had won the right to claim life for the novel only upon condition of not claiming for it much power.

I do not believe that the novel is dead. And yet particular forms of the creative imagination may indeed die—English poetic drama stands as the great witness of the possibility—and there might at this time be an advantage in accepting the proposition as an hypothesis which will lead us to understand under what conditions the novel may live.

If we consent to speak of the novel as dead, three possible

explanations of the fact spring at once to mind. The first is
simply that the genre has been exhausted, worked out in the
way that a lode of ore is worked out—it can no longer yield
a valuable supply of its natural matter. The second explanation is that the novel was developed in response to certain
cultural circumstances which now no longer exist but have
given way to other circumstances which must be met by
other forms of the imagination. The third explanation is that
although the circumstances to which the novel was a response
do still exist we either lack the power to use the form,[1] or no
longer find value in the answers that the novel provides, because the continuing circumstances have entered a phase of
increased intensity.

The first theory was put forward by Ortega in his essay
"Notes on the Novel." It is an explanation which has its clear
limitations, but it is certainly not without its cogency. We have
all had the experience of feeling that some individual work of
art, or some canon of art, or a whole idiom of art, has lost,
temporarily or permanently, its charm and power. Sometimes
we weary of the habitual or half-mechanical devices by which
the artist warms up for his ideas or by which he bridges the
gap between his ideas; this can happen even with Mozart.
Sometimes it is the very essence of the man's thought that
fatigues; we feel that his characteristic insights can too easily
be foreseen and we become too much aware of how they
exist at the expense of blindness to other truths; this can happen even with Dostoevski. And so with an entire genre of art
—there may come a moment when it cannot satisfy one of
our legitimate demands, which is that it shall surprise us.
This demand, and the liability of our artistic interests to
wear out, do not show us to be light-minded. Without them
our use of art would be only ritualistic, or commemorative of
our past experiences; and although there is nothing wrong in
using art for ritual and commemoration, still these are not
the largest uses to which it can be put. Curiosity is as much
an instinct as hunger and love, and curiosity about any particular thing may be satisfied.

Then we must consider that technique has its autonomy
and that it dictates the laws of its own growth. Aristotle

[1] This might seem to beg the cultural question; yet certain technical
abilities do deteriorate or disappear for reasons which although theo-
retically ascertainable are almost beyond practical determination.

speaks of Athenian tragedy as seeking and finding its fulfillment, its entelechy, and it may be that we are interested in
any art only just so long as it is in process of search; that
what moves us is the mysterious energy of quest. At a certain
point in the development of a genre, the practitioner looks
back and sees all that has been done by others before him
and knows that no ordinary effort can surpass or even match
it; ordinary effort can only repeat. It is at this point that, as
Ortega says, we get the isolated extraordinary effort which
transcends the tradition and brings it to an end. This, no
doubt, is what people mean when they speak of Joyce and
Proust bringing the novel to its grave.

Here is the case, as strongly as I can put it, for the idea
that a genre can exhaust itself simply by following the laws
of its own development. As an explanation of the death of
the novel it does not sufficiently exfoliate or sufficiently connect with the world. It can by no means be ignored, but of
itself it cannot give an adequate answer to our question.

TWO

So we must now regard the novel as an art form contrived to
do a certain kind of work, its existence conditioned by the
nature of that work. In another essay [2] I undertook to say
what the work of the novel was—I said that it was the investigation of reality and illusion. Of course the novel does not
differ in this from all other highly developed literary forms; it
differs, however, in at least one significant respect, that it
deals with reality and illusion in relation to questions of social class, which in relatively recent times are bound up with
money.

In Western civilization the idea of money exercises a great
fascination—it is the fascination of an actual thing which has
attained a metaphysical ideality or of a metaphysical entity
which has attained actual existence. Spirits and ghosts are
beings in such a middling state of existence; and money is
both real and not real, like a spook. We invented money and
we use it, yet we cannot either understand its laws or control
its actions. It has a life of its own which it properly should
not have; Karl Marx speaks with a kind of horror of its inde-

2 "Manners, Morals, and the Novel."

cent power to reproduce, as if, he says, love were working in
its body. It is impious, being critical of existent social realities, and it has the effect of lessening their degree of reality.
The social reality upon which it has its most devastating effect
is of course that of class. And class itself is a social fact
which, whenever it is brought into question, has like money a
remarkable intimacy with metaphysics and the theory of
knowledge—I have suggested how for Shakespeare any derangement of social classes seems always to imply a derangement of the senses in madness or dream, some elaborate joke
about the nature of reality. This great joke is the matter of
the book which we acknowledge as the ancestor of the modern novel, *Don Quixote;* and indeed no great novel exists
which does not have the joke at its very heart.

In the essay to which I refer I also said that, in dealing
with the questions of illusion and reality which were raised
by the ideas of money and class, the novel characteristically
relied upon an exhaustive exploitation of manners. Although
I tried to give a sufficiently strong and complicated meaning
to the word *manners,* I gather that my merely having used
the word, or perhaps my having used it in a context that
questioned certain political assumptions of a pious sort, has
led to the belief that I am interested in establishing a new
genteel tradition in criticism and fiction. Where misunderstand-
ing serves others as an advantage, one is helpless to make
oneself understood; yet to guard as well as I can against this
imputation, I will say not only that the greatest exploitation
of manners ever made is the *Iliad,* but also that *The Possessed* and *Studs Lonigan* are works whose concern with
manners is of their very essence.

To these characteristics of the novel—the interest in illusion and reality as generated by class and money, this interest
expressed by the observation of manners—we must add the
unabashed interest in ideas. From its very beginning the
novel made books the objects of its regard. Nowadays we are
inclined to see the appearance of a literary fact in a novel as
the sign of its "intellectuality" and specialness of appeal, and
even as a sign of decadence. But Joyce's solemn literary discussions in *A Portrait of the Artist as a Young Man,* or his
elaborate literary play in the later works, or Proust's critical
excursions, are in the direct line of *Don Quixote* and *Tom
Jones,* which are works of literary criticism before they are
anything else. The Germans had a useful name for a certain
kind of novel which they called a *Kulturroman;* actually

every great novel deserves that name, for it is hard to think of one that is not precisely a romance of culture. By culture we must mean not merely the general social condition to which the novel responds but also a particular congeries of formulated ideas. The great novels, far more often than we remember, deal explicitly with developed ideas, and although they vary greatly in the degree of their explicitness, they tend to be more explicit rather than less—in addition to the works already mentioned one can adduce such diverse examples as *Lost Illusions, The Sentimental Education, War and Peace, Jude the Obscure,* and *The Brothers Karamazov.* Nowadays the criticism which descends from Eliot puts explicit ideas in literature at a discount, which is one reason why it is exactly this criticism that is most certain of the death of the novel, and it has led many of us to forget how in the novel ideas may be as important as character and as essential to the given dramatic situation.

This, then, as I understand it is the nature of the novel as defined by the work it does. Of these defining conditions how many are in force today?

I think it is true to say that money and class do not have the same place in our social and mental life that they once had. They have certainly not ceased to exist, but certainly they do not exist as they did in the nineteenth century or even in our own youth. Money of itself no longer can engage the imagination as it once did; it has lost some of its impulse, and certainly it is on the defensive; it must compete on the one hand with the ideal of security and on the other hand with the ideal of a kind of power which may be more directly applied. And for many to whom the ideal of mere security is too low and to whom the ideal of direct political power is beyond the reach of their imagination, money, in order to be justified, must be involved with virtue and with the virtuous cultivation of good taste in politics, culture, and the appointments of the home—money is terribly ashamed of itself. As for class, in Europe the bourgeoisie together with its foil the aristocracy has been weakening for decades. It ceased some time ago to be the chief source of political leaders; its nineteenth-century position as ideologue of the world has vanished before the ideological strength of totalitarian communism; the wars have brought it to the point of economic ruin. In England the middle class is in process of liquidating itself. In this country the real basis of the novel has never existed —that is, the tension between a middle class and an aristocracy which brings manners into observable relief as the living representation of ideals and the living comment on ideas. Our class structure has been extraordinarily fluid; our various upper classes have seldom been able or stable enough to establish their culture as authoritative. With the single exception of the Civil War, our political struggles have not had the kind of cultural implications which catch the imagination, and the extent to which this one conflict has engaged the American mind suggests how profoundly interesting conflicts of culture may be. (It is possible to say that the Cromwellian revolution appears in every English novel.) For the rest, the opposition between rural and urban ideals has always been rather factitious; and despite a brief attempt to insist on the opposite view, the conflict of capital and labor is at present a contest for the possession of the goods of a single way of life, and not a cultural struggle. Our most fervent interest in manners has been linguistic, and our pleasure in drawing distinctions between a presumably normal way of speech and an "accent" or a "dialect" may suggest how simple is our national notion of social difference.[3] And of recent years, although we grow more passionately desirous of status and are bitterly haunted by the ghost of every status-conferring ideal, including that of social class, we more and more incline to show our status-lust not by affirming but by denying the reality of social difference.

I think that if American novels of the past, whatever their merits of intensity and beauty, have given us very few substantial or memorable people, this is because one of the things which makes for substantiality of character in the

[3] Lately our official egalitarianism has barred the exploitation of this interest by our official arts, the movies and the radio; there may be some social wisdom in this; yet it ignores the fact that at least certain forms and tones of the mockery of their speech habits are a means by which "extraneous" groups are accepted. Mention of this naturally leads to the question of whether the American attitude toward "minority" groups, particularly Negroes and Jews, is not the equivalent of class differentiation. I think it is not, except in a highly modified way. And for the purposes of the novel it is not the same thing at all, for two reasons: it involves no real cultural struggle, no significant conflict of ideals, for the excluded group has the same notion of life and the same aspirations as the excluding group, although the novelist who attempts the subject naturally uses the tactic of showing that the excluded group has a different and better ethos; and it is impossible to suppose that the novelist who chooses this particular subject will be able to muster the satirical ambivalence toward both groups which marks the good novel even when it has a social *parti pris*.

novel is precisely the notation of manners, that is to say, of class traits modified by personality. It is impossible to imagine a Silas Wegg or a Smerdyakov or a Félicité (of *A Simple Heart*) or a Mrs. Proudie without the full documentation of their behavior in relation to their own class and to other classes. All great characters exist in part by reason of the ideas they represent. The great characters of American fiction, such, say, as Captain Ahab and Natty Bumppo, tend to be mythic because of the rare fineness and abstractness of the ideas they represent; and their very freedom from class gives them a large and glowing generality; for what I have called *substantiality* is not the only quality that makes a character great. They are few in number and special in kind; and American fiction has nothing to show like the huge, swarming, substantial population of the European novel, the substantiality of which is precisely a product of a class existence. In fiction, as perhaps in life, the conscious realization of social class, which is an idea of great power and complexity, easily and quickly produces intention, passion, thought, and what I am calling substantiality. The diminution of the reality of class, however socially desirable in many respects, seems to have the practical effect of diminishing our ability to see people in their difference and specialness.

Then we must be aware of how great has been the falling-off in the energy of ideas that once animated fiction. In the nineteenth century the novel followed the great lines of political thought, both the conservative and the radical, and it documented politics with an original and brilliant sociology. In addition, it developed its own line of psychological discovery, which had its issue in the monumental work of Freud. But now there is no conservative tradition and no radical tradition of political thought, and not even an eclecticism which is in the slightest degree touched by the imagination; we are in the hands of the commentator. On the continent of Europe political choice may be possible but political thought is not, and in a far more benign context the same may be said of England. And in the United States, although for different reasons, there is a similar lack of political intelligence: all over the world the political mind lies passive before action and the event. In psychological thought we find a strange concerted effort of regression from psychoanalysis, such as the reformulations of the analytical psychology which Dr. Horney and Dr. Sullivan make in the name of reason and society and progress, which are marked by the most astonishing weakness of mind, and which appeal to the liberal intellectual by an exploitation of the liberal intellectual's fond belief that he suspects "orthodoxy." Nor really can it be said that Freudian psychology itself has of late made any significant advances.

This weakness of our general intellectual life is reflected in our novels. So far as the novel touches social and political questions it permits itself to choose only between a cheery or a sour democratism; it is questionable whether any American novel since *Babbitt* has told us a new thing about our social life. In psychology the novel relies either on a mechanical or a clinical use of psychiatry or on the insights that were established by the novelists of fifty years ago.

It is not then unreasonable to suppose that we are at the close of a cultural cycle, that the historical circumstances which called forth the particular intellectual effort in which we once lived and moved and had our being is now at an end, and that the novel as part of that effort is as deciduous as the rest.

THREE

But there is an explanation of the death of the novel which is both corollary and alternative to this. Consider a main intellectual preoccupation of the period that ends with Freud and begins with Swift or with Shakespeare's middle period or with Montaigne—it does not matter just where we set the beginning so long as we start with some typical and impressive representation, secular and not religious, of man's depravity and weakness. Freud said of his own theories that they appealed to him as acting, like the theories of Darwin and Copernicus, to diminish man's pride, and this intention, carried out by means of the discovery and demonstration of man's depravity, has been one of the chief works of the human mind for some four hundred years. What the mind was likely to discover in this period was by and large much the same thing, yet mind was always active in the enterprise of discovery; discovery itself was a kind of joy and sometimes a hope, no matter how great the depravity that was turned up; the activity of the mind was a kind of fortitude. Then too there was reassurance in the resistance that was offered to the assaults of mind upon the strong texture of the social façade of humanity. That part of the mind which delights in discovery was permitted its delight by the margin that existed between speculation and proof; had the mind been able fully to prove

what it believed, it would have fainted and failed before its
own demonstration, but so strongly entrenched were the
forces of respectable optimism and the belief in human and
social goodness that the demonstration could never be finally
established but had to be attempted over and over again.
Now, however, the old margin no longer exists; the façade is
down; society's resistance to the discovery of depravity has
ceased; now everyone knows that Thackeray was wrong,
Swift right. The world and the soul have split open of themselves and are all agape for our revolted inspection. The simple eye of the camera shows us, at Belsen and Buchenwald,
horrors that quite surpass Swift's powers, a vision of life
turned back to its corrupted elements which is more disgust-
ing than any that Shakespeare could contrive, a cannibalism
more literal and fantastic than that which Montaigne ascribed
to organized society. A characteristic activity of mind is
therefore no longer needed. Indeed, before what we now
know the mind stops; the great psychological fact of our time
which we all observe with baffled wonder and shame is that
there is no possible way of responding to Belsen and Buchenwald. The activity of mind fails before the incommunicability
of man's suffering.

This may help to explain the general deterioration of our
intellectual life. It may also help to explain an attitude to our
life in general. Twenty-five years ago Ortega spoke of the
"dehumanization" of modern art. Much of what he said
about the nature of modern art has, by modern art, been
proved wrong, or was wrong even when he said it. But
Ortega was right in observing of modern art that it expresses
a dislike of holding in the mind the human fact and the
human condition, that it shows "a real loathing of living
forms and living beings," a disgust with the "rounded and
soft forms of living bodies"; and that together with this revulsion, or expressed by it, we find a disgust with history and
society and the state. Human life as an aesthetic object can
perhaps no longer command our best attention; the day
seems to have gone when the artist who dealt in representation could catch our interest almost by the mere listing of the
ordinary details of human existence; and the most extreme
and complex of human dilemmas now surely seem to many
to have lost their power to engage us. This seems to be supported by evidence from those arts for which a conscious ex-
altation of humanistic values is stock-in-trade—I mean advertising and our middling novels, which, almost in the degree

that they celebrate the human, falsify and abstract it; in the very business of expressing adoration of the rounded and soft forms of living bodies they expose the disgust which they really feel.

FOUR

At this point we are in the full tide of those desperate perceptions of our life which are current nowadays among thinking and talking people, which even when we are not thinking and talking haunt and control our minds with visions of losses worse than that of existence—losses of civilization, personality, humanness. They sink our spirits not merely because they are terrible and possible but because they have become so obvious and cliché that they seem to close for us the possibility of thought and imagination.

And at this point too we must see that if the novel is dead or dying, it is not alone in its mortality. The novel is a kind of summary and paradigm of our cultural life, which is perhaps why we speak sooner of its death than of the death of any other form of thought. It has been of all literary forms the most devoted to the celebration and investigation of the human will; and the will of our society is dying of its own excess. The religious will, the political will, the sexual will, the artistic will—each is dying of its own excess. The novel at its greatest is the record of the will acting under the direction of an idea, often an idea of will itself. All else in the novel is but secondary, and those examples which do not deal with the will in action are but secondary in their genre. Sensibility in the novel is but notation and documentation of the will in action. Again *Don Quixote* gives us our first instance. In its hero we have the modern conception of the will in a kind of wry ideality. Flaubert said that Emma Bovary was Quixote's sister, and in her we have the modern will in a kind of corruption. Elizabeth Bennet and Emma Woodhouse and Jane Eyre are similarly related to all the Karamazovs, to Stavrogin, and to that Kirillov who was led by awareness of the will to assert it ultimately by destroying it in himself with a pistol shot.

Surely the great work of our time is the restoration and the reconstitution of the will. I know that with some the opinion prevails that, apart from what very well *may* happen by way of Apocalypse, what *should* happen is that we advance farther and farther into the darkness, seeing to it that the will finally exhausts and expends itself to the end that we purge our minds of all the old ways of thought and feeling, giving up all hope of ever reconstituting the great former will of humanism, which, as they imply, has brought us to this pass. One must always listen when this opinion is offered in true passion. But for the vision and ideal of apocalyptic renovation one must be either a particular kind of moral genius with an attachment to life that goes beyond attachment to any particular form of life—D. H. Lawrence was such a genius—or a person deficient in attachment to life in any of its forms. Most of us are neither one nor the other, and our notions of renovation and reconstitution are social and pragmatic and in the literal sense of the word conservative. To the restoration and reconstitution of the will thus understood the novelistic intelligence is most apt.

When I try to say on what grounds I hold this belief, my mind turns to a passage in Henry James's preface to *The American*. James has raised the question of "reality" and "romance," and he remarks that "of the men of largest resounding imagination before the human scene, of Scott, of Balzac, even of the coarse, comprehensive, prodigious Zola, we feel, I think, that the reflexion toward either quarter has never taken place"; they have never, that is, exclusively committed themselves either to "reality" or to "romance" but have maintained an equal commerce with both. And this, James goes on to say, is the secret of their power with us. Then follows an attempt to distinguish between "reality" and "romance," which defines "reality" as "the things we cannot possibly not know," and then gives us this sentence: "The romantic stands . . . for the things that, with all the facilities in the world, all the wealth and all the courage and all the wit and all the adventure, we never *can* directly know; the things that can reach us only through the beautiful circuit of thought and desire."

The sentence is perhaps not wholly perspicuous, yet, if I understand it at all, it points to the essential moral nature of the novel. Julien Sorel eventually acquired all the facilities in the world; he used "all the wealth and all the courage and all the wit and all the adventure" to gain the things that are to be gained by their means; what he gained was ashes in his mouth. But what in the end he gained came to him in prison not by means of the "facilities" but through the beautiful circuit of thought and desire, and it impelled him to make his great speech to the Besançon jury in which he threw away his life; his happiness and his heroism came, I think, from his will having exhausted all that part of itself which naturally turns to the inferior objects offered by the social world and from its having learned to exist in the strength of its own knowledge of its thought and desire. I have said that awareness of the will in its beautiful circuit of thought and desire was the peculiar property of the novel, yet in point of fact we find it long before the novel came into existence and in a place where it always surprises us, in the *Inferno*, at the meetings of Dante with Paolo and Francesca, with Brunetto Latini and with Ulysses, the souls who keep the energy of thought and desire alive and who are therefore forever loved however damned. For James the objects of this peculiarly human energy go by the name of "romance." The word is a risky one and therefore it is necessary to say that it does not stand for the unknowable, for what is vulgarly called "the ideal," let alone for that which is pleasant and charming because far off. It stands for the world of unfolding possibility, for that which, when brought to actuality, is powerfully operative. It is thus a synonym for the will in its creative aspect, especially in its aspect of *moral* creativeness, as it subjects itself to criticism and conceives for itself new states of being. The novel has had a long dream of virtue in which the will, while never abating its strength and activity, learns to refuse to exercise itself upon the unworthy objects with which the social world tempts it, and either conceives its own right objects or becomes content with its own sense of its potential force—which is why so many novels give us, before their end, some representation, often crude enough, of the will unbroken but in stasis.

It is the element of what James calls "romance," this operative reality of thought and desire, which, in the novel, exists side by side with the things "we cannot possibly not know," that suggests to me the novel's reconstitutive and renovating power.

FIVE

If there is any ground for my belief that the novel can, by reason of one of its traditional elements, do something in the work of reconstituting and renovating the will, there may be some point in trying to say under what particular circumstances of its own nature and action it may best succeed.

I think it will not succeed if it accepts the latest-advanced theory of the novel, Jean-Paul Sartre's theory of "dogmatic realism." According to the method of this theory, the novel is to be written as if without an author and without a personal voice and "without the foolish business of storytelling." The reader is to be subjected to situations as nearly equivalent as possible to those of life itself; he is to be prevented from falling out of the book, kept as strictly as possible within its confines and power by every possible means, even by so literal a means as the closest approximation of fictional to historical time, for the introduction of large periods of time would permit the reader to remember that he is involved in an illusion; he is, in short, to be made to forget that he is reading a book. We all know the devices by which the sensations of actual life, such as claustrophobia and fatigue, are generated in the reader; and although the novels which succeed in the use of these devices have had certain good effects, they have had bad effects too. By good and bad effects I mean, as Sartre means, good and bad social effects. The banishment of the author from his books, the stilling of his voice, have but reinforced the faceless hostility of the world and have tended to teach us that we ourselves are not creative agents and that we have no voice, no tone, no style. no significant existence. Surely what we need is the opposite of this, the opportunity to identify ourselves with a mind that willingly admits that it is a mind and does not pretend that it is History or Events or the World but only a mind thinking and planning—possibly planning our escape.

There is not very much that is actually original in Sartre's theory, which seems to derive from Flaubert at a not very great remove. Flaubert himself never could, despite his own theory, keep himself out of his books; we always know who is there by guessing who it is that is kept out—it makes a great difference just which author is kept out of a novel, and Flaubert's absence occupies more room than Sartre's, and is a much more various and impressive thing. And Flaubert's mind, in or out of his novels, presents itself to us as an ally —although, as I more and more come to think, the alliance it offers is dangerous.

As for what Sartre calls "the foolish business of storytelling," I believe that, so far from giving it up, the novel will have to insist on it more and more. It is exactly the story that carries what James calls "romance," which is what the theologians call "faith," and in the engaged and working literature which Sartre rightly asks for this is an essential element. To

know a story when we see one, to know it *for* a story, to
know that it is not reality itself but that it has clear and effective relations with reality—this is one of the great disciplines
of the mind.

In speaking against the ideal of the authorless novel I am
not, of course, speaking in behalf of the "personality" of the
author consciously displayed—nothing could be more frivo-
lous—but only in behalf of the liberating effects that may be
achieved when literature understands itself to be literature
and does not identify itself with what it surveys. (This is as
intellectually necessary as for science not to represent itself as
a literal picture of the universe.) The authorial minds that in
Tom Jones and *Tristram Shandy* play with events and the
reader in so nearly divine a way become the great and
strangely effective symbols of liberty operating in the world
of necessity, and this is more or less true of all the novelists
who *contrive* and *invent*.

Yet when I speak in defense of the salutary play of the
mind in the controlled fantasy of storytelling I am not defending the works of consciously literary, elaborately styled
fantasy in the manner of, let us say, *Nightwood,* which in
their own way subscribe to the principles of Sartre's dogmatic
realism, for although the conscious literary intention of the
author is always before us, yet style itself achieves the claus-
tral effect which Sartre would manage by the representation
of events.

Mr. Eliot praises the prose of *Nightwood* for having so
much affinity with poetry. This is not a virtue, and I believe
that it will not be mistaken for a virtue by any novel of the
near future which will interest us. The loss of a natural prose,
one which has at least a seeming affinity with good common
speech, has often been noted. It seems to me that the observation of the loss has been too complacently made and that
its explanations, while ingenious, have had the intention of
preventing it from being repaired in kind. A prose which approaches poetry has no doubt its own value, but it cannot
serve to repair the loss of a straightforward prose, rapid, masculine, and committed to events, making its effects not by the
single word or by the phrase but by words properly and naturally massed. I conceive that the creation of such a prose
should be one of the conscious intentions of any novelist.[4]

[4] The question of prose is as important as that of prosody and we
never pay enough attention to it in criticism. I am far from thinking that
my brief paragraph even opens the subject adequately. The example of

And as a corollary to my rejection of poetic prose for the novel, I would suggest that the novelist of the next decades will not occupy himself with questions of form. The admitted weakness of the contemporary novel, the far greater strength of poetry, the current strong interest in the theory of poetry, have created a situation in which the canons of poetical perfection are quite naturally but too literally applied to the novel. These canons have not so much reinforced as displaced the formal considerations of Flaubert and James, which have their own dangers but which were at least conceived for the novel itself. I make every expectable disclaimer of wishing to depreciate form and then go on to say that a conscious preoccupation with form at the present time is almost certain to lead the novelist, particularly the young novelist, into limitation. The notions of form which are at present current among even those who are highly trained in literature—let alone among the semiliterary, who are always very strict about enforcing the advanced ideas of forty years ago —are all too simple and often seem to come down to nothing more than the form of the sonata, the return on the circle with appropriate repetitions of theme. For the modern highly trained literary sensibility, form suggests completeness and the ends tucked in; resolution is seen only as all contradictions equated, and although form thus understood has its manifest charm, it will not adequately serve the modern experience. A story, like the natural course of an emotion, has its own form, and I take it as the sign of our inadequate trust of story and of our exaggerated interest in sensibility that we have begun to insist on the precise ordering of the novel.

Then I venture the prediction that the novel of the next decades will deal in a very explicit way with ideas. The objections to this will be immediate. Everybody quotes Mr. Eliot's remark about Henry James having a mind so fine that no idea could violate it, which suggests an odd, violent notion of the relation of minds and ideas, not at all the notion that James himself held; and everybody knows the passage in which Mr. Eliot insists on the indifferent connection which

---

Joyce has been urged against what I have just said. It seems to me that whenever the prose of *A Portrait of the Artist* becomes what we call poetic, it is in a very false taste; this has been defended as being a dramatic device, an irony against the hero. *Ulysses* may be taken as making a strong case against my own preference, yet I think that its basic prose, which is variously manipulated, is not without its affinities with the prose I ask for. The medium of *Finnegans Wake* may, without prejudice, be said to be something other than prose in any traditional sense; if it should establish a tradition it will also establish new criteria and problems.

Dante and Shakespeare had with the intellectual formulations of their respective times. I think I can understand—and sympathetically as well as sociologically—Mr. Eliot's feeling for a mode of being in which the act and tone of ideation are not dominant, just as I can understand something of the admiration which may be felt for a society such as Yeats celebrated, which expresses its sense of life not by means of words but by means of houses and horses and by means of violence, manners, courage, and death. But I do not understand what Mr. Eliot means when he makes a sharp distinction between ideas and emotions in literature; I think that Plato was right when in *The Symposium* he represented ideas as continuous with emotions, both springing from the appetites.

It is a prevailing notion that a novel which contains or deals with ideas is bound to be pallid and abstract and intellectual. As against this belief here is an opinion from the great day of the novel: "There are active souls who like rapidity, movement, conciseness, sudden shocks, action, drama, who avoid discussion, who have little fondness for meditation and take pleasure in results. From such people comes what I should call the Literature of Ideas." This odd definition, whose seeming contradictions we will not pause over, was made by Balzac in the course of his long review of *The Charterhouse of Parma,* and it is Stendhal whom Balzac mentions as the great exemplar of the literature of ideas. And we know what ideas are at work in *The Charterhouse* and *The Red and the Black:* they are the ideas of Rousseau and they are named as such. These ideas are not to be separated from the passions of Julien and Fabrice; they are reciprocally expressive of each other. To us it is strange that ideas should be expressed so, and also in terms of prisons and rope ladders, pistols and daggers. It should not seem strange, for it is in the nature of ideas to be so expressed.

Yet although these two great examples support much of my view of the place of ideas in the novel, they do not support all of it. They make for me the point of the continuity of ideas and emotions, which in our literary context is forgotten. And they remind us forcibly of the ideological nature of institutions and classes. But in Stendhal's novels the ideas, although precisely identified, are chiefly represented by character and dramatic action, and although this form of representation has of course very high aesthetic advantages, yet I would claim for the novel the right and the necessity to deal with ideas by means other than that of the "objective correlative," to deal with them as directly as it deals with people or terrain of social setting.

There is an obvious social fact which supports this claim. No one who is in the least aware of our social life today can miss seeing that ideas have acquired a new kind of place in society. Nowadays everyone is involved in ideas—or, to be more accurate, in ideology. The impulse of novelists, which has been much decried, to make their heroes intellectuals of some sort was, however dull it became, perfectly sound: they wanted people of whom it was clear that ideas were an important condition of their lives. But this limitation to avowed intellectuals is no longer needed; in our society the simplest person is involved with ideas. Every person we meet in the course of our daily life, no matter how unlettered he may be, is groping with sentences toward a sense of his life and his position in it; and he has what almost always goes with an impulse to ideology, a good deal of animus and anger. What would so much have pleased the social philosophers of an earlier time has come to pass—ideological organization has cut across class organization, generating loyalties and animosities which are perhaps even more intense than those of class. The increase of conscious formulation, the increase of a certain kind of consciousness by formulation, makes a fact of modern life which is never sufficiently estimated. This is a condition which has been long in developing, for it began with the movements of religious separatism; now politics, and not only politics but the requirements of a whole culture, make verbal and articulate the motive of every human act: we eat by reason, copulate by statistics, rear children by rule, and the one impulse we do not regard with critical caution is that toward ideation, which increasingly becomes a basis of prestige.

This presents the novel with both an opportunity and a duty. The opportunity is a subject matter. Social class and the conflicts it produces may not be any longer a compelling subject to the novelist, but the organization of society into ideological groups presents a subject scarcely less absorbing. Ideological society has, it seems to me, nearly as full a range of passion and nearly as complex a system of manners as a society based on social class. Its promise of comedy and tragedy is enormous; its assurance of relevance is perfect. Dostoevski adequately demonstrated this for us, but we never had in this country a sufficiently complex ideological situation to support it in our own practice of the novel. We have it now.

This opportunity of the novel clearly leads to its duty. Ideology is not ideas; ideology is not acquired by thought but by breathing the haunted air. The life in ideology, from which none of us can wholly escape, is a strange submerged life of habit and semihabit in which to ideas we attach strong passions but no very clear awareness of the concrete reality of their consequences. To live the life of ideology with its special form of unconsciousness is to expose oneself to the risk of becoming an agent of what Kant called "the Radical Evil," which is "man's inclination to corrupt the imperatives of morality so that they may become a screen for the expression of self-love." [5] But the novel is a genre with a very close and really a very simple relation to actuality, to the things we cannot possibly not know—not if they are pointed out to us; it is the form in which the things we cannot possibly not know live side by side with thought and desire, both in their true and beautiful state and in their corrupt state; it is the form which provides the perfect criticism of ideas by attaching them to their appropriate actuality. No less than in its infancy, and now perhaps with a greater urgency and relevance, the novel passionately concerns itself with reality, with appearance and reality.

SIX

But I must not end on a note so high—it would falsify my present intention and my whole feeling about the novel. To speak now of "duty" and, as I earlier did, of the work the novel may do in the reconstitution and renovation of the will, to formulate a function and a destiny for the novel, is to put it into a compromised position where it has been far too long already. The novel was better off when it was more humbly conceived than it is now; the novelist was in a far more advantageous position when his occupation was misprized, or when it was estimated by simpler minds than his own, when he was nearly alone in his sense of wonder at the possibilities of his genre, at the great effects it might be made to yield. The novel was luckier when it had to compete with the ser-

---

[5] Reinhold Niebuhr, *The Nature and Destiny of Man,* Vol. I, p. 120: " 'This evil is radical,' [Kant] declares, 'because it corrupts the very basis of all maxims.' In analyzing the human capacity for self-deception and its ability to make the worse appear the better reason for the sake of providing a moral façade for selfish actions, Kant penetrates into spiritual intricacies and mysteries to which he seems to remain completely blind in his *Critique of Practical Reason.*"

mon, with works of history, with philosophy and poetry and with the ancient classics, when its social position was in question and like one of its own poor or foundling or simple heroes it had to make its way against odds. Whatever high intentions it may have had, it was permitted to stay close to its own primitive elements from which it drew power. Believing this, I do not wish to join in the concerted effort of contemporary criticism to increase the superego of the novel, to conspire with our sense of cultural crisis to heap responsibilities upon it, to hedge it about with prescribed functions and spiked criteria; as things are, the novel feels quite guilty enough.

A sentence in Aristotle's *Ethics* has always been memorable, perhaps because I have never wholly understood it. Aristotle says, "There is a sense in which Chance and Art have the same sphere; as Agathon says, 'Art fosters Fortune; Fortune fosters Art.'" Taken out of its context, and merely as a gnomic sentence, this says much. It says something about the reciprocation which in the act of composition exists between form and free invention, each making the other, which even the most considerate criticism can never really be aware of and often belies. *Fortune fosters Art:* there is indeed something fortuitous in all art, and in the novel the element of the fortuitous is especially large. The novel achieves its best effects of art often when it has no concern with them, when it is fixed upon effects in morality, or when it is simply reporting what it conceives to be objective fact. The converse is of course also true, that the novel makes some of its best moral discoveries or presentations of fact when it is concerned with form, when it manipulates its material merely in accordance with some notion of order or beauty, although it must be stipulated that this is likely to occur only when what is manipulated resists enough, the novel being the form whose aesthetic must pay an unusually large and simple respect to its chosen material. This predominance of fortuitousness in the novel accounts for the roughness of grain, even the coarseness of grain as compared with other arts, that runs through it. The novel is, as many have said of it, the least "artistic" of genres. For this it pays its penalty and it has become in part the grave as well as the monument of many great spirits who too carelessly have entrusted their talents to it. Yet the headlong, profuse, often careless quality of the novel, though no doubt wasteful, is an aspect of its bold and immediate grasp on life.

But from this very sense of its immediacy to life we have come to overvalue the novel. We have, for example, out of awareness of its power, demanded that it change the world; no genre has ever had so great a burden of social requirement put upon it (which, incidentally, it has very effectively discharged), or has been so strictly ordered to give up, in the fulfillment of its assigned function, all that was unconscious and ambivalent and playful in itself. Our sense of its comprehensiveness and effectiveness have led us to make a legend of it: one of the dreams of a younger America, continuing until recently, was of *the* Great American Novel, which was always imagined to be as solitary and omniseminous as the Great White Whale. Then we have subjected it to criteria which are irrelevant to its nature—how many of us happily share the horror which John Gould Fletcher expressed at the discovery that Trollope thought of novel-writing as a trade. The overvaluation of love is the beginning of the end of love; the overvaluation of art is the beginning of the end of art.

What I have called the roughness of grain of the novel, and praised as such, corresponds with something in the nature of the novelists themselves. Of all practitioners of literature, novelists as a class have made the most aggressive assault upon the world, the most personal demand upon it, and no matter how obediently they have listened to their daemons they have kept an ear cocked at the crowd and have denounced its dullness in not responding with gifts of power and fame. This personal demand the haughtiest reserve of Flaubert and James did not try to hide. The novelists have wanted much and very openly; and with great simplicity and naïveté they have mixed what they personally desired with what they desired for the world and have mingled their mundane needs with their largest judgments. Then, great as their mental force has been, they have been touched with something like stupidity, resembling the holy stupidity which Pascal recommends: its effects appear in their ability to maintain ambivalence toward their society, which is not an acquired attitude of mind, or a weakness of mind, but rather the translation of a biological datum, an extension of the pleasure-pain with which, in a healthy state, we respond to tension and effort; the novelist expresses this in his coexistent hatred and love of the life he observes. His inconsistency of intellectual judgment is biological wisdom.

It is at this point that I must deal with a lapse in my argument of which I am aware. My statement of belief that the

novel is not dead, together with what I have said about what
the novel should or should not do, very likely does not weigh
against those circumstances in our civilization which I have
adduced as accounting for the hypothetical death of the
novel. To me certainly these circumstances are very real. And
as I describe the character of the novelist they inevitably
occur to me again. For it is exactly that character and what it
suggests in a culture that the terrible circumstances of our
time destroy. The novelist's assertion of personal demand and
his frank mingling of the mundane and personal with the
high and general, his holy stupidity, or as Keats called it,
"negative capability," which is his animal faith—can these
persist against the assaults which the world now makes on
them? If the novel cannot indeed survive without ambivalence, does what the world presents us with any longer permit
ambivalence? The novelist could once speak of the beautiful
circuit of thought and desire which exists beside the daily
reality, but the question is now whether thought and desire
have any longer a field of possibility. No answer can soon be
forthcoming. Yet, "as Agathon says, 'Art fosters Fortune;
Fortune fosters Art.'" There is both an affirmation and an
abdication in that sentence; the abdication is as courageous as
the affirmation, and the two together make up a good deal of
wisdom. If anything of the old novelistic character survives
into our day, the novelist will be sufficiently aware of Fortune, of Conditions, of History, for he is, as Fielding said, the
historian's heir; but he will also be indifferent to History,
sharing the vital stupidity of the World-Historical Figure, who
of course is not in the least interested in History but only in
his own demands upon life and thus does not succumb to
History's most malign and subtle trick, which is to fix and
fascinate the mind of men with the pride of their foreknowl-
edge of doom. There are times when, as the method of Perseus with the Medusa suggests, you do well not to look
straight at what you are dealing with but rather to see it in
the mirror-shield that the hero carried. Which is to say, "Art
fosters Fortune."

But the shrug which is implied by the other half of the
sentence is no less courageous. It does not suggest that we
compare our position with what appears to be the more favored situation of the past, or keep in mind how History has
robbed the novelist of a great role. What a demand upon the
guarantees of History this would imply! What an overvaluation of security, and of success and the career, and of art,

and of life itself, which must always be a little undervalued if
it is to be lived. Rather should the phrase suggest both the fortuitous and the gratuitous nature of art, how it exists beyond
the reach of the will alone, how it is freely given and not always for good reason, and for as little reason taken away. It
is not to be demanded or prescribed or provided for. The understanding of this cannot of itself assure the existence of the
novel but it helps toward establishing the state of the soul in
which the novel becomes possible.

1948

The mystery of personality
in the novel

HERBERT GOLD

THE novelist's boldest address to himself says: "I must master the most powerful sense of human life on earth, that of individual striving in a world clotted with both trouble and joy; I mean to commit myself to love and ambition and the frustrating of mortality."

The timorous wee clerk within replies: "Who, *you?*"

"Yes," says the novelist, "and don't interrupt. I will reflect the movement of men in society in order to give an example of the glory of desire."

The inner clerk, snuffling righteously before so much rhetoric, says: "Watch out! That's very difficult."

And so it is. And so ensues a struggle. Generally the clerk wins. Often the dialogue is never quite argued through. Occasionally, a few times in each generation, the novelist wins against his other self.

In the first case there is the sleek and pure pseudo-novelist, faking passion, faking life, the opportunist of problems, the Herman Wouks and Sloan Wilsons and Cameron Hawleys, with their deep affirmations for those who admire the editorials in *Life*. In the second case there is an uneasy, unfulfilled writer, often precious, satisfied with aspects and insights and partial comfort. And in the third case, when the novelist never abandons his deepest hopes, well, there is the possibility of a masterpiece. He gives us the stories for which we hunger, rich with people we love in mortal danger; his way of telling, his angle of vision, his perspective—this is what we mean by style—give us the judgment married to perception which defines both the whole man and the artist. Sensitive

Reprinted from *The Age of Happy Problems* by Herbert Gold. Copyright © 1952, 1954, 1957, 1958, 1959, 1960, 1961, 1962 by Herbert Gold, and used by permission of the publisher, The Dial Press, Inc.

and brave at the same time—what a monster!—he joins plot and perspective in a way that finally, without exhortation, suggests a vision of the good life.

This is the critical maximum which no individual can reach.

But although it is more pleasant to talk of success, I would like first to name some of the ways by which novelists evade the possibilities of their art. They construct a mannered style of arbitrary perspectives, with the intention that neither they nor their readers will be obliged to venture into the huge mystery of personality. The aim is simple: If you restrict your world, then the world is reduced in size and manageable. Hide what is difficult; trim what does not fit; make it neat. The great novelist is committed to a world without horizons, manifested first of all by a large and lyric sense for his heroes. The mediocre or tertiary writer limits and limits and limits, and so we have, sometimes overlapping, the following contemporary types:

The Forthright Brutes: Ernest Hemingway and imitators. They are bewitched boys, newly discovering verbs and nouns, physical sensation, zip-pow-wham of weather, drink, sex, war, bulls. They are too scared of what goes on inside an intelligence, inside a memory, inside a group of people to be able to face these matters except by smashing physical symbols like fists across the page. Sometimes they have sensitive nerves in their fists, but the nerve endings are stunned before making contact with the complex congeries of will and desire within.

Hemingway's resolution of the necessary tension of conception in fiction can be examined in the light of the traditional philosphical concept of Universals and Particulars. In one tradition "reality" is defined by abstract forms outside time, and the specific ever-changing events of our world are flickering shadows through fire on the wall of the cave, imperfect imitations of the ideal forms. In the other tradition, it is these particular events which are "real," and general statements are inaccurate, merely useful summaries of the only knowable reality—the fact in the here and now. The terms *Idealism* and *Materialism* are approximate, somewhat misleading labels for these opposing world views.

The novel as a form is obviously empirical, working toward whatever large statements it has to offer about men in society, love, death, ambition, and so on, through specific instances of *a* man, *a* love, *a* death, *an* ambition, a specific society in a specific time and place. Not merely in general approach but in method also the novelist tends to be empirical. He does not say, "She was beautiful." He describes a particular lovely creature with all her lovely attachments and gadgets, and then leaves us with one of the formal summaries which are part of the reader's active participation in a fiction: "Wow! Beautiful!" The novelist seeks what T. S. Eliot has called, in a famous phrase, the "objective correlative" of emotion.

This objectifying in Hemingway goes very far. It is as if he were a too-literal student of some early physical scientist, over-skeptical about what he can learn. The abstention from analysis, deduction, conjecture, the bold hunch—these risks which are taken by the great scientist, too—in favor of a minute noting of symptoms, has a certain animal simplicity, grace, and power. But even the most graceful and powerful bull hangs from a very small head, which he uses mainly for battering, and little of what one bull learns needs to be passed on to another. He has opted for a pathetic lowering of the eyes, a doomed charge, a sword in the heart, and an occasional chance to gore before thumping in the dust with his life running out. *El pobre toro!* His head admits not enough to understanding.

A passion for objectifying emotion through physical sensation and act spins off to mania in the lesser work of Hemingway and in his fleas. The details become more and more ritual; the general emotion and sense which is supposed to emerge from the details has to be supplied entirely by the reader. In its own way, this is a highly "literary" manner, depending on knowledge of other stories, other stages in the life of the maestro, rather than on the work at hand itself: "It was hot. He took a cigarette. It was very hot. He took a drink. He went upstairs. Christ, it was hot."

This type of minimal statement in Hemingway goes very far toward forgetting that thoughts, fantasies, memories, projects, the constant inner monologue and the unspoken conversations among people are also facts in the world, facts of being human. That we think defines our humanity. We are remembering, reasoning, political creatures, constantly responding to others and constantly willing ourselves into relation with others. Eliminate these actions in the guise of objective reporting and the writer eliminates the properly human, just as at the opposite extreme, in the precious and private writer, he eliminates social meaning by signifying nothing but his own obsession. The force of an obsession cannot be communicated; the obsessed person clings to his loneliness. Hemingway's compulsion toward objectivity links him with the obsessively subjective writer: they both fail to give us sufficient criteria for judgment, sufficient material for a full participation in the life of large human beings. They bind their projections of men in action to limited conceptions of the possibilities of being human.

Obviously, however, Hemingway has found an adequate stance for expressing the sadness of the basically uncommunicative soul and for giving glory to its instants of lonely courage. When he depicts the isolated man, he knows whereof he speaks and the simplistic prose manner which he derives from Gertrude Stein serves him well. (He was a nice boy, a good pupil, she notes maliciously.) He describes a static condition, not an act of becoming. His "moments of truth" are plateaus. The consequence of revelation is a fortified stoic acceptance of mortality. He gives us a partial truth about the human condition.

Why then does so much of his work make us feel like a rainy Sunday afternoon? What depresses us finally is this vision of human possibility—one of violent compartmentalization, strict limits, and no growth possible. On the occasions when he seeks to express a sense of people coming meaningfully together, he falls into an embarrassing purple rhetoric, as in the sleeping-bag scenes of *For Whom the Bell Tolls* or in the biography of the battered old love-hungry soldier in *Across the River and into the Trees*. This is not to derogate his great achievement, the one which is responsible for his popularity and his enduring projection of an aspect of life in the twentieth century. From beginning to end, he has spun out a continuous moral romance about the lonely man striving for dignity, grace, and compassion within a world populated by real sharks and imaginary tender boys and girls.

The Cataloguers: John O'Hara is a good example. They observe. They make the discovery of the trivial—it is *most* important; in fact, even the important is merely trivial; the trivial tells us all we need to know. They soothe us with sociology. They lay us to rest with details of tailoring and brand names. Their predominant cast of mind is a sentimental passivity toward the dead weight of facts, which are seen quantitatively, and the contents of a closet are given the same loyal inventory as the two-headed contents of a bed.

The Outer-Essence Girls: Truman Capote and the chattering poets of decoration. A paragraph is a hammock in which words copulate prettily. Society is a meeting of birds on the wing. Put more formally, they do what bad poets do: They use words as if they were things and not signs representing acts and things. They drop the object of narrative prose, which is to make sense about human action, and replace it with a prettifying function. They are interior decorators for sentences. We can't all be William Faulkner, Katherine Anne Porter, or even Carson McCullers, but each and every one of us can aspire to be Speed Lamkin.

The Daintily Involved Observers of Aspects: This is *The New Yorker* fashion, although its best writers, such as John Cheever and Robert Coates, do something more. It is a variety of corporate prose less solemn-chuckly than the *Time-Life* product, but no more able to bear the full weight of experience. *The New Yorker* stylists are marvelously shy about the world. They blush before experience, but have learned graceful ways toward it, with shrewd notings of intonation and the vagaries of expression. Parts stand for wholes, although there seems to be a law of expression—the smaller the part, the larger the whole. Finally summoning up their courage before fleeing, these writers offer a pox on life in the last paragraph.

The Common-Style Fellas: Herman Wouk proudly claims to write "the common style." This cottony diction, also worked with varying degrees of efficiency by Sloan Wilson and Cameron Hawley, is the great current success. These people are the just-plain-Bills of literature, producing an upper-middle-class soap opera for the readers of Luce magazines and subscribers to the Book-of-the-Month Club's service. They love what-is, whether it be the Navy, the suburb, or the corporation, and come forward to swear their allegiance without quaver or quibble. There may be some touch of nonsense in the process, for the flesh is weak, but they rinse and bleach it all for us in the end.

It is the latter, the "common style," which enjoys the greatest success today. By the phrase "common style" is meant uninvolved, unambitious, "traditional" English diction, without

excesses of feeling or rhetoric, suitable to describing the lives
of people who want nothing to change, nothing to stop, just
let's all pull together, hup-two-three, on to America's last
frontier—Adjustment. Those who write the common style
show us how to avoid adventure, giving us just enough of it
along the way to keep us titillated. It is a manner of withdrawal. They use the tricks of plot to replace action, the display of hysteria to justify emotions treated by Equanil, the
questioning of moral assumptions in order to tell us that
these questions can be avoided. The method consists in the
ejaculatio praecox of drama. Clear out before we feel something! The result here too, of course, is a safe but jaded withdrawal from feeling, which is seen as dangerous. (Passion
builds and renews only *after* we have submitted to it utterly.)

The artisans of the common style often, like all good engi-
neers, borrow techniques. Particularly they have mastered the
cataloguing skill; occasionally they seem for paragraphs at a
time almost as delicate as the *New Yorker* stylists; more
rarely they imitate a Hemingway growl or a Capote fruiti-
ness. But they turn these methods to their own ends, and go
plodding on through their scenarios for adjustment. Flat-
footed sentence dogs flat-footed sentence; limp paragraph
folds into limp paragraph; the rhythm of phrase prepares us
for the denouement, which is a calculated marriage, a comfortable job, a saving of the company.

Form follows function.

The function is to assure us that the lowest common denominator of personality and experience is all we need. The
common-style artisans give us an ideal of comfortable con-
forming ways. The package is all wrapped up and ready to
wear, in fact, as easy as old shoes.

The mysterious longing of individuals to create and renew
is excised with an almost surgical brutality and precision—although funnily enough, the American reader can teach these
writers much about that of which the novelist is supposed to
have special knowledge. American readers are drinkers and
sometimes addicts; Americans love jazz and fast driving and
secluded corners; with all the itch to conform, Americans are
still trying to burst the bonds of isolation by various sorts of
violent experiences, including art.

Why then do so many readers find comfort in the dry
apotheosis of Marjorie Morningstar's frigidity? How can
Sloan Wilson get away with a billion copies of his pettish

smugness in the job, the house, the rich aunt, the old wartime affair "talked out" between husband and wife? The great novelists have always given us, before anything else, before all morality and sociology, a sense of the richness of possibility. Why do so many novelists fear the mystery of personality?

Well, first of all, they always have. Besides, life is hard enough without going out looking for challenges. In an impoverished time, palliated by plenty but worried all the same, there is a generalized loss of the sense for creative activity. Nothing more than anxiety inhibits the power to do, to make, to invent, to admit. When your belly is constricted by worry, oatmeal goes down most comfortably. Novelists are human beings more than they are anything else. The mystery of personality is a mystery: isolation, incomprehension, brusque flashes of lightning, cold and hot, danger, danger, danger. To enter into a dark place involves the risk of coming out where you won't see things as they were. In novels as in life, we cannot eliminate emotion utterly and remain human; but we can replace deep involvements by passing safely from the stage of titillation to that of being jaded without crossing through commitment. We live this way, we write these books, we read them in order to say: *I'm safe, I really am, and I'm pleased about it!* (We keep on renewing the experience because secretly we are not pleased.) Thus Sloan Wilson can declare that his novel expresses his sense for a world which has treated him "pretty well"—wars, bombs, a third of a nation watching Ed Sullivan, all of it. Better forget about adventuring, he means to say; better accept a stereotyped image of desire; better be attentive to the media and take the profit in subsidiary rights.

The novel at its best is a large perspective on life in society —large because the hero's doings are important and because the novelist is deeply concerned with the careers of his people. *Ulysses,* for example, has difficulties of manner, but is not in its conception hermetic. Leopold Bloom is a representative, poignant, and troubling instance of city-dwelling man; his fretting and wandering in Dublin bring to us the challenge and limitations of our own intelligence, ambition, and ability to love. James Joyce's personal voice here is many-focused, as true personality always is, not the pale self-contemplation, blank and onanistic, which the seventeen-year-old thinks of as the pursuit of himself; nor is it the

cruelly partial view of the writer fleeing his largest intelligence. It is a lyric reverie *in the light of* the wide world of
society.

What is that grit out of a unique individual which somehow provokes the novel of largest general significance? The
nature of the writer's involvement with his material (which
consists of all that he knows of life) suggests another clue.
For complex psychological reasons, many novelists have been
unavowed Platonists, philosophical idealists, possessed of a
spectator theory of reality. That is, life has meaning as the
shadows on Plato's cave have meaning—as flickering
glimpses through fire of something beyond life, something
perfect and unchanging and finally unknowable by men.
Their world is a system deduced from unknown premises.
Unknown—this paradox torments them. How can deductions
be made without defined terms? Therefore they look for
moral abstractions, categories, faiths, anything that can place
them outside the tormenting flux of time and sensuality. Perhaps they become doctrinaire religionists or Marxists. They
take their stand as viewers, as unwinders. What is the effect
on their novels? Well, some of these writers are great ones,
like Proust and Henry James, engaged in enterprises of passive integration in order to give some "symbolic" sense to the
unruly factness of life. They shrink; still they cannot avoid
rendering this dense, combative, time-ridden teeming. Despite
their static position, Proust and James at their best project a
moving image of desire.

But in anything less than a master, the type of self-absorp-
tion in moody fantasies is crippling. We may be hypnotized
by it; we all have deep impulses to passivity before the fright
of time; but an aspiration to perfection expressed as static
clutching leads finally to paralysis. We stiffen; we are isolated.
Platonism here parallels what the psychoanalysts call "fixa-
tion"—a retreat to impossibly perfect and unchanging gratifi-
cations or frustrations. We sneeze, we wheeze, our bodies
protest.

Let us now set the empirical novelist against the deductive
one. "Love" is not an abstraction to be encompassed by definition: it is this Jack and Jane, that Bud and Joy—look and
see! The novelist is *not* studying shadows for some ultimate
reality beyond earth; he accepts that the shadows themselves
give him all that he can know; in fact, that they are enough;
in fact, they are not shadows—they are thick reality itself
and a marvel to behold.

There is the lesson of a Welsh phrase: "The rent that's due to love"—you must pay and pay and pay, relentlessly giving yourself and making others give, too. The category "Love" does not exist; it can be merely rented, never owned; it is unpossessable in any final way. Like the medieval cathedral, like a child, like love, the great novel gives a sense of not yet completed life within whatever its perfections of design. Attempting to offer the sense of life, a novel is always in process. You can't step in the same story twice. When the writer sits down to his desk in the morning, there is nothing so safe and deadly as knowing exactly what comes next. If he is a real novelist by temper of imagination, but weakly hopes to have the security of a controlled symmetry, he will find that his characters shake their fists into the crooks of their elbows, set his schemes on their tails, ruthlessly rewrite him. All that he is makes his people all that they are, but they are endowed with the kind of independence which defiant children have when they leave a good home. Fortified by their parents to make their own way, they are most loyal in being most free.

The mystery of personality can be defined again and again, and then redefined: that's what mysteries are for. A jittery scientist has defined personality as "the index of inefficiency." Machines are both efficient and free of caprice, he assures himself; therefore personality is a negative quantity with respect to intention, plan, goals; therefore the ideal of Science must be the elimination of personality in favor of socially governed ends. How are the ends to be determined? By what criteria are they judged? By the efficient, impersonal needs of the smoothly running society. Needs? *Needs?* Why, for Plato's sake, pal, that's more circular (in logical terms) and hysterical (in psychological lingo) than any aesthetic rant.

Personality is prickly against definition. Let us return to the novel. In novels the mystery will make itself manifest as an individual, unsocialized perception, compassion, hatred, and love—a congeries of unique relationships with unique creatures and events. Despite the difficulties of definition, we know that the lonely, self-devouring ego is not personality and neither is the busy radar-flaunting opportunist: they are both flights from that mystery. They are willed, not willing; worked on, not working. They are not mysterious, either: they are explainable products. They can be comic and pathetic, even typical of a society—never heroic, tragic, or representative of aspiration (which is also a part of the twentieth century archetype).

However, the man moving in consciousness and contemplation of his will—really conscious and watching, really moving and committed—is the personality capable of defining freedom for all of us. His is the will which, in type, reaches to the divine maximum, where God made something from nothing, the heavens and earth popping out of his pride in six days, not seven—on the seventh day He gloated. At a slightly less monstrous level, Balzac created *Père Goriot* in fifty-eight days, complete with Vautrin swarming over Rastignac's soul. Love, ambition, power under the sun of mortality! These are the issues; the great heroes of fiction meet their risks head-on, as we all must do, but too often we do it also faces down.

The novelist must reach for the grown-up, risking, athletic personality, surely must in some way be this person, in order to find a hero who gives the sense of men at their best on earth: and catch him finally where his great gifts do not suffice: this is tragedy. American life is rich in suggestions of tragic themes: The man in politics is cracked by his ambition —but really involved, not floating above politics; the man in business fails against the fierce appetite of the devouring business world—but really struggling and pretty fierce himself while not mistaking the business world for the whole of life; the lover is lost by love, as it is perhaps still possible to be, but by a love which is health and desire for a woman worth desiring and defeated by the natural strangeness of human beings. It would not be stretching the essential definition of tragedy to show the possibilities of individual triumph in all these struggles.

Personality is a key, not a twitch.

Without personality, manifested by what is called style, there is no significant touching.

Personality in the novel leads to communion with others, a meaningful individual participation in the common career. Otherwise, despite all brilliance, emotion is reduced to the self-loathing of a Celine or the self-aggrandizement of the crippled perspectives mentioned earlier. The individual is more than the common style's stock-figure cartoon of Everyman in gray flannel. And of course the individual is more than the cracked-up romantic poet at three o'clock in the morning in the dark night of his soul.

We should expect the fragmentation of self in the modern novel, just as we expect it in the man bound to a factory or office, within a social structure which cannot use the largest capacities of millions of individuals. Writers are responsive people: the complexities of being an American in 1957 are enough to tempt all of us to turn to partial, limited, maybe soothing half-views. What a dangerous thing to be all present and awake before the front page of the daily newspaper!

Can some novelists stand up against their confusion and fright?

Yes, and even with courage, humor, and a will to do good work. Without naming specific writers, I suggest that the contemporary American novel is still the best place to look for instances of lives which seek to be whole and unafraid. Confidence and freedom of style are good signs of a writer's taking the chance. A style which attempts to use all a writer knows to tell all he can imagine involves a moral stance in favor of intelligence and liberty and risk-taking. With their varying defects and capacities, such writers have this in common: they are individuals, not products; they are making a way, not accepting a road; they do not flinch before the mystery of personality, or when they do, they give signs of knowing that there is something vital left out. Their failures are peculiarly ungracious: they intend otherwise. They will try again next time.

At its best, the art of the novel tells us more than we can find out elsewhere about love and death. We commune together before a guiding image of the always unfulfilled possibilities of life on earth. We are therefore in continual need of the dangerous, destructive moralist which the great novelist is.

1957

The alone generation

a comment on the
fiction of the fifties

ALFRED KAZIN

THE other day a prominent American publisher advertised a
book of stories by a Continental writer who died some time
ago: "These stories, never before published in English, could
only have been written by a great writer who flourished before World War II. They are stamped by that unobtrusive assurance, perfect sympathy with their subjects, and resonant
tone which have become, it would seem, lost secrets in almost
all the fiction of the immediate present." Not very encourag-
ing, what? Yet I must admit that while I see a host of brilliantly talented writers all around me, I don't often get a very
profound satisfaction out of the novels they write.

I am tired of reading for compassion instead of pleasure.
In novel after novel I am presented with people who are so
soft, so wheedling, so importunate, that the actions in which
they are involved are too indecisive to be interesting or to develop those implications which are the lifeblood of narrative.
The age of "psychological man," of the herd of aloners, has
finally proved the truth of Tocqueville's observation that in
modern times the average man is absorbed in a very puny object, himself, to the point of satiety. The whole interest of the
reader seems to be summoned toward "understanding" and

tolerance of the leading characters. We get an imaginative universe limited to the self and its detractors. The old-fashioned novel of sensitive souls, say Somerset Maugham's *Of Human Bondage* or even Sinclair Lewis' *Main Street,* showed a vulnerable hero or heroine battling it out (*a*) for principles which he identified with himself and (*b*) against social enemies who were honestly opposed to the protagonist's demand of unlimited freedom. Now we get novels in which society is merely a backdrop to the aloneness of the hero. People are not shown in actions that would at least get us to see the conditions of their personal struggle. Carson McCullers' beautiful first novel, *The Heart Is a Lonely Hunter,* characterized a stagnant society in the silent relationship between two mutes; in her third novel, *The Member of the Wedding,* the adolescent loneliness of Frankie fills up the scene, becomes the undramatic interest of the book, to the point where the reader feels, not that he is witnessing a drama, but that he is being asked to respond to a situation.

American society is remarkable for the degree of loneliness (not solitude) in which the individual can find himself. In our mass age, the individual's lack of privacy, his unlimited demand for self-satisfaction, his primary concern with his own health and well-being have actually thrown him back on himself more than before. Our culture is stupefyingly without support from tradition, and has become both secular and progressive in its articulation of every discontent and ambition; the individual now questions himself constantly because his own progress—measured in terms of the social norms—is his fundamental interest. The kind of person who in the nineteenth-century novel was a "character" now regards himself in twentieth-century novels as a problem; the novel becomes not a series of actions which he initiates because of *who* he is, but a series of disclosures, as at a psychoanalyst's, designed to afford him the knowledge that may heal him. It is astonishing how many novels concerned with homosexuality, on the order of Truman Capote's *Other Voices, Other Rooms,* are apologies for abnormality, designed to make us sympathize with the twig as it is bent the wrong way.

I would suspect that it is the intention of extracting "understanding" that accounts for the extraordinary number of children and adolescents in American fiction; at least in the imaginative society of fiction they can always be objects of concern. Even in a good writer like Capote, to say nothing of a bad writer like Gore Vidal, the movement of the book comes to a standstill in the grinding machinery of sensibility. As in James Baldwin's *Giovanni's Room,* sympathetic justice is always accorded homosexuals. No Vautrin as in Balzac, no Charlus as in Proust, no honest homosexual villains! The immediate result is the immobilization of narrative, the fashionable mistiness of prose; first the hero is cherished to the point of suffocation, then the style. *Other Voices, Other Rooms* is a brilliant effort of will, but it is unmoving rather than slow, retrospective rather than searching. In the past the movement of fiction was more energetic than life; now fiction becomes vaguer, dimmer, an "exercise" in "craft."

TWO

This demand on our compassion is not limited to the quivering novels of sensibility by overconscious stylists; it is the very essence of the deliberately churned up novels of the Beat Generation. I mention Jack Kerouac here only because his novels, in which he has increasingly developed the trick of impersonating spontaneity by bombarding the reader with a mass of deliberately confused impressions, depend on a naked and unashamed plea for "love," understanding, fellowship, and are read and enjoyed only because this pleading so answers to our psychological interest in fiction that we indulge Kerouac without knowing why we do. Nothing human is now alien to us; after all, the fellow's problem could be our problem! It is ridiculous that novels can now be sent off as quickly as they are written and published immediately afterward in order to satisfy the hopped-up taste of people who, when they open a novel, want to feel that they are not missing a thing. The sluttishness of a society whose mass ideal seems to be unlimited consumption of all possible goods and services is the reason for the "success" of writers whose literary strategy is to paint America as an unlimited supply of sex, travel, liquor—and lonely yearners. The individual who is concerned entirely with his aloneness will inevitably try to invade society, "the other" in his universe, by writing stormily, angrily, lashing the reader with a froth of words. But we are at fault in allowing the addict quality of such books to stand for "intensity" in fiction. More and more we judge novels by their emotional authenticity, not their creative achievement; we read them as the individual testifying for himself in a confused and troubling time. But the testimony is so self-concerned that we equate this glibness of feeling with recklessness of style. And here I come to another complaint, the increasing slovenliness, carelessness, and plain cowardice of style in fiction today.

We were wrong when we thought that the ghost of Henry James had put his too, too careful hand on our young 'uns. It is true that some of the new professor-novelists, Benjamin DeMott in *The Body's Cage* or Monroe Engel in *The Visions of Nicholas Solon,* like Capote himself in his first book and his stories, can remind us of the rage of style in the fiction of the forties. So talented a writer as Jean Stafford has of late years often seemed to bury herself in fine phrases. It is a rare professor-novelist, Robie Macauley in *The Disguises of Love,* who can escape the ostentatious carefulness, the jogging of the reader: *Please don't lose sight of my arm as I put together this beautiful edifice of words.* But actually, the increasing fussiness of our social ideals and the plain boredom of a period in which writers so often feel incapable of imagining decisive roles for their characters have led to the opposite quality. John Wain recently wrote:

"At the moment, the literary mind of the West seems to be swamped in one of its periodic waves of what George Orwell once called 'sluttish antinomianism,' which he defined as 'lying in bed drinking Pernod.' "

What we get now is not the style of pretended fineness— the *New Yorker* ladies with every tuck in place—but the imitation of anger, the leer of the desperado. You can't fool us with your genteel learning, we're young American men who have been around and who have a punch! So I read in an article on fiction, by Herbert Gold, that something-or-other is like kissing a girl with spinach on her teeth. Wow, bang, and slam. Kerouac and whoever it is who follows *him* are "wild" in the hope of getting out of themselves, in finding some person, thing, or cause to latch onto. Gold is slovenly in the hope of sounding "cool"; he is understandably alarmed by the softness that threatens young novelists in so self-pitying an age as this. In England the young men are angry because still made to feel inferior; in America young novelists get angry because they hope to sound belligerent and positive, *alive,* against the doldrums of the Eisenhower age.

One root of their difficulty is the irresistible example of Saul Bellow's *The Adventures of Augie March.* Anyone who has read his first two novels, *Dangling Man* and *The Victim,*

knows that Bellow began with an almost excessive nobility of
style, that the open and comically pretentious style in which
Augie talks is a tour de force. Bellow has always been fascinated by characters who, in the deep Existentialist sense, are
conscious of being *de trop*, excessive of themselves and their
society, insatiable in their demands on life. All his representative men, in the phrase of Henderson the rain king, cry, *"I
want! I want!"* This excess of human possibility over social
goals, of the problem, man, over his intended satisfactions,
led to a prose in *Augie* which is rapturously, not whiningly,
faithful to all the signs and opportunities of experience. "If
you've seen a winter London open thundering mouth in its
awful last minutes of river light or have come with cold
clanks from the Alps into Torino in December white steam
then you've known like greatness of place." In *Augie,* Bellow
attained a rosy deliverance from the grip of his past, he discovered himself equal to the excitement of the American experience, he shook himself all over and let himself go. "I am
an American, Chicago born—Chicago, that somber city—and
go at things as I have taught myself, free-style, and will make
the record in my own way. . . ."

But just as no poet should attempt free verse who has not
performed in traditional forms and meters, so no novelist
should identify toughness with "free-style":

> He brought his hand with the horny nail of his index
> finger in a wide circle, swinging an invisible lassoo, looping
> their belly-eyed gaze and taking it at his eye. They were
> caught first at the spongy wart on his nose and then in
> his eyes, working it for themselves now like the flies
> caught wriggling in sticky-paper. That wart made a stiff
> flop when he tossed his head in beckon and hitch toward
> the pungent foot-darkened sawdust at the door of Grack's
> Zoo, a gobble of cajolery up from his throat and the
> swollen Adam's apple.

This is from Gold's most admired book, *The Man Who
Was Not With It,* and makes me think of what was once
scrawled on a student paper at Harvard by ancient Dean
Briggs: "falsely robust." I think I understand where such
worked-up militancy of phrase comes from: from the novelist's honest need, in the spirit of Henry James, to have language do the work of characterization. There is so much for
a novelist to put together before he can invite people into the
world of his imagination; there are so many things to say

about human beings who, in the absence of public beliefs, appear arbitrary to themselves and to everyone else. The novelist feels he has to work ten times harder than he used to, falls into despair, and tries to ram it all home. Things aren't as clear as they used to be, and there's no kidding ourselves that they are. The true novelist wants only to set the stage, to get people going, to tell his story, but as Augie March says, "You do all you can to humanize and familiarize the world, and suddenly it becomes stranger than ever." The sense of that strangeness is vivid despite the murky powers of contemporary novelists; no wonder, having to make language work all the time for them, that they often escape into an assumed violence and negligence of tone.

Sometimes the language of violence fits. Ralph Ellison's *Invisible Man* is a series of episodes, but the screaming crescendo on which the book opens—the hero in his Harlem cellar, all the stolen lights ablaze, collaring the reader and forcing him to notice and to hear—is an unforgettably powerful expression, at the extreme of racial experience, of the absurdity, the feeling of millions that the world is always just out of their reach. I don't care for novelists who ignore what H. G. Wells himself called the "queerness" that has come into contemporary life since the bomb. The ways of escape from this queerness are legion, but let me name some who don't try to escape it. Paul Bowles doesn't, although his values are so skittery that he sometimes seems to escape from horror into a Fitzpatrick travelogue. The American writer is so likely to see more of the world, and to experience it more openly, that, like Hemingway at the end of *Death in the Afternoon*, he always wants to get in after the bell all the sensuous travel notes he hadn't been able to fit into his book. Bowles tends to fall into this sophisticated romanticism; sometimes he reports North Africa and Asia instead of setting his imagination in them. On the other hand, the landscape in *The Sheltering Sky* itself represents the inhumanity of people who can no longer communicate with one another, the coldness of a world that now seems to put man off. What minimizes the symbolic values in *The Sheltering Sky* and deprives us of the "resonance" we used to get in fiction is the aloneness of people who are concerned entirely with the search for their own sexual satisfaction. The slightly depressing atmosphere of anxiety that hangs over Bowles's novel is characteristic of the effort to find an identity for oneself in sexual relationships. Norman Mailer, a writer with so much more native power than Bowles, with so much more ability to confront American life directly than he seems to acknowledge, has created in *The Deer Park* the same essential atmosphere of paralysis, of the numbness that results when people feel themselves to be lost in the pursuit of compulsions.

Mailer's novels, at least for me, personify the dilemma of novelists who are deeply concerned with history but dangerously oversimplify it; if they seem consumed by their interest in sex, it is because they are always seeking some solution for "the times." In many ways Mailer seems to me the most forceful and oddly objective novelist of his age, objective in the sense that he is most capable of imagining objects to which a reader can give himself. You see this, despite the obvious debts to older writers, in *The Naked and the Dead* and in the satire behind the wonderful exchanges between the producer and his son-in-law in *The Deer Park*. Yet Mailer's interest in the external world has dwindled to the point where the theme of sexual power and delight—which Mailer feels to be a lost secret in contemporary life—has become a labyrinthine world in itself. Mailer now seems bent on becoming the American Marquis de Sade, where once he seemed to be another Dos Passos. Yet the energy, the often unconscious yet meticulous wit, above all the eery and totally unexpected power of concrete visualization are curious because Mailer is able to make more of a world out of his obsessions than other writers are able to make out of the given materials of our common social world.

Here I come to the heart of my complaint. I complain of the dimness, the shadowiness, the flatness, the paltriness, in so many reputable novelists. I confess that I have never been able to get very much from Wright Morris, though he is admired by influential judges. In reading Morris' *The Field of Vision*, I thought of George Santayana's complaint that contemporary poets often give the reader the mere suggestion of a poem and expect him to finish the poem for them. Morris' many symbols, his showy intentions, his pointed and hinted significances, seem to me a distinct example of the literary novel which professors like to teach and would like to write: solemnly meaningful in every intention but without the breath or extension of life.

There are many writers, like J. D. Salinger, who lack strength but who are competent and interesting. He identifies himself too fussily with the spiritual aches and pains of his characters; in some of his recent stories, notably "Zooey" and "Seymour: An Introduction," he has overextended his line, thinned it out, in an effort to get the fullest possible significance out of his material. Salinger's work is a perfect example of the lean reserves of the American writer who is reduced to "personality," even to the "mystery of personality," instead of the drama of our social existence. It is the waveriness, the effort at control, that trouble me in Salinger; the professional hand is there, the ability to create an imaginative world, plus almost too much awareness of what he can and can't do. Only, it *is* thin, and peculiarly heartbreaking at times; Salinger identifies the effort he puts out with the vaguely spiritual "quest" on which his characters are engaged, which reminds me of Kierkegaard's saying that we have become "pitiful," like the lace-makers whose work is so flimsy. The delicate balances in Salinger's work, the anxious striving, inevitably result in beautiful work that is rather too obviously touching, and put together on a frame presented to it by *The New Yorker*.

But I must admit that the great majority of stories I read in magazines seem only stitchings and joinings and colorings of some original model. No wonder that in so much contemporary fiction we are excited by the intention and tolerate the achievement. We are so hungry for something new in fiction that the intention, marked early in the handling of a story, will often please us as if it were the dramatic emotion accomplished by the story; the intuition of hidden significance that usually waits for us at the end of a Salinger story is both a reward to the reader and the self-cherished significance of the story to the writer himself.

Salinger's characters are incomparably larger and more human than those of John Cheever, but Cheever has a gift for being more detached and at the same time more open to what *is*—to the ever-present danger and the half-felt queerness of contemporary existence. It is a pity in a way—I am thinking here of Cheever's stories, not his novel—that contemporary American fiction must derive so much of its strength from the perishable value of social information. James Jones wrote a really extraordinary documentary novel in *From Here to Eternity*, and ever since, like so many Americans who wrote extraordinary first novels directly out of experience, he has had the look of someone trying to invent things that once were conferred on him. So Cheever, in *The New Yorker* style, sometimes takes such easy refuge in the details of gardens, babysitters, parks, dinners, apartment houses, clothes, that he goes to the opposite extreme of the Beat writers (who present the sheer emptiness of life when human beings are not attached to a particular environment): he falls into mechanical habits of documentation, becomes a slyer John O'Hara. It is as if he were trying to get back to the social reportage and satire that worked in our fiction so long as the people writing these stories, like Sinclair Lewis or Scott Fitzgerald, knew what values they could oppose to the "rich." As one can see from O'Hara's novels, which get more pointless as they get bigger and sexier, it is impossible to remain an old-fashioned "realist" unless you can portray a class or an individual opposed to the dominant majority. (James Gould Cozzens was able to do exactly this in *Guard of Honor* but not in *By Love Possessed,* which is more of an aggrieved complaint against the destruction of values.) O'Hara's *Appointment in Samarra* was an exciting book because it involved the real conflict of classes in America; *From the Terrace* suggests that the transformation of our society has proceeded beyond the power of a commonplace mind to describe it deeply. For depth of description demands that the writer identify himself with a social force to which he can give symbolic significance, that he can discern a pattern in history, that he can not only plot his way through it but recognize himself to be a figure in it.

This social intelligence is now lacking to our novelists—except to those brilliant Southern writers, like William Styron and Flannery O'Connor, who can find the present meaningful because they find the past so. But other Southern writers run the risk of being as confused as anyone else once they get off that safe subject, the betrayal of the past, which has been Faulkner's great theme. The bigger, richer, and more anxious the country becomes, the more writers in the traditional mode, like O'Hara, or writers who are now formidably "hip," like Mailer, find themselves trying to find in sex as individual appetite the drama of society in which they can see themselves as partisans and judges. This lack of breadth and extent and dimension I have been complaining of: what is it but the uncertainty of these writers about their connection with that part of reality which other novelists include in their work simply because they are always aware of it—not because they have strained to know it? What many writers feel today is that reality is not much more than what *they* say it

is. This is a happy discovery only for genius. For most writers today, the moral order is created, step by step, only
through the clarifications achieved by art and, step by step,
they refuse to trust beyond the compass of the created work.
There has probably never been a time when the social nature
of the novel was so much at odds with the felt lack of order
in the world about us. In the absence of what used to be
given, the novelist must create a wholly imaginary world—or
else he must have the courage, in an age when personal willfulness rules in every sphere, to say that we are *not* alone,
that the individual does not have to invent human values but
only to rediscover them. The novel as a form will always demand a commonsense respect for life and interest in society.

THREE

Whatever my complaints, I never despair of the novel.
As someone said, it is more than a form, it is a literature. I
hope never to overlook the positive heroism of those writers
who believe in the novel and in the open representation of experience that is its passion and delight—who refuse to believe
that there can be an alternative to it for an age like ours. And
it does seem to me that the tangibility, the felt reverberations
of life that one finds in a writer like Bernard Malamud, spring
from his belief that any imaginative "world," no matter how
local or strange, *is* the world, and that for the imaginative
writer values must be considered truths, not subjective fancies.
It is really a kind of faith that accounts for Malamud's "perfect sympathy" with *his* characters in *The Assistant* and *The
Magic Barrel.* Though it is difficult for the alone to sympathize with each other, it is a fact that fiction can elicit and
prove the world we share, that it can display the unforeseen
possibilities of the human—even when everything seems dead
set against it.

1959

Mass society and post-modern fiction

IRVING HOWE

RASKOLNIKOV is lying on his bed: feverish, hungry, despondent. The servant Nastasya has told him that the landlady plans to have him evicted. He has received a letter from his mother in which she writes that for the sake of money his sister Dounia is to marry an elderly man she does not love. And he has already visited the old pawnbroker and measured the possibility of murdering her.

There seems no way out, no way but the liquidation of the miserly hunchback whose disappearance from the earth would cause no one any grief. Tempted by the notion that the strong, simply because they are strong, may impose their will upon the weak, Raskolnikov lies there, staring moodily at the ceiling. It must be done: so he tells himself and so he resolves.

Suddenly—but here I diverge a little from the text—the doorbell rings. A letter. Raskolnikov tears it open:

Dear Sir,

It is my pleasure to inform you, on behalf of the Guggenheim Foundation, that you have been awarded a fellowship for the study of color imagery in Pushkin's poetry and its relation to the myths of the ancient Muscovites. If you will be kind enough to visit our offices, at Nevsky Prospect and Q Street, arrangements can be made for commencing your stipend immediately.

(signed) Moevsky

From *Partisan Review*, Summer 1959, pp. 420-436. Reprinted by permission.

Trembling with joy, Raskolnikov sinks to his knees and bows his head in gratitude. The terrible deed he had contemplated can now be forgotten; he need no longer put his theories to the test; the way ahead, he tells himself, is clear.

But Dostoevsky: is the way now clear for him? May not Raskolnikov's salvation prove to be Dostoevsky's undoing? For Dostoevsky must now ask himself: how, if the old pawnbroker need no longer be destroyed, can Raskolnikov's pride be brought to a visible dramatic climax? The theme remains, for we may imagine that Raskolnikov will still be drawn to notions about the rights of superior individuals; but a new way of realizing this theme will now have to be found.

It is a common assumption of modern criticism that Dostoevsky's ultimate concern was not with presenting a picture of society, nor merely with showing us the difficulties faced by an impoverished young intellectual in czarist Russia. He was concerned with the question of what a human being, acting in the name of his freedom or disenchantment, may take upon himself. Yet we cannot help noticing that the social setting of his novel "happens" to fit quite exactly the requirements of his theme: it is the situation in which Raskolnikov finds himself that embodies the moral and metaphysical problems which, as we like to say, form Dostoevsky's deepest interest.

The sudden removal of Raskolnikov's poverty, as I have imagined it a moment ago, does not necessarily dissolve the temptation to test his will through killing another human being; but it does eliminate the immediate cause for committing the murder. Gliding from fellowship to fellowship, Raskolnikov may now end his life as a sober Professor of Literature. Like the rest of us, he will occasionally notice in himself those dim urges and quavers that speak for hidden powers beyond the assuagement of reason. He may remember that once, unlikely as it has now come to seem, he was even tempted to murder an old woman. But again like the rest of us, he will dismiss these feelings as unworthy of a civilized man.

The case is not hopeless for Dostoevsky: it never is for a writer of his stature. He can now invent other ways of dramatizing the problem that had concerned him in the novel as it was to be, the novel before Moevsky's letter arrived; but it is questionable whether even he could imagine circumstances —imagine circumstances, as distinct from expressing sentiments—which would lead so persuasively, so inexorably to a revelation of Raskolnikov's moral heresy as do those in what I am tempted to call the unimproved version of *Crime and Punishment*.

From which it will not be concluded, I hope, that a drop in our standard of living is needed in order to provide novelists with extreme or vivid situations. I am merely trying to suggest that in reading contemporary fiction one sometimes feels that the writers find themselves in situations like the one I have here fancied for Dostoevsky.

TWO

Let us assume for a moment that we have reached the end of one of those recurrent periods of cultural unrest, innovation, and excitement that we call "modern." Whether we really have no one can say with assurance, and there are strong arguments to be marshalled against such a claim. But if one wishes to reflect upon some—the interesting minority—of the novels written in America during the past 15 years, there is a decided advantage in regarding them as "postmodern," significantly different from the kind of writing we usually call modern. Doing this helps one to notice the distinctive qualities of recent novels: what makes them new. It tunes the ear to their distinctive failures. And it lures one into patience and charity.

That modern novelists—those, say, who began writing after the early work of Henry James—have been committed to a peculiarly anxious and persistent search for values, everyone knows. By now this search for values has become not only a familiar but an expected element in modern fiction; that is, a tradition has been established in which it conspicuously figures, and readers have come, somewhat unhistorically, to regard it as a necessary component of the novel. It has been a major cause for that reaching, sometimes a straining toward moral surprise, for that inclination to transform the art of narrative into an act of cognitive discovery, which sets modern fiction apart from a large number of 18th- and even 19th-century novels.

Not so frequently noticed, however, is the fact that long after the modern novelist had come to suspect and even assault traditional values there was still available to him—I would say, until about the Second World War—a cluster of stable assumptions as to the nature of our society. If the question, "How shall we live?" agitated the novelists without rest, there was a remarkable consensus in their answers to the question, "How do we live?"—a consensus not so much in explicit opinion as in a widely shared feeling about Western society.

Indeed, the turn from the realistic social novel among many of the modern writers would have been most unlikely had there not been available such a similarity of response to the familiar social world. At least some of the novelists who abandoned realism seem to have felt that modern society had been exhaustively, perhaps even excessively portrayed (so D.H. Lawrence suggests in one of his letters) and that the task of the novelist was now to explore a chaotic multiplicity of meanings rather than to continue representing the surfaces of common experience.

No matter what their social bias, and regardless of whether they were aware of having any, the modern novelists tended to assume that the social relations of men in the world of capitalism were established, familiar, knowable. If Joyce could write of Stephen Dedalus that "his destiny was to be elusive of social or religious orders," that was partly because he knew and supposed his readers to know what these orders were. If Lawrence in his later works could write a new kind of novel that paid as little attention to the external phenomena of the social world as to the fixed conventions of novelistic "character," that was partly because he had already registered both of these—the social world and the recognizable solid characters—in *Sons and Lovers*. The observations of class relationships in the earlier novels are not discarded by Lawrence in the later ones; they are tacitly absorbed to become a basis for a new mode of vision.

Values, as everyone now laments, were in flux; but society, it might be remembered, was still there: hard, tangible, ruled by a calculus of gain. One might not know what to make of this world, but at least one knew what was happening in it. Every criticism that novelists might direct against society had behind it enormous pressures of evidence, enormous accumulations of sentiment; and this, one might remark to those literary people who bemoan the absence of "tradition," this is the tradition that has been available to and has so enriched modern fiction. A novelist like F. Scott Fitzgerald, whose gifts for conceptual thought were rather meager, could draw to great advantage upon the social criticism that for over a century had preceded him, the whole lengthy and bitter assault upon bourgeois norms that had been launched by the spokesmen for culture. That Fitzgerald may have known little more than the names of these spokesmen, that he drew upon their work with only a minimum of intellectual awareness, serves merely to confirm my point. The rapidity with which such criticism was accumulated during the nineteenth century, whether by Marx or Carlyle, Nietzsche or Mill, enabled the modern novelists to feel they did not need to repeat the work of Flaubert and Dickens, Balzac and Zola: they could go beyond them.

Between radical and conservative writers, as between both of these and the bulk of nonpolitical ones, there were many bonds of shared feeling—a kinship they themselves were often unable to notice but which hindsight permits us to see. The sense of the banality of middle-class existence, of its sensuous and spiritual meanness, is quite the same among the conservative as the radical writers, and their ideas about the costs and possibilities of rising in the bourgeois world are not so very different either.

If one compares two American novelists so different in formal opinion, social background, and literary method as Theodore Dreiser and Edith Wharton, it becomes clear that in such works as *Sister Carrie* and *The House of Mirth* both are relying upon the same crucial assumption: that values, whether traditional or modernist, desirable or false, can be tested in a novel by dramatizing the relationships between mobile characters and fixed social groups. Neither writer felt any need to question, neither would so much as think to question, the presence or impact of these social groups as they formed part of the examined structure of class society. In both novels "the heart of fools is in the house of mirth," the heartbreak house of the modern city; and as Carrie Meeber and Lily Bart make their way up and down the social hierarchy, their stories take on enormous weights of implication because we are ready to assume *some* relationship —surely not the one officially proclaimed by society, nor a mere inversion of it, but still some complex and significant relationship—between the observed scale of social place and the evolving measure of moral value. It is this assumption that has been a major resource of modern novelists; for without some such assumption there could not occur the symbolic compression of incident, the readiness to assume that X stands for Y, which is a prerequisite for the very existence of the novel.

Beset though they might be by moral uncertainties, the modern novelists could yet work through to a relative assurance in their treatment of the social world; and one reason for this assurance was that by the early years of our century the effort to grasp this world conceptually was very far advanced. The novelists may not have been aware of the various theories concerning capitalism, the city, and modern industrial society; it does not matter. These ideas had so thoroughly penetrated the consciousness of thinking men, and even the folklore of the masses, that the novelists could count on them without necessarily being able to specify or elaborate them. In general, when critics "find" ideas in novels, they are transposing to a state of abstraction those assumptions which had become so familiar to novelists that they were able to seize them as sentiments.

Part of what I have been saying runs counter to the influential view that writers of prose fiction in America have written romances and not novels because, in words of Lionel Trilling that echo a more famous complaint of Henry James, there has been in this country "no sufficiency of means for the display of a variety of manners, no opportunity for the novelist to do his job of searching out reality, not enough complication of appearance to make the job interesting." I am not sure that this was ever true of American fiction—the encounter between Ishmael and Queequeg tells us as much about manners (American manners), and through manners about the moral condition of humanity, as we are likely to find in a novel by Jane Austen or Balzac. But even if it is granted that the absence of clearcut distinctions of class made it impossible in the nineteenth century to write novels about American society and encouraged, instead, a species of philosophical romance, this surely ceased to be true by about 1880. Since then, at least, there has been "enough complication of appearance to make the job interesting."

Nor am I saying—what seems to me much more dubious —that the presumed absence in recent years of a fixed, stratified society or of what one critic, with enviable naïveté, calls "an agreed picture of the universe" makes it impossible to study closely our social life, or to develop (outside of the South) human personalities rooted in a sense of tradition, or to write good novels dealing with social manners and relationships. That all of these things can be done we know, simply because they have been done. I wish merely to suggest that certain assumptions concerning modern society, which

have long provided novelists with symbolic economies and
dramatic conveniences, are no longer quite so available as
they were a few decades ago. To say this is not to assert that
we no longer have recognizable social classes in the United
States or that distinctions in manners have ceased to be significant. It is to suggest that the modern theories about society—theories which for novelists have usually been present as
tacit assumptions—have partly broken down; and that this
presents a great many new difficulties for the younger writers.
New difficulties, which is also to say: new possibilities.

THREE

In the last two decades there has occurred a series of changes
in American life, the extent, durability, and significance of
which no one has yet measured. No one can. We speak of
the growth of a "mass society," a term I shall try to define in
a moment; but at best this is merely a useful hypothesis, not
an accredited description. It is a notion that lacks common
consent, for it does not yet merit common consent. Still, one
can say with some assurance that the more sensitive among
the younger writers, those who feel that at whatever peril to
their work and careers they must grapple with something new
in contemporary experience, even if, like everyone else, they
find it extremely hard to say what that "newness" consists of
—such writers recognize that the once familiar social categories and place marks have now become as uncertain and
elusive as the moral imperatives of the nineteenth century
seemed to novelists of fifty years ago. And the something new
which they notice or stumble against is, I would suggest, the
mass society.

By the mass society we mean a relatively comfortable, half
welfare and half garrison society in which the population
grows passive, indifferent, and atomized; in which traditional
loyalties, ties, and associations become lax or dissolve entirely; in which coherent publics based on definite interests
and opinions gradually fall apart; and in which man becomes
a consumer, himself mass-produced like the products, diver-
sions, and values that he absorbs.

No social scientist has yet come up with a theory of mass
society that is entirely satisfying; no novelist has quite cap-
tured its still amorphous symptoms—a peculiar blend of
frenzy and sluggishness, amiability and meanness. I would

venture the guess that a novelist unaware of the changes in our experience to which the theory of mass society points, is a novelist unable to deal successfully with recent American life; while one who focused only upon those changes would be unable to give his work an adequate sense of historical depth.

This bare description of the mass society can be extended by noting a few traits or symptoms:

1) Social classes continue to exist, and the society cannot be understood without reference to them; yet the visible tokens of class are less obvious than in earlier decades and the correlations between class status and personal condition, assumed both by the older sociologists and the older novelists, become elusive and problematic—which is not, however, to say that such correlations no longer exist.

2) Traditional centers of authority, like the family, tend to lose some of their binding-power upon human beings; vast numbers of people now float through life with a burden of freedom they can neither sustain nor legitimately abandon to social or religious groups.

3) Traditional ceremonies that have previously marked moments of crisis and transition in human life, thereby helping men to accept such moments, are now either neglected or debased into mere occasions for public display.

4) Passivity becomes a widespread social attitude: the feeling that life is a drift over which one has little control and that even when men do have shared autonomous opinions they cannot act them out in common.

5) As perhaps never before, opinion is manufactured systematically and "scientifically."

6) Opinion tends to flow unilaterally, from the top down, in measured quantities: it becomes a market commodity.

7) Disagreement, controversy, polemic are felt to be in bad taste; issues are "ironed out" or "smoothed away"; reflection upon the nature of society is replaced by observation of its mechanics.

8) The era of "causes," good or bad, comes to an end; strong beliefs seem anachronistic; and as a result, agnostics have even been known to feel a certain nostalgia for the rigors of belief.

9) Direct and firsthand experience seems to evade human beings, though the quantity of busy-ness keeps increasing

and the number of events multiplies with bewildering
speed.

10) The pressure of material need visibly decreases, yet
there follows neither a sense of social release nor a feeling of personal joy; instead, people become increasingly
aware of their social dependence and powerlessness.

Now this is a social cartoon and not a description of
American society; but it is a cartoon that isolates an aspect of
our experience with a suggestiveness that no other mode of
analysis is likely to match. Nor does it matter that no actual
society may ever reach the extreme condition of a "pure"
mass society; the value of the theory lies in bringing to our
attention a major historical drift.

If there is any truth at all in these speculations, they should
help illuminate the problems faced by the novelists whose
work began to appear shortly after the Second World War.
They had to confront not merely the chronic confusion of
values which has gripped our civilization for decades. In a
sense they were quite prepared for that—the whole of modern literature taught them to expect little else. But they had
also to face a problem which, in actually composing a novel,
must have been still more troublesome: our society no longer
lent itself to assured definition, one could no longer assume
as quickly as in the recent past that a spiritual or moral difficulty could find a precise embodiment in a social conflict.
Raskolnikov, fellowship in hand, might still be troubled by
the metaphysical question of what a human being can allow
himself; but Raskolnikov as a graduate student with an anxious young wife and a two-year-old baby—what was the novelist to make of him? Something fresh and valuable, no
doubt; but only if he were aware that this new Raskolnikov
had to be seen in ways significantly different from those of
the traditional modern novelists.

How to give shape to a world increasingly shapeless and an
experience increasingly fluid; how to reclaim the central assumption of the novel that telling relationships can be discovered between a style of social behavior and a code of moral
judgment, or if that proves impossible, to find ways of imaginatively projecting the code in its own right—these were the
difficulties that faced the young novelists. It was as if the
guidelines of both our social thought and literary conventions
were being erased. Or as a young German writer has recently
remarked:

There's no longer a society to write about. In former years you knew where you stood: the peasants read the Bible; the maniacs read *Mein Kampf*. Now people no longer have any opinions; they have refrigerators. Instead of illusions we have television, instead of tradition, the Volkswagen. The only way to catch the spirit of the times is to write a handbook on home appliances.

Taken literally, this is close to absurd; taken as half-comic hyperbole, it reaches a genuine problem.

The problem, in part, is the relationship between the writer and his materials. Some years ago Van Wyck Brooks had spoken of the conflict between the life of the spirit and the life of commerce, and had called upon American writers to make their choice. Most of them did. Almost every important writer in twentieth century America, whether or not he read Brooks, implicitly accepted his statement as the truth and chose, with whatever lapses or qualifications, to speak for the life of the spirit.

But was the conflict between spirit and commerce, between culture and society still so acute during the postwar years? Was not a continued belief in this conflict a stale and profitless hangover from the ideologies of the thirties? Might there not be ground for feeling, among the visible signs of our careless postwar prosperity, that a new and more moderate vision of society should inform the work of our novelists? It hardly matters which answers individual writers gave to these questions; the mere fact that they were now being seriously raised had a profound impact upon their work.

Those few who favored a bluntly "positive" approach to American society found it hard to embody their sentiments in vibrant—or even credible—fictional situations. The values of accommodation were there for the asking, but they seemed, perversely, to resist creative use. For almost two decades now there has been an outpouring of "affirmative" novels about American businessmen—Executive Suites in various shades; but I do not know of a single serious critic who finds these books anything but dull and mediocre. At least in our time, the novel seems to lend itself irrevocably to the spirit of criticism; as Camus has remarked, it "is born simultaneously with the spirit of rebellion and expresses, on the esthetic plane, the same ambition."

But what has been so remarkable and disconcerting is that those writers who wished to preserve the spirit of rebellion also found it extremely hard to realize their sentiments in novels dealing with contemporary life. Most of them were unable, or perhaps too shrewd, to deal with the postwar experience directly; they preferred tangents of suggestion to frontal representation; they could express their passionate, though often amorphous, criticism of American life not through realistic portraiture but through fable, picaresque, prophecy, and nostalgia.

Morally the young novelists were often more secure than their predecessors. Few of them were as susceptible to money and glitter as Fitzgerald; few had Hemingway's weakness for bravado and swagger; few succumbed to hallucinatory rhetoric in the manner of Faulkner. Yet, as novelists, they were less happily "placed" than the writers who began to publish in the twenties and early thirties. They lacked the pressure of inevitable subjects as these take shape in situations and locales. They lacked equivalents of Fitzgerald's absorption with social distinctions, Hemingway's identification with expatriates, Faulkner's mourning over the old South. Sentiments they had in abundance and often fine ones; but to twist a remark of Gertrude Stein's, literature is not made of sentiments.

Literature is not made of sentiments; yet a good portion of what is most fresh in recent American fiction derives from sentiments. Better than any other group of literate Americans, our novelists resisted the mood of facile self-congratulation which came upon us during the postwar years. To be novelists at all, they had to look upon our life without ideological delusions; and they saw—*often better than they could say*—the hovering sickness of soul, the despairing contentment, the prosperous malaise. They were not, be it said to their credit, taken in. Yet the problem remained: how can one represent malaise, which by its nature is vague and without shape? It can be done, we know. But to do it one needs to be Chekhov; and that is hard.

My point, let me hasten to add, is not that novelists need social theories or philosophical systems. They do, however, need to live in an environment about which they can make economical assumptions that, in some ultimate way, are related to the ideas of speculative thinkers. Let me borrow a useful distinction that C. Wright Mills makes between troubles and issues. Troubles signify a strong but unfocused sense of disturbance and pain, while issues refer to troubles that have been articulated as general statements. Novelists, as a rule, concern themselves with troubles, not issues. But to write with assurance and economy about troubles, they need to be working in a milieu where there is at least some awareness of issues. And in the troubled years after the Second World War it was precisely this awareness that was often lacking.

A few serious writers did try to fix in their novels the amorphous "troubledness" of postwar American experience. In *The Violated*, an enormous realistic narrative about some ordinary people who reach adulthood during the war, Vance Bourjaily seemed consciously to be dramatizing a view of American society quite similar to the one I have sketched here. He chose to write one of those full-scale narratives composed of parallel strands of plot—a technique which assumes that society is distinctly articulated, that its classes are both sharply visible and intrinsically interesting, and that a novelist can arrange a conflict between members of these classes which will be dramatic in its own right and emblematic of larger issues. But for the material Bourjailly chose—the lives of bewildered yet not uncharacteristic drifters during the past two decades—these assumptions could not operate with sufficient force; and as his characters, in the sameness of their misery, melted into one another, so the strands of his narrative, also having no inevitable reason for separate existence, collapsed into one another.

Norman Mailer, trying in *The Deer Park* to compose a novel about the malaise of our years, avoided the cumbersomeness of the traditional social novel but could find no other structure that would give coherence to his perceptions. Mailer tried to embody his keen if unstable vision in a narrative about people whose extreme dislocation of experience and feeling would, by the very fact of their extreme dislocation, come to seem significant. But in its effort to portray our drifting and boredom full-face, in its fierce loyalty to the terms of its own conception, *The Deer Park* tended to become a claustrophobic work, driving attention inward, toward its own tonal peculiarities, rather than outward, as an extending parable. Throughout the novel Mailer had to fall back upon his protagonist, through whom he tried to say that which he found hard to show.

FOUR

A whole group of novelists, among the best of recent years, has found itself responding to immediate American experi-

ence by choosing subjects and locales that are apparently far
removed from that experience yet, through their inner quality, very close to it. These writers are sensitive to the moods
and tones of postwar American life; they know that something new, different, and extremely hard to describe has been
happening to us. Yet they do not usually write about postwar
experience *per se:* they do not confront it as much as they
try to ambush it. The film critic Stanley Kaufmann has noted
a similar phenomenon:

> When Vittorio de Sica was asked why so many of his
> films deal with adultery, he is said to have replied, "But
> if you take adultery out of the lives of the bourgeoisie,
> what drama is left?" It is perhaps this belief that has im-
> pelled Tennessee Williams into the areas that his art in-
> habits. He has recognized that most of contemporary life
> offers limited dramatic opportunities . . . so he has left
> "normal" life to investigate the highly neurotic, the
> violent and the grimy. It is the continuing problem of the
> contemporary writer who looks for great emotional issues
> to move him greatly. The anguish of the advertising ex-
> ecutive struggling to keep his job is anguish indeed, but
> its possibilities in art are not large-scale. The writer who
> wants to "let go" has figuratively to leave the urban and
> suburban and either go abroad, go into the past, or go
> into those few pockets of elemental emotional life left in
> this country.

Abroad, the past, or the few pockets of elemental emotional life:—many of our best writers have pursued exactly
these strategies in order to suggest their attitudes toward contemporary experience. In *The Assistant* Bernard Malamud
has written a somber story about a Jewish family during the
Depression years, yet it soon becomes clear that one of his
impelling motives is a wish to recapture intensities of feeling
we have apparently lost but take to be characteristic of an
earlier decade. Herbert Gold's *The Man Who Was Not With
It* is an account of marginal figures in a circus as they teeter
on the edge of *lumpen* life; but soon one realizes that he
means his story to indicate possibilities for personal survival
in a world increasingly compressed. The precocious and bewildered boy in J.D. Salinger's *The Catcher in the Rye* expresses something of the moral condition of adolescents today
—or so they tell us; but clearly his troubles are not meant to
refer to his generation alone. In *A Walk on the Wild Side*
Nelson Algren turns to down-and-outers characteristic of an

earlier social moment, but if we look to the psychic pressures breaking through the novel we see that he is really searching for a perspective for estrangement that will be relevant to our day. In *The Field of Vision* Wright Morris moves not backward in time but sideways in space: he contrives to bring a dreary Nebraskan middle-class family to a Mexican bullfight so that the excitement of the blood and ritual will stir it to self-awareness. And while, on the face of it, Saul Bellow's *The Adventures of Augie March* is a picaresque tale about a cocky Jewish boy moving almost magically past the barriers in American society, it is also a kind of paean to the idea of personal freedom in hostile circumstances. Bellow's most recent novel, *Henderson the Rain King*, seems an even wilder tale about an American millionaire venturing into deepest Africa, in part, the deepest Africa of boys' books; but when he writes that men need a shattering experience to "wake the spirit's sleep," we soon realize that his ultimate reference is to America, where many spirits sleep.

Though vastly different in quality, these novels have in common a certain obliqueness of approach. They do not represent directly the postwar American experience, yet refer to it constantly. They tell us rather little about the surface tone, the manners, the social patterns of recent American life, yet are constantly projecting moral criticism of its essential quality. They approach that experience on the sly, yet are colored and shaped by it throughout. And they gain from it their true subject: the recurrent search—in America, almost a national obsession—for personal identity and freedom. In their distance from fixed social categories and their concern with the metaphysical implications of that distance these novels constitute what I would call "post-modern" fiction.

But the theme of personal identity, if it is to take on fictional substance, needs some kind of placement, a setting in the world of practical affairs. And it is here that the "post-modern" novelists run into serious troubles: the connection between subject and setting cannot always be made, and the "individual" of their novels, because he lacks social definition and is sometimes a creature of literary or even ideological fiat, tends to be not very individualized. Some of the best postwar novels, like *Invisible Man* and *The Adventures of Augie March*, are deeply concerned with the fate of freedom in a mass society; but the assertiveness of idea and vanity of style which creep into such books are the result, I think, of willing a subject onto a novel rather than allowing it to grow

out of a sure sense of a particular moment and place. These
novels merit admiration for defending the uniqueness of
man's life, but they suffer from having to improvise the terms
of this uniqueness. It is a difficulty that seems, at the moment, unavoidable and I have no wish to disparage writers
who face it courageously. Still, it had better be said that the
proclamation of personal identity in recent American fiction
tends, if I may use a fashionable phrase, to be more a product of the will than of the imagination.

It may help strengthen my point—critics ought not to
strengthen such points too much—if I turn for a moment to
the two most-discussed literary groups of the last few years:
the "angry young men" in England and the "beat generation"
writers of San Francisco.

Partly because they write in and about England, Kingsley
Amis, John Braine and John Wain are blessed with something utterly precious to a writer: a subject urgently, relentlessly imposing itself upon their imaginations. They have
earned the scorn of a good many American critics—notable,
of course, for asceticism—who point out that it is not clear
whether it is a better or just a bigger share of the material
and cultural goods in contemporary England that these writers want. But while you can feel righteous or even hostile toward Amis and Braine, you can hardly deny that in their
novels one finds something of the focused desire, the quick
apprehension and notation of contemporary life which, for
reasons I have tried to suggest, has become somewhat rare in
serious American fiction. These English writers face a predicament of the welfare state: it rouses legitimate desires in people of the "lower orders"; it partly satisfies these desires; but
it satisfies them only to the point of arousing new demands
beyond its power of meeting. For society this may be irk-
some; for writers it is exhilarating. Gripes can be transformed
into causes, ambitions cloaked as ideals. And the "angry
young men" are particularly fortunate in that their complaints lead them to deal with some of the traditional materials of the novel: frustrated ambition, frozen snobbery, fake
culture, decaying gentility. Through comedy they are able to
structure their complaints. Their work touches upon sore
spots in English life, hurting some people and delighting others. It threatens the Establishment, perhaps its survival, more
likely its present leaders. It creates tension, opposition, a di-

alectic of interests. All of which is to say: it rests upon an articulated, coherent though limited vision of English social relations.

By contrast, the young men in San Francisco seem largely a reflex of the circumstances of mass society. They are suffering from psychic and social disturbance: and as far as that goes, they are right—there is much in American life to give one a pain. But they have no clear sense of why or how they are troubled, and some of them seem opposed in principle to a clear sense of anything. The "angry young men" in England, even if their protest will prove to be entirely opportunistic and momentary, can say what it is that hurts. The San Francisco writers fail to understand, as Paul Goodman has remarked, that

> It is necessary to have some contact with institutions and people in order to be frustrated and angry. They [the San Francisco writers] have the theory that to be affectless, not to care, is the ultimate rebellion, but this is a fantasy; for right under the surface is burning shame, hurt feelings, fear of impotence, speechless and powerless tantrum, cowering before papa, being rebuffed by mama; and it is these anxieties that dictate their behavior in every crisis.

These writers, I would contend, illustrate the painful though not inevitable predicament of rebellion in a mass society: they are the other side of the American hollow. In their contempt for mind they are at one with the middle-class suburbia they think they scorn. In their incoherence of feeling and statement they mirror the incoherent society that clings to them like a mocking shadow. In their yearning to keep "cool" they sing out an eternal fantasy of the shopkeeper. Feeling themselves lonely and estranged, they huddle together in gangs, create a Brook Farm of Know-Nothings, and send back ecstatic reports to the squares: Having a Wonderful Time, Having Wonderful Kicks! But alas, all the while it is clear that they are terribly lost, and what is more pitiable, that they don't even have the capacity for improvising vivid fantasies. As they race meaninglessly back and forth across the continent, veritable mimics of the American tourist, they do not have a Wonderful Time. They do not get happily drunk, many of them preferring milk shakes and tea; and their sexual revelations, particularly in Kerouac's *The Subterraneans,* are as sad as they are unintentional. They can't, that is, dream themselves out of the shapeless nightmare of California; and for that, perhaps we should not blame them, since it is not certain that anyone can.

No wonder, then, that in Kerouac's novels one is vaguely aware that somewhere, in the unmapped beyond, a society does exist: a society with forms, requirements, burdens, injustices, duties and pleasures; but that in the space of the novels themselves we can only find a series of distraught and compulsive motions. The themes of what I have called "postmodern" fiction are reflected in the San Francisco writers as caricature and symptom; for if you shun consciousness as if it were a plague, then a predicament may ravage you but you cannot cope with it.

Where finally does this leave us? In the midst, I hope, of the promise and confusion of American writing today. No settled ending is possible here, because the tendencies I have been noticing are still in flux, still open to many pressures and possibilities. But it may not be too rash to say that the more serious of the "post-modern" novelists—those who grapple with problems rather than merely betraying their effects—have begun to envisage that we may be on the threshold of enormous changes in human history. These changes, merely glanced by the idea of the "mass society," fill our novelists with a sense of foreboding; and through the strategy of obliqueness, they bring to bear a barrage of moral criticisms, reminders of human potentiality, and tacit exhortations.

The possibilities that appear to them are those which struck at T. E. Lawrence when he returned from Arabia and discovered that he did not know how or why to live. One such possibility is that we are moving toward a quiet desert of moderation where men will forget the passion of moral and spiritual restlessness that has characterized Western society. That the human creature, no longer a Quixote or a Faust, will become a docile attendant to an automated civilization. That the "aura of the human" will be replaced by the nihilism of satiety. That the main question will no longer be the conditions of existence but existence itself. That high culture as we understand it will become increasingly problematical and perhaps reach some point of obsolescence.

But before such prospects—they form the bad dreams of

thoughtful men, the nightmares our "post-modern" novelists are trying to exorcise—the mind grows dizzy and recalcitrant. It begins to solace itself with rumblings about eternal truths, and like the exacerbated judge in Faulkner's *The Hamlet,* cries out, "I can't stand no more . . . This case is adjourned!"

1959

Writing american fiction

PHILIP ROTH

SEVERAL winters back, while I was living in Chicago, the city was shocked and mystified by the death of two teen-age girls. So far as I know the populace is mystified still; as for the shock, Chicago is Chicago, and one week's dismemberment fades into the next's. The victims this particular year were sisters. They went off one December night to see an Elvis Presley movie, for the sixth or seventh time we are told, and never came home. Ten days passed and fifteen and twenty, and then the whole bleak city, every street and alley, was being searched for the missing Grimes girls, Pattie and Babs. A girl friend had seen them at the movie, a group of boys had had a glimpse of them afterward getting into a black Buick; another group said a green Chevy, and so on and so forth, until one day the snow melted and the unclothed bodies of the two girls were discovered in a roadside ditch in a forest preserve on the West Side of Chicago. The coroner said he didn't know the cause of death and then the newspapers took over. One paper, I forget which one, ran a drawing of the girls on the back page, in bobby socks and Levi's and babushkas: Pattie and Babs a foot tall, and in four colors, like Dixie Dugan on Sundays. The mother of the two girls wept herself right into the arms of a local newspaper lady, who apparently set up her typewriter on the Grimes's front porch and turned out a column a day, telling us that these

Reprinted from *Commentary*, by permission; copyright © 1961 by the American Jewish Committee.

had been good girls, hardworking girls, average girls, church-going girls, et cetera. Late in the evening one could watch television interviews featuring schoolmates and friends of the Grimes sisters: the teen-age girls look around, dying to giggle; the boys stiffen in their leather jackets. "Yeah, I knew Babs, yeah she was all right, yeah, she was popular. . . ." On and on until at last comes a confession. A Skid Row bum of thirty-five or so, a dishwasher, a prowler, a no-good named Benny Bedwell, admits to killing both girls after he and a pal had cohabited with them for several weeks in various flea-bitten hotels. Hearing the news, the mother weeps and cries and tells the newspaper lady that the man is a liar—her girls, she insists now, were murdered the night they went off to the movie. The coroner continues to maintain (with rumblings from the press) that the girls show no signs of having had sexual intercourse. Meanwhile, everybody in Chicago is buying four papers a day, and Benny Bedwell, having supplied the police with an hour-by-hour chronicle of his adventures, is tossed in jail. Two nuns, teachers of the girls at the school they attended, are sought out by the newspapermen. They are surrounded and questioned and finally one of the sisters explains all. "They were not exceptional girls," the sister says, "they had no hobbies." About this time some good-natured soul digs up Mrs. Bedwell, Benny's mother, and a meeting is arranged between this old woman and the mother of the slain teen-agers. Their picture is taken together, two overweight, overworked American ladies, quite befuddled but sitting up straight for the photographers. Mrs. Bedwell apologizes for her Benny. She says, "I never thought any boy of mine would do a thing like that." Two weeks later, or maybe three, her boy is out on bail, sporting several lawyers and a new one-button roll suit. He is driven in a pink Cadillac to an out-of-town motel where he holds a press conference. Yes—he barely articulates—he is the victim of policy brutality. No, he is not a murderer; a degenerate maybe, but even that is going out the window. He is changing his life—he is going to become a carpenter (a carpenter!) for the Salvation Army, his lawyers say. Immediately Benny is asked to sing (he plays the guitar) in a Chicago night spot for two thousand dollars a week, or is it ten thousand? I forget. What I remember is that suddenly there is a thought that comes flashing into the mind of the spectator, or newspaper reader: is this all Public Relations? But of course not—two girls are dead. At any rate, a

song begins to catch on in Chicago, "The Benny Bedwell
Blues." Another newspaper launches a weekly contest: "How
Do You Think the Grimes Girls Were Murdered?" and a
prize is given for the best answer (in the opinion of the
judges). And now the money begins; donations, hundreds of
them, start pouring in to Mrs. Grimes from all over the city
and the state. For what? From whom? Most contributions are
anonymous. Just money, thousands and thousands of dollars
—the *Sun-Times* keeps us informed of the grand total. Ten
thousand, twelve thousand, fifteen thousand. Mrs. Grimes
sets about refinishing and redecorating her house. A strange
man steps forward, by the name of Shultz or Schwartz—I
don't really remember, but he is in the appliance business and
he presents Mrs. Grimes with a whole new kitchen. Mrs.
Grimes, beside herself with appreciation and joy, turns to her
surviving daughter and says, "Imagine me in that kitchen!"
Finally the poor woman goes out and buys two parakeets (or
maybe another Mr. Shultz presented them as a gift); one par-
akeet she calls "Babs," the other, "Pattie." At just about this
point, Benny Bedwell, doubtless having barely learned to
hammer a nail in straight, is extradited to Florida on the
charge of having raped a twelve-year-old girl there. Shortly
thereafter I left Chicago myself, and so far as I know, though
Mrs. Grimes hasn't her two girls, she has a brand-new dishwasher and two small birds.

And what is the moral of so long a story? Simply this: that
the American writer in the middle of the 20th century has his
hands full in trying to understand, and then describe, and
then make *credible* much of the American reality. It stupe-
fies, it sickens, it infuriates, and finally it is even a kind of
embarrassment to one's own meager imagination. The actuality is continually outdoing our talents, and the culture tosses
up figures almost daily that are the envy of any novelist. Who
for example, could have invented Charles Van Doren? Roy
Cohn and David Schine? Sherman Adams and Bernard Gold-
fine? Dwight David Eisenhower? Several months back most
of the country heard one of the candidates for the presidency
of the United States, the office of Jefferson, Lincoln, and
FDR, say something like, "Now if you feel that Senator Kennedy is right, then I sincerely believe you should vote for
Senator Kennedy, and if you feel that I am right, I humbly
submit that you vote for me. Now I feel, and this is certainly
a personal opinion, that I am right. . . ." and so on. Though it

did not appear quite this way to some thirty-four million voters, it still seems to me a little easy to pick on Mr. Nixon as someone to ridicule, and it is not for that reason that I have bothered to paraphrase his words here. If one was at first amused by him, one was ultimately astonished. As a literary creation, as some novelist's image of a certain kind of human being, he might have seemed believable, but I myself found that on the TV screen, as a real public image, a political fact, my mind balked at taking him in. Whatever else the television debates produced in me, I should like to point out, as a literary curiosity, that they also produced a type of professional envy. All the machinations over makeup, rebuttal time, all the business over whether Mr. Nixon should look at Mr. Kennedy when he replied, or should look away—all of it was so beside the point, so fantastic, so weird and astonishing, that I found myself beginning to wish I had invented it. That may not, of course, be a literary fact at all, but a simple psychological one—for finally I began to wish that *someone* had invented it, and that it was not real and with us.

The daily newspapers then fill one with wonder and awe: is it possible? is it happening? And of course with sickness and despair. The fixes, the scandals, the insanities, the treacheries, the idiocies, the lies, the pieties, the noise. . . . Recently, in *Commentary*, Benjamin DeMott wrote that the "deeply lodged suspicion of the times [is] namely, that events and individuals are unreal, and that power to alter the course of the age, of my life and your life, is actually vested nowhere." There seems to be, said DeMott, a kind of "universal descent into unreality." The other night—to give a benign example of the descent—my wife turned on the radio and heard the announcer offering a series of cash prizes for the three best television plays of five minutes' duration written by children. At such moments it is difficult to find one's way around the kitchen; certainly few days go by when incidents far less benign fail to remind us of what DeMott is talking about. When Edmund Wilson says that after reading *Life* magazine he feels that he does not belong to the country depicted there, that he does not live in that country, I think I understand what he means.

However, for a writer of fiction to feel that he does not really live in the country in which he lives—as represented by *Life* or by what he experiences when he steps out his front door —must certainly seem a serious occupational impediment.

For what will be his subject? His landscape? It is the tug of reality, its mystery and magnetism, that leads one into the writing of fiction—what then when one is not mystified, but stupefied? not drawn but repelled? It would seem that what we might get would be a high proportion of historical novels or contemporary satire—or perhaps just nothing. No books. Yet the fact is that almost weekly one finds on the bestseller list another novel which is set in Mamaroneck or New York City or Washington, with people moving through a world of dishwashers and TV sets and advertising agencies and senatorial investigations. It all *looks* as though the writers are still turning out books about our world. There is *Cash McCall* and *The Man in the Gray Flannel Suit* and *Marjorie Morningstar* and *The Enemy Camp* and *Advise and Consent,* and so on. But what is crucial, of course, is that these books aren't very good. Not that these writers aren't sufficiently horrified with the landscape to suit me—quite the contrary. They are generally full of concern for the world about them; finally, however, they just don't seem able to imagine the corruptions and vulgarities and treacheries of American public life any more profoundly than they can imagine human character—that is, the country's private life. All issues are generally solvable, which indicates that they are not so much wonderstruck or horror-struck or even plain struck by a state of civilization as they are provoked by some topical controversy. *Controversial* is a common word in the critical language of this literature as it is, say, in the language of the TV producer. But it is clear that though one may refer to a "problem" as being controversial, one does not usually speak of a state of civilization as controversial, or a state of the soul.

It is hardly news that in bestsellerdom we frequently wind up with the hero coming to terms and settling down in Scarsdale, or wherever, knowing himself. And on Broadway, in the third act, someone says, "Look, why don't you just love each other?" and the protagonist, throwing his hand to his forehead, cries, "Oh, God, why didn't *I* think of that!" and before the bulldozing action of love, all else collapses—verisimilitude, truth, and interest. It is like "Dover Beach" ending happily for Matthew Arnold, and for us, because the poet is standing at the window with a woman who understands him. If the investigation of our times and the impact of these times upon human personality were to become the sole property of Wouk, Weidman, Sloan Wilson, Cameron Hawley, and the theatrical *amor-vincit-omnia* boys, it would indeed be unfortunate, for it would be somewhat like leaving sex to the pornographers, where again there is more to what is happening than first meets the eye.

And of course the times have not yet been left completely to lesser minds and talents. There is Norman Mailer. And he is an interesting example, I think, of one in whom our era has provoked such a magnificent disgust that dealing with it in fiction has almost come to seem, for him, beside the point. He has become an actor in the cultural drama, the difficulty of which, I should guess, is that it leaves one with considerably less time to be a writer. For instance, to defy the Civil Defense authorities and their H-bomb drills, you have to take off a morning from the typewriter and go down and stand outside of City Hall; then if you're lucky and they toss you in jail, you have to give up an evening at home and your next morning's work as well. To defy Mike Wallace, or challenge his principle-less aggression, or simply use him or straighten him out, you must first go on the program—there's one night shot. Then you may well spend the next two weeks (I am speaking from memory) disliking yourself for having gone, and then two more writing an article (or a confession to a gentle friend) in which you attempt to explain why you did it and what it was like. "It's the age of the slob," says a character in William Styron's new novel. "If we don't watch out they're going to drag us under. . . ." And the dragging under, as we see, takes numerous forms. We get, for instance, from Mailer a book like *Advertisements for Myself,* a chronicle for the most part of why I did it and what it was like—and who I have it in for: life as a substitute for fiction. An infuriating, self-indulgent, boisterous, mean book, not much worse than most advertising we have to put up with, I think —but also, taken as a whole, a curiously moving book, moving in its revelation of the connection between one writer and the times that have given rise to him, in the revelation of a despair so great that the man who bears it, or is borne by it, seems for the time being—out of either choice or necessity —to have given up on making an imaginative assault upon the American experience, and has become instead the champion of a kind of public revenge. Unfortunately, however, what one is champion of one day, one may wind up victim of the next; that is everybody's risk. Once having written *Adver-*

tisements for Myself, I don't see that you can write it again. Mr. Mailer probably now finds himself in the unenviable position of having to put up or shut up. Who knows—maybe it's where he wanted to be. My own feeling is that times are tough for a writer when he takes to writing letters to his newspaper rather than those complicated, disguised letters to himself, which are stories.

The last is not meant to be a sententious or a condescending remark, or even a generous one. However one suspects Mailer's style or his reasons, one sympathizes with the impulse that leads him to be—or to want to be—a critic, a reporter, a sociologist, a journalist, a figure, or even Mayor of New York. For what is particularly tough about the times is writing about them, as a serious novelist or storyteller. Much has been made, much of it by the writers themselves, of the fact that the American writer has no status and no respect and no audience: the news I wish to bear is of a loss more central to the task itself, a loss of subject; or if not a loss, if to say that is, romantically and inexactly and defensively, an attempt to place most of the responsibility outside the writer for what may finally be nothing more than the absence of genius in our times—then let me say a voluntary withdrawal of interest by the writer of fiction from some of the grander social and political phenomena of our times.

Of course there have been writers who have tried to meet these phenomena head-on. It seems to me I have read several books or stories in the past few years in which one character or another starts to talk about "The Bomb," and the conversation generally leaves me feeling half convinced, and in some extreme instances, even with a certain amount of sympathy for fallout; it is like people in college novels having long talks about what kind of generation they are. But what then? What can the writer do with so much of the American reality as it is? Is the only other possibility to be Gregory Corso and thumb your nose at the whole thing? The attitude of the Beats (if such a phrase has meaning) is not in certain ways without appeal. The whole thing is a kind of joke. America, ha-ha. The only trouble is that such a position doesn't put very much distance between Beatdom and its sworn enemy, bestsellerdom—not much more, at any rate, than what it takes to get from one side of a nickel to the other: for what is America, ha-ha, but the simple reverse of America, hooray?

* * *

It is possible that I have exaggerated both the serious writer's response to our cultural predicament, and his inability or unwillingess to deal with it imaginatively. There seems to me little, in the end, to be used as proof for an assertion having to do with the psychology of a nation's writers, outside, that is, of their books themselves. So, with this particular assertion, the argument may appear to be somewhat compromised in that the evidence to be submitted is not so much the books that have been written, but the ones that have been left unwritten and unfinished, and those that have not even been considered worthy of the attempt. Which is not to say that there have not been certain literary signs, certain obsessions and innovations and concerns, to be found in the novels of our best writers, supporting the notion that the world we have been given, the society and the community, has ceased to be as suitable or as manageable a subject for the novelist as it once may have been.

Let me begin with some words about the man who, by reputation at least, is *the* writer of the age. The response of college students to the works of J. D. Salinger should indicate to us that perhaps he, more than anyone else, has not turned his back on the times, but instead has managed to put his finger on what is most significant in the struggle going on today between the self (all selves, not just the writer's) and the culture. *The Catcher in the Rye* and the recent stories in *The New Yorker* having to do with the Glass family surely take place in the social here and now. But what about the self, what about the hero? This question seems to me of particular interest here, for in Salinger more than in most of his contemporaries, there has been an increasing desire of late to place the figure of the writer himself directly in the reader's line of vision, so that there is an equation, finally, between the insights of the narrator as, say, brother to Seymour Glass, and as a man who is a writer by profession. And what of Salinger's heroes? Well, Holden Caulfield, we discover, winds up in an expensive sanitarium. And Seymour Glass commits suicide finally, but prior to that he is the apple of his brother's eye—and why? He has learned to live in this world—but how? By not living in it. By kissing the soles of little girls' feet and throwing rocks at the head of his sweetheart. He is a saint, clearly. But since madness is undesirable and sainthood, for most of us, out of the question, the problem of how to live *in* this world is by no means answered; unless the answer is that one cannot. The only advice we seem to get from Salinger is to be charming on the way to the loony bin. Of course, Salinger is under no burden to supply us, writers or readers, with advice, though I must admit that I find myself growing more and more curious about this professional writer, Buddy Glass, and how *he* manages to coast through this particular life in the arms of sanity.

It is not Buddy Glass, though, in whom I do not finally believe, but Seymour himself. Seymour is as unreal to me as his world, in all its endless and marvelous detail, is decidedly credible. I am touched by the lovingness that is attributed to him, as one is touched by so many of the gestures and attitudes in Salinger, but this lovingness, in its totality and otherworldliness, becomes for me in the end an attitude of the writer's, a cry of desperation, even a program, more than an expression of character. If we forgive this lapse, it is, I think, because we understand the depth of the despairing.

There is, too, in Salinger the suggestion that mysticism is a possible road to salvation; at least some of his characters respond well to an intensified, emotional religious belief. Now my own involvement with Zen is slight, but as I understand it in Salinger, the deeper we go into this world, the further we can get away from it. If you contemplate a potato long enough, it stops being a potato in the usual sense; unfortunately, though, it is the usual sense that we have to deal with from day to day. For all the loving handling of the world's objects, for all the reverence of life and feeling, here seems to me, in the Glass family stories as in *The Catcher,* a spurning of life as it is lived in this world, in this reality—this place and time is seen as unworthy of those few precious people who have been set down in it only to be maddened and destroyed.

A spurning of our world—though of a much different order —seems to occur in another of our most talented writers, Bernard Malamud. Even, one recalls, when Malamud writes a book about baseball, a book called *The Natural,* it is not baseball as it is played in Yankee Stadium, but a wild, wacky baseball, where a player who is instructed to knock the cover off the ball promptly steps up to the plate and knocks it off; the batter swings and the inner hard string core of the ball goes looping out to center field, where the confused fielder commences to tangle himself in the unwinding sphere; then the shortstop runs out, and with his teeth, bites the center fielder and the ball free from one another. Though *The Natural* is not Malamud's most successful, nor his most significant book, it is at any rate our introduction to his world, which has a kind of historical relationship to our own but is by no means a replica of it. By historical I mean that there are really things called baseball players and really things called Jews, but there much of the similarity ends. The Jews of *The Magic Barrel* and the Jews of *The Assistant*, I have reason to suspect, are not the Jews of New York City or Chicago. They are a kind of invention, a metaphor to stand for certain human possibilities and certain human promises, and I find myself further inclined to believe this when I read of a statement attributed to Malamud which goes, "All men are Jews." In fact we know this is not so; even the men who are Jews aren't sure they're Jews. But Malamud, as a writer of fiction, has not shown specific interest in the anxieties and dilemmas and corruptions of the modern American Jew, the Jew we think of as characteristic of our times; rather, his people live in a timeless depression and a placeless Lower East Side; their society is not affluent, their predicament not cultural. I am not saying—one cannot, of Malamud—that he has spurned life or an examination of the difficulties of being human. What it is to be human, to be humane, is his subject; connection, indebtedness, responsibility, these are his moral concerns. What I do mean to point out is that he does not—or has not yet—found the contemporary scene a proper or sufficient backdrop for his tales of heartlessness and heartache, of suffering and regeneration.

Now Malamud and Salinger do not speak, think, or feel for all writers, and yet their fictional response to the world about them—what they choose to mention, what they choose to avoid—is of interest to me on the simple grounds that they are two of our best. Surely there are other writers around, and capable ones too, who have not taken the particular roads that these two have; however, even with some of these others, I wonder if we may not be witnessing a response to the times, perhaps not so dramatic as in Salinger and Malamud, but a response nevertheless.

Let us take up the matter of prose style. Why is everybody so bouncy all of a sudden? Those who have been reading in the works of Saul Bellow, Herbert Gold, Arthur Granit, Thomas Berger, Grace Paley, and others will know to what I am referring. Writing recently in the *Hudson Review*, Harvey Swados said that he saw developing "a nervous muscular prose perfectly suited to the exigencies of an age which seems at once appalling and ridiculous. These are metropolitan writers, most of them are Jewish, and they are specialists in a kind of prose-poetry that often depends for its effectiveness as much on how it is ordered, or how it looks on the printed page, as it does on what it is expressing. This is risky writing, . . ." Swados added, and perhaps it is in its very riskiness that we can discover some kind of explanation for it. I should like to compare two short descriptive passages, one from Bellow's *The Adventures of Augie March,* the other from Gold's new novel, *Therefore Be Bold,* in the hope that the differences revealed will be educational.

As has been pointed out by numerous people before me, the language of *Augie March* is one that combines a literary complexity with a conversational ease, a language that joins the idiom of the academy with the idiom of the streets (not all streets—certain streets); the style is special, private, and energetic, and though occasionally unwieldy and indulgent, it generally, I believe, serves the narrative, and serves it brilliantly. Here for instance is a description of Grandma Lausch:

> With the [cigarette] holder in her dark little gums between which all her guile, malice, and command issued, she had her best inspirations of strategy. She was as wrinkled as an old paper bag, an autocrat, hard-shelled and jesuitical, a pouncy old hawk of a Bolshevik, her small ribboned gray feet immobile on the shoe-kit and stool Simon had made in the manual-training class, dingy old wool Winnie [the dog] whose bad smell filled the flat on the cushion beside her. If wit and discontent don't necessarily go together, it wasn't from the old woman that I learned it.

Herbert Gold's language has also been special, private, and energetic. One will notice in the following passage from *Therefore Be Bold* that here too the writer begins by recognizing a physical similarity between the character described and some unlikely object, and from there, as in Bellow's Grandma Lausch passage, attempts to move into a deeper, characterological description, to wind up, via the body, making a discovery about the soul. The character described is named Chuck Hastings.

In some respects he resembled a mummy—the shriveled yellow skin, the hand and head too large for a wasted body, the bottomless eye sockets of thought beyond the Nile. But his agile Adam's apple and point-making finger made him less the Styx-swimmer dog-paddling toward Coptic limbos than a high school intellectual intimidating the navel-eyed little girl.

First I must say that the grammar itself has me baffled: ". . . bottomless eye sockets of thought beyond the Nile." Is the thought beyond the Nile, or are the eye sockets? What does it mean to be beyond the Nile anyway? The agrammaticality of the sentence has little in common with the ironic inversion with which Bellow's description begins: "With the holder in her dark little gums between which all her guile, malice, and command issued. . . ." Bellow goes on to describe Grandma Lausch as "an autocrat," "hard-shelled," "jesuitical," "a pouncy old hawk of a Bolshevik"—imaginative terms certainly, but toughminded, exact, and not exhibitionistic. Of Gold's Chuck Hastings, however, we learn, "His agile Adam's-apple and point-making finger made him less the Styx-swimmer dog-paddling toward Coptic limbos etc. . . ." Is this language in the service of the narrative, or a kind of literary regression in the service of the ego? In a recent review of *Therefore Be Bold*, Granville Hicks quoted this very paragraph in praise of Gold's style. "This is high-pitched," Mr. Hicks admitted, "but the point is that Gold keeps it up and keeps it up." I take it that Mr. Hicks's sexual pun is not deliberate; nevertheless, it should remind us all that showmanship and passion are not, and never have been, one and the same. What we have here, it seems to me, is not so much stamina or good spirits, but reality taking a backseat to personality—and not the personality of the character described, but of the writer who is doing the describing. Bellow's description seems to arise out of a firm conviction on the part of the writer about the character: Grandma Lausch IS. Behind the description of Chuck Hastings there seems to me the conviction—or the desire for us to be convinced—of something else: Herbert Gold IS. I am! I am! In short: look at me, I'm writing.

Because Gold's work serves my purposes, let me say a word or two more about him. He is surely one of our most productive and most respected novelists, and yet he has

begun to seem to me a writer in competition with his own
fiction. Which is more interesting—my life or my work? His
new book of stories, *Love and Like,* is not over when we
have finished reading the last narrative. Instead we go on to
read several more pages in which the author explains why
and how he came to write each of the preceding stories. At
the end of *Therefore Be Bold* we are given a long listing of
the various cities in which Gold worked on this book, and the
dates during which he was living or visiting in them. It is all
very interesting if one is involved in tracing lost mail, but the
point to be noted here is that how the fiction has come to be
written is supposed to be nearly as interesting as what is written. Don't forget, ladies and gentlemen, that behind each and
every story you have read here tonight is—me. For all Gold's
delight with the things of this world—and I think that his
prose, at its best, is the expression of that delight—there is
also a good deal of delight in the work of his own hand. And,
I think, with the hand itself.

Using a writer for one's own purposes is of course to be unfair to him (nearly as unfair as the gambit that admits to
being unfair); I confess to this, however, and don't intend to
hang a man for one crime. Nevertheless, Gold's extravagant
prose, his confessional tone (the article about divorce; then
the several prefaces and appendices about his own divorce—
my ex-wife says this about me, etc.; then finally the story
about divorce)—all of this seems to have meaning to me in
terms of this separation I tried to describe earlier, the not-so-
friendly relationship between the writer and the culture. In
fact, it is paradoxical really, that the very prose style which, I
take it, is supposed to jolt and surprise us, and thereby produce a new and sharper vision, turns back upon itself, and
the real world is in fact veiled from us by this elaborate and
self-conscious language-making. I suppose that in a way one
can think of it as a sympathetic, or kinetic, response to the
clamor and din of our mass culture, an attempt to beat the
vulgar world at its own game. I am even willing to entertain
this possibility. But it comes down finally to the same thing:
not so much an attempt to understand the self, as to assert it.

I must say that I am not trying to sell selflessness. Rather, I
am suggesting that this nervous muscular prose that Swados
talks about may perhaps have to do with the unfriendliness
between the self of the writer and the realities of the culture.
The prose suits the age, Swados suggests, and I wonder if it

does not suit it, in part, because it rejects it. The writer pushes before our eyes—it is in the very ordering of our sentences—personality, in all its separateness and specialness. Of course the mystery of personality is nothing less than the writer's ultimate concern; and certainly when the muscular prose is revelatory of character—as in *Augie March*—then it is to be appreciated; at its worst, however, as a form of literary onanism, it seriously curtails the fictional possibilities, and may perhaps be thought of, and sympathetically so, as a symptom of the writer's loss of the community as subject.

True, the bouncy style can be understood in other ways as well. It is not surprising that most of these writers Swados sees as its practitioners are Jewish. When writers who do not feel much of a connection to Lord Chesterfield begin to realize that they are under no real obligation to try and write like that distinguished old stylist, they are quite likely to go out and be bouncy. Also, there is the matter of the spoken language which these writers have heard, as our statesmen might put it, in the schools, in the homes, in the churches and the synagogues; I should even say that when the bouncy style is not an attempt to dazzle the reader, or one's self, but to incorporate into written prose the rhythms, the excitements, the nuances and emphases of urban speech, or immigrant speech, the result can sometimes be a language of new and rich emotional subtleties, with a kind of backhanded grace and irony all its own, as say the language of Mrs. Paley's book of stories, *The Little Disturbances of Man.*

But whether the practitioner is Gold or Bellow or Paley, there is one more point to be made about bounciness, and that is that it is an expression of pleasure. One cannot deny that there is that in it. However, a question arises: if the world is as crooked and unreal as I think it is becoming, day by day; if one feels less and less power in the face of this unreality, day by day; if the inevitable end is destruction, if not of all life, then of much that is valuable and civilized in life—then why in God's name is the writer pleased? Why don't all of our fictional heroes wind up in institutions like Holden Caulfield, or suicides like Seymour Glass? Why is it, in fact, that so many of our fictional heroes—not just the heroes of Wouk and Weidman, but of Bellow, Gold, Styron, and others—wind up affirming life? For surely the air is thick these days with affirmation, and though we shall doubtless get this year our annual editorial from *Life* calling for affirmative

novels, the plain and simple fact is that more and more books
by serious writers seem to end on a note of celebration. Not
just the tone is bouncy, but the moral is bouncy too. In *The
Optimist,* another novel of Gold's, the hero, having taken his
lumps, cries out at the conclusion, "More. More. More!
More! More!" This is the book's last line. Curtis Harnack's
novel, *The World of an Ancient Hand,* ends with the hero
filled with "rapture and hope" and saying aloud, "I believe in
God." And Saul Bellow's *Henderson the Rain King* is a book
which is given over to celebrating the regeneration of a man's
heart, feelings, blood, and general health. Of course it is of
crucial importance, I think, that the regeneration of Henderson takes place in a world that is thoroughly and wholly
imagined *but does not really exist;* that is, it is not a part of
that reality which we all read about and worry over—this is
not the tumultuous Africa of the newspapers and the United
Nations discussions that Eugene Henderson visits. There is
nothing here of nationalism or riots or *apartheid.* But, then,
why should there be? There is the world, but there is also the
self. And the self, when the writer turns upon it all his attention and talent, is revealed to be a remarkable thing. First off,
it exists, it's real. *I am,* the self cries, and then, taking a nice
long look, it adds, *and I am beautiful.*

At the conclusion of Bellow's book, the hero, Eugene Henderson, a big, sloppy millionaire, is returning to America,
coming home from a trip to Africa where he has been
plague-fighter, lion-tamer, and rainmaker; he is bringing back
with him a real lion. Aboard the plane he befriends a small
Persian boy, whose language he cannot understand. Still,
when the plane lands at Newfoundland, Henderson takes the
child in his arms and goes out onto the field. And then:

> Laps and laps I galloped around the shining and riveted
> body of the plane, behind the fuel trucks. Dark faces
> were looking from within. The great, beautiful propellers
> were still, all four of them. I guess I felt it was my turn
> now to move, and so went running—leaping, leaping,
> pounding, and tingling over the pure white lining of the
> gray Arctic silence.

And so we leave Henderson, a very happy man. Where? In
the Arctic. This picture has stayed with me since I read the
book a year or so ago: of a man who finds energy and joy in

an imagined Africa, and celebrates it on an unpeopled, ice-bound vastness.

Earlier I quoted from Styron's new novel, *Set This House on Fire*. Now Styron's book, like Bellow's, is also the story of the regeneration of a man, and too of an American who leaves his own country and goes abroad for a while to live. But where Henderson's world is removed from our own, not about riots or nationalism, Kinsolving, Styron's hero, inhabits a planet we immediately recognize. The book is drenched in details that twenty years from now will surely require foot-notes to be thoroughly understood. The hero of the book is an American painter who has taken his family to live in a small town on the Amalfi coast. Cass Kinsolving detests America, and himself to boot. Throughout most of the book he is taunted and tempted and disgraced by Mason Flagg, a fellow countryman, rich, boyish, naive, licentious, indecent, and finally cruel and stupid. Kinsolving, by way of his attach-ment to Flagg, spends most of the book choosing between liv-ing and dying, and at one point, in a language and tone that are characteristic, he says this, concerning his expatriation:

> . . . . the man I had come to Europe to escape [why he's] the man in all the car advertisements, you know, the young guy waving there—he looks so beautiful and edu-cated and everything, and he's got it *made,* Penn State and a blonde there, and a smile as big as a billboard. And he's going places. I mean electronics. Politics. What they call communication. Advertising. Saleshood. Outer space. God only knows. And he's as ignorant as an Al-banian peasant.

However, at the end of the book, for all his disgust with what the American public life does to a man's private life, Kinsolving, like Henderson, has come back to America, hav-ing opted for existence. But the America that we find him in seems to me to be the America of his childhood, and, if only in a metaphoric way, of all our childhoods: he tells his story while he fishes from a boat in a Carolina stream. The affirma-tion at the conclusion is not as go-getting as Gold's "More! More!" nor as sublime as Harnack's, "I believe in God," nor as joyous as Henderson's romp on the Newfoundland airfield. "I wish I could tell you that I had found some belief, some rock . . ." Kinsolving says, "but to be truthful, you see, I can only tell you this: that as for being and nothingness, the only thing I did know was that to choose between them was simply to choose being. . . ." Being. Living. Not where one lives or with whom one lives—but that one lives.

And now, alas, what does all of this add up to? It would certainly be to oversimplify the art of fiction, and the complex relationship between a man and his times, to ignore the crucial matters of individual talent, history, and character, to say that Bellow's book, or Styron's, or even Herbert Gold's prose style, arise naturally out of our distressing cultural and political predicament. However, that our communal predicament is a distressing one, is a fact that weighs upon the writer no less, and perhaps even more, than his neighbor—for to the writer the community is, properly, both his subject and his audience. And it may be that when the predicament produces in the writer not only feelings of disgust, rage, and melancholy but impotence, too, he is apt to lose heart and finally, like his neighbor, turn to other matters or to other worlds; or to the self, which may, in a variety of ways, become his subject or even the impulse for his technique. What I have tried to point out is that the sheer fact of self, the vision of self as inviolable, powerful, and nervy, self as the only real thing in an unreal environment, that that vision has given to some writers joy, solace, and muscle. Certainly to have come through a holocaust in one piece, to have survived, is nothing to be made light of, and it is for that reason, say, that Styron's hero manages to engage our sympathies right down to the end. However, when survival itself becomes one's *raison d'être*, when one cannot choose but be ascetic, when the self can only be celebrated as it is excluded from society, or as it is exercised and admired in a fantastic one, we then, I think, do not have much reason to be cheery. Finally there is for me something hollow and unconvincing about Henderson up there on top of the world dancing around that airplane. Consequently, it is not with this image that I should like to conclude, but instead with the image that Ralph Ellison gives to us of his hero at the end of *Invisible Man*. For here too the hero is left with the simple stark fact of himself. He is as alone as a man can be. Not that he hasn't gone out into the world; he has gone out into it, and out into it, and out into it—but at the end he chooses to go underground, to live there and to wait. And it does not seem to him a cause for celebration either.

1961

Some notes on recent american fiction

SAUL BELLOW

GERTRUDE Stein is supposed to have explained to Hemingway that "remarks are not literature." Here I am offering
some remarks, and I make no claim for them whatever. A
writer's views on other writers may have a certain interest, but
it should be clear that he reads what they write almost always
with a special attitude. If he should be a novelist, his own
books are also a comment on his contemporaries and reveal
that he supports certain tendencies and rejects others. In his
own books he upholds what he deems necessary, and usually
by the method of omission he criticizes what he understands
as the errors and excesses of others.

I intend to examine the view taken by recent American
novelists and short-story writers of the individual and his society, and I should like to begin with the title of the new
book by Wylie Sypher: *Loss of the Self in Modern Literature
and Art*. I do not propose to discuss it; I simply want to cite
the title, for in itself it tells us much about the common acceptance of what the Spanish critic Ortega y Gasset described
some years ago as "the dehumanisation of the arts." One
chapter is devoted to the Beats, but, for the most part, Sypher
finds, as we might have expected, that the theme of annihila-
tion of Self, and the description of an "inauthentic" life
which can never make sense, is predominantly European and
particularly French. The names he most often mentions are

Copyright © 1963 by Saul Bellow. From *Encounter*, November 1963,
pp. 22-29. (This essay was also delivered as a lecture in Washington,
D.C., under the auspices of the Gertrude Clarke Whittall Poetry and
Literature Fund. Reprinted by permission.)

those of André Gide, Sartre, Beckett, Sarraute, and Robbe-
Grillet: writers whose novels and plays are derived from definite theories which make a historical reckoning of the human
condition and are peculiarly responsive to new physical, psychological, and philosophical theories. American writers,
when they are moved by a similar spirit to reject and despise
the Self, are seldom encumbered by such intellectual baggage,
and this fact pleases their European contemporaries, who find
in them a natural, that is, a brutal or violent acceptance of
the new universal truth by minds free from intellectual pre-
conceptions.

In the early twenties D. H. Lawrence was delighted to dis-
cover a blunt, primitive virtue in the first stories of Ernest
Hemingway, and twenty years later André Gide praised
Dashiell Hammett as a good barbarian.

European writers take strength from German phenom-
enology and from the conception of entropy in modern
physics in order to attack a romantic idea of the Self, trium-
phant in the 19th century but intolerable in the 20th. The
feeling against this idea is well-nigh universal. The First
World War with its millions of corpses gave an aspect of the
horrible to romantic overvaluation of the Self. The leaders of
the Russian Revolution were icy in their hatred of bourgeois
individualism. In the Communist countries millions were sacrificed in the building of socialism, and almost certainly the
Lenins and the Stalins, the leaders who made these decisions,
serving the majority and the future, believed they were rejecting a soft, nerveless humanism which attempted in the face
of natural and historical evidence to oppose progress.

A second great assault on the separate Self sprang from
Germany in 1939. Just what the reduction of millions of
human beings into heaps of bone and mounds of rag and hair
or clouds of smoke betokened, there is no one who can
plainly tell us, but it is at least plain that something was being
done to put in question the meaning of survival, the meaning
of pity, the meaning of justice and of the importance of
being oneself, the individual's consciousness of his own existence.

It would be odd, indeed, if these historical events had made
no impression on American writers, even if they are not on
the whole given to taking the historical or theoretical view.
They characteristically depend on their own observations and
appear at times obstinately empirical.

But the latest work of writers like James Jones, James Baldwin, Philip Roth, John O'Hara, J. F. Powers, Joseph Bennett, Wright Morris, and others shows the individual under a great strain. Laboring to maintain himself, or perhaps an idea of himself (not always a clear idea), he feels the pressure of a vast public life, which may dwarf him as an individual while permitting him to be a giant in hatred or fantasy. In these circumstances he grieves, he complains, rages, or laughs. All the while he is aware of his lack of power, his inadequacy as a moralist, the nauseous pressure of the mass media, and the weight of money and organization, of cold war and racial brutalities.

Adapting Gresham's theorem to the literary situation, one might say that public life drives private life into hiding. People begin to hoard their spiritual valuables. Public turbulence is largely coercive, not positive. It puts us into a passive position. There is not much we can do about the crises of international politics, the revolutions in Asia and Africa, the rise and transformation of masses. Technical and political decisions, invisible powers, secrets which can be shared only by a small élite, render the private will helpless and lead the individual into curious forms of behavior in the private sphere.

Public life, vivid and formless turbulence, news, slogans, mysterious crises, and unreal configurations dissolve coherence in all but the most resistant minds, and even to such minds it is not always a confident certainty that resistance can ever have a positive outcome. To take narcotics has become in some circles a mark of rebellious independence, and to scorch one's personal earth is sometimes felt to be the only honorable course. Rebels have no bourgeois certainties to return to when rebellions are done. The fixed points seem to be disappearing. Even the Self is losing its firm outline.

One recent American novel deals openly and consciously with these problems: *The Thin Red Line* by James Jones, a book which, describing the gross and murderous conditions of jungle combat, keeps a miraculously sensitive balance and does not weary us with a mere catalogue of horrors. What Mr. Jones sees very precisely is the fluctuation in the value of the life of the individual soldier. Childhood in some cases ends for the fighting man as he accepts the lesson of realism. The attitude of Storm, one of the older soldiers, toward Fife, a younger man, is described as follows: "He [Fife] was a good enough kid. He just hadn't been away from home long enough. And Storm, who had started off bumming during the

Depression when he was only fourteen, couldn't find kids like
that very interesting." Storm, the mess sergeant, tolerates the
inexperienced Fife, but First Sergeant Welsh has no such tolerance. He cannot abide softness and the lack of realism, and
he cruelly and punitively teaches the hard lesson to his unde-
veloped subordinates. Real knowledge as he sees it is brutal
knowledge and it must be painfully and brutally learned. The
heart of the lesson, as Welsh understands it, is that it matters
little—it matters, therefore, not at all—whether any single
man survives or falls. Welsh offers no indulgence to anyone
and asks none for himself. His message to mankind is that
you must cast the cold eye on life, on death.

Mr. Jones shrewdly understands that the philosophy of
Welsh is not ultimately hard. Toward himself the sergeant is
not fanatically severe, and his toughness betrays a large degree of self-pity. What Jones describes here is the casting off
of a childish or feminine or false virtue, despised because it
cannot meet the test of survival. In apprehending what is
real, Jones' combat soldiers learn a bitter and leveling truth
and in their realism revenge themselves on the slothful and
easy civilian conception of the Self. The new idea cruelly as-
sails the old, exposing its conventionality and emptiness.
Young Fife, after he has gone the rugged course, kills like
the rest, becomes quarrelsome, drinks and brawls, and casts
off his hesitant, careful, and complaining childishness.

A very different sort of novel, in a peaceful sphere far removed from the explosions and disembowelings of Guadalca-
nal, is J. F. Power's *Morte d'Urban,* which does not so much
study as brood over the lives of priests belonging to the
Order of St. Clement. Father Urban, a well-known preacher
and a man of some talent, is transferred for reasons not
clearly understood from Chicago, where he has worked effectively, to a new Foundation of the Order in Duesterhaus,
Minnesota. To Urban, a sociable and civilized priest, this
transfer can only be seen as a mysterious banishment, and he
is described by Mr. Powers looking from the train windows
at the empty country beyond Minneapolis.

> . . . flat and treeless, Illinois without people. It didn't
> attract, it didn't repel. He saw more streams than he'd
> see in Illinois, but they weren't working. November was
> winter here. Too many white frame farmhouses, not new
> and not old, not at all what Father Urban would care to

come to for Thanksgiving or Christmas. Rusty implements. Brown dirt. Grey skies. Ice. No snow. A great
deal of talk about this on the train. Father Urban
dropped entirely out of it after an hour or so. The Voya-
geur arrived in Duesterhaus a few minutes before eleven
that morning, and Father Urban was the only passenger
to get off.

In more ways than one, Father Urban is viewed as the
only passenger. At the new Foundation he is, without complaint, in a solitary situation. In charge of the Duesterhaus
Foundation is Father Wilfred ". . . who, on account of his
broad nose and padded cheeks, had been called Bunny in the
Novitiate. Bunny Bestudik." Father Wilfred's concerns are all
of a practical nature. His interests are the interests of any
Midwestern American who has to run a place efficiently; he
watches the fuel bills, thinks about the pickup truck and its
rubber, the cost of paint, and is anxious to have good public
relations. This religious Order is described as a community of
consumers. It is the American and average character of activ-
ities whose ultimate aim is religious that Mr. Powers wants to
describe. His tone is dry and factual as he tells of the discussions of the Fathers who have to heat, paint, and renovate
their buildings, sand the floors, tear up old linoleum, lay new
tiles in the bathrooms, and this light and dry comedy cannot
be maintained through such a long account of the effort to fill
up a great emptiness with activity which is insufficiently purposeful. The religion of Father Urban is expressed in steadi-
ness and patience, in endurance, not in fiery strength. His resistance to the prolonged barrenness and vacant busyness of
this thoroughly American Order is made in a spirit of mild
and decent martyrdom. Indeed the only violent and passionate person in the book is a certain Billy Cosgrove. Billy is
rich and generous. He gives lavishly to the Order but he expects also to have his way. He and Father Urban eat shish
kebab and drink champagne, play golf and go fishing. With
Billy one talks of cars and sailing boats. Urban gets along
rather well with spoiled and boisterous Billy until Billy tries
to drown a deer in the water of Bloodsucker Lake. Billy has
been fishing and is in an ugly mood because his luck has been
bad. Seeing a swimming deer, he decides to seize it by the
antlers and hold its head under water. As hungry for trophies
as the soldiers in *The Thin Red Line,* Billy wants those antlers. Father Urban, who cannot bear his cruelty, starts up

the motor of the boat, and Billy falls into the water. For this outrage Billy will never forgive him.

What Father Urban had been thinking just before the appearance of the deer was that in the Church there was perhaps too great an emphasis on dying for the faith and winning the martyr's crown.

> How about living for the faith? Take Lanfranc and William the Conqueror—of whom it was written (in the Catholic Encyclopædia and Father Urban's notes on a book he might write some day): "He was mild to good men of God and stark beyond all bounds to those who withsaid his will."

Billy Cosgrove turns out to occupy the position of the Conqueror. He is stark beyond all bounds, and Urban is never again to see his face. Nor does Urban seem destined to write his book. He goes to the Novitiate of the Order as Father Provincial, there to deal with practical matters to the best of his ability. But he appears to be succumbing to a brain injury he received while playing golf. He had been struck in the head by a golf ball in Minnesota and is now subject to fits of dizziness. A martyr's crown seems to be waiting Urban as the book ends.

Powers does not look at the issue of the single Self and the multitude as nakedly as Jones does, and it is a pity that he chose not to do so, for he might have been able to offer us a more subtle development of the subject. He would have been examining what Mr. Sypher calls "Loss of the Self" from the point of view of a Christian, that is, from the point of view of one who believes in the existence of something more profound than the romantic or secular idea of selfhood, namely, a soul. But there is curiously little talk of souls in this book about a priest. Spiritually, its quality is very thin. That perhaps is as Mr. Powers meant it to be. Even at play Father Urban is serving the Church, and, if he is hit in the head by a golf ball, we can perhaps draw our own conclusions from that about the present age viewed as a chapter in the spiritual history of mankind. Here great things will only be dimly apprehended even by the most willing servant of God. Still this seems to me unsatisfactory, and I am not sure that I can bring myself to admire such meekness. A man might well be meek in his own interests, but furious at such abuses of the soul and eager to show what is positive and powerful in his faith. The lack of such power makes faith itself shadowy, more like obscure tenacity than spiritual conviction. In this sense Mr. Powers' book is disappointing.

The individual in American fiction often comes through to us, especially among writers of "sensibility," as a colonist who has been sent to a remote place, some Alaska of the soul. What he has to bring under cultivation, however, is a barren emptiness within himself. This is, of course, what writers of sensibility have for a long time been doing and what they continue to do. The latest to demonstrate his virtuosity with exceptional success is John Updike, who begins the title story of his new collection, *Pigeon Feathers,*

> When they moved to Firetown, things were upset, displaced, rearranged.

The rearrangement of things in new and hostile solitude is a common theme with writers of sensibility. David, the only child of a family which has moved to the country, is assailed by terror when he reads in H. G. Wells' *The Outline of History* that Jesus was nothing more than a rather communistic Galilean, ". . . an obscure political agitator, a kind of hobo in a minor colony of the Roman Empire." The effect of this is to open the question of death and immortality. David is dissatisfied with answers given by the Reverend Dobson and by his parents. He cannot understand the pleasure his mother takes in her solitary walks along the edge of the woods. ". . . to him the brown stretches of slowly rising and falling land expressed only a huge exhaustion."

" 'What do you want Heaven to be?' " asks David's mother. "He was becoming angry, sensing her surprise at him. She had assumed that Heaven had faded from his head long ago. She had imagined that he had already entered, in the secrecy of silence, the conspiracy that he now knew to be all around him."

Young David in the end resolves the problem for himself æsthetically. Admiring the beauty of pigeon feathers he feels consoled by the sense of a providence. ". . . the God who had lavished such craft upon these worthless birds would not destroy His whole Creation by refusing to let David live forever." The story ends with a mild irony at the expense of the boy. Nevertheless, there is nothing to see here but the writer's

reliance on beautiful work, on an æsthetic discipline and
order. And sensibility, in such forms, incurs the dislike of
many because it is perceptive inwardly, and otherwise blind.
We suspect it of a stony heart because it functions so
smoothly in its isolation. The writer of sensibility assumes
that only private exploration and inner development are possible, and accepts the opposition of public and private as
fixed and indissoluble.

We are dealing with modern attitudes toward the ancient idea
of the individual and the many, the single Self in the midst of
the mass or species. In modern times the idea of the unique
Self has become associated with the name of Rousseau.
Nietzsche identified the Self with the God Apollo, the god of
light, harmony, music, reason and proportion, and the many,
the tribe, the species, the instincts and passions, with Dionysus. Between these two principles, the individual and the generic, men and civilizations supposedly work out their destinies. It is to Nietzsche, too, that we owe the concept of the
"last man." His "last man" is an obituary on the unitary and
sufficient Self produced by a proud bourgeois and industrial
civilization. Dostoevsky's Underground Man is an analogous
figure. Atheism, rationalism, utilitarianism, and revolution are
signs of a deadly sickness in the human soul, in his scheme of
things. The lost Selves whose souls are destroyed he sees as
legion. The living soul clearly discerns them. It owes this illumination to Christ the Redeemer. More optimistically, an
American poet like Walt Whitman imagined that the single
Self and the democratic mass might complement each other.
But on this side of the Atlantic, also, Thoreau described men
as leading lives of quiet desperation, accepting a deadly common life: the individual retires from the community to define
or redefine his real needs in isolation beside Walden Pond.

Still later a French poet tells us, *"Je est un autre."* Rimbaud
and Jarry launch their bombs and grenades against the tight
little bourgeois kingdom of the Self, that sensitive sovereign.
Darwin and the early anthropologists unwittingly damage his
sovereignty badly. Then come the psychologists, who explain
that his Ego is a paltry shelter against the unendurable storms
that rage in outer reality. After them come the logicians and
physical scientists who tell us that "I" is a grammatical
expression. Poets like Valéry describe this Self as a poor fig-
ment, a thing of change, and tell us that consciousness is in-

terested only in what is eternal. Novelists like Joyce turn
away from the individualism of the romantics and the hu-
manists to contemplate instead qualities found in dreams and
belonging to the entire species—Earwicker is everybody.
Writers like Sartre, Ionesco, and Beckett or like our own William Burroughs and Allen Ginsberg are only a few of the active campaigners on this shrinking front against the Self. One
would like to ask these contemporaries, "After nakedness,
what?" "After absurdity, what?"

But, on the whole, American novels are filled with complaints over the misfortunes of the sovereign Self. Writers
have inherited a tone of bitterness from the great poems and
novels of this century, many of which lament the passing of a
more stable and beautiful age demolished by the barbarous
intrusion of an industrial and metropolitan society of masses
or proles who will, after many upheavals, be tamed by bu-
reaucracies and oligarchies in brave new worlds, human ant-
hills.

These works of the first half of our century nourish the imagination of contemporary writers and supply a tonal background of disillusion or elegy.

There are modern novelists who take all of this for granted
as fully proven and implicit in the human condition and who
complain as steadily as they write, viewing modern life with a
bitterness to which they themselves have not established clear
title, and it is this unearned bitterness that I speak of. What is
truly curious about it is that often the writer automatically
scorns contemporary life. He bottles its stinks artistically.
But, seemingly, he does not need to study it. It is enough for
him that it does not allow his sensibilities to thrive, that it
starves his instincts for nobility or for spiritual qualities.

But what the young American writer most often appears to
feel is his *own* misfortune. The injustice is done to *his* talent
if life is brutish and ignorant, if the world seems overcome
by spam and beer, or covered with detergent lathers and poi-
sonous monoxides. This apparently is the only injustice he
feels. Neither for himself nor for his fellows does he attack
power and injustice directly and hotly. He simply defends his
sensibility.

Perhaps the reason for this is the prosperity and relative
security of the middle class from which most writers come.
In educating its writers it makes available to them the radical
doctrines of all the ages, but these in their superabundance

only cancel one another out. The middle-class community trains its writers also in passivity and resignation and in the double enjoyment of selfishness and goodwill. They are taught that they can have it both ways. In fact they are taught to expect to enjoy everything that life can offer. They can live dangerously while managing somehow to remain safe. They can be both bureaucrats and bohemians, they can be executives but use pot, they can raise families but enjoy bohemian sexuality, they can observe the laws while in their hearts and in their social attitudes they may be as subversive as they please. They are both conservative and radical. They are everything that is conceivable. They are not taught to care genuinely for any man or any cause.

A recent novel like Philip Roth's *Letting Go* is a consummate example of this. Roth's hero, Gabriel, educated to succeed in this world and to lead a good life come hell or high water, is slightly uncomfortable in his selfishness. But nevertheless he wants his, as the saying goes, and he gets his. But he feels obscurely the humiliation of being a private bourgeois Self, the son of an unhappy but prosperous dentist, and he senses that a "personal life" with its problems of personal adjustment and personal responsibility and personal happiness, its ostensibly normal calculations of profit and loss, safety and danger, lust and prudence is a source of shame. But Gabriel's middle-class parents sent him into life to make the grade and that is precisely, with tough singlemindedness, what he does. His shame therefore becomes a province of his sensibility, and it is something he can be rather proud of as he does what he was going to do anyway.

Roth's hero clings to the hope of self-knowledge and personal improvement, and he concludes that, with all his faults, he loves himself still. His inner life, if it may be called that, is a rather feeble thing of a few watts. Conceivably it may guide him to a more satisfactory adjustment, but it makes me think of the usher's flashlight in the dark theater guiding the single ticket-holder to his reserved seat. We are supposed to feel that Gabriel is unusually sensitive, but what we find is that he is a tough young man who cannot be taken in and who will survive the accidents of life that madden or kill genuinely sensitive young men.

I would like now to list the categories suggested by my reading of current novels: the documentation of James Jones, the partially Christian approach of Powers, the sensibility of Updike, and the grievance of Philip Roth. I do not retract my earlier statement that in American novels—for I have decided rather arbitrarily to limit myself to examining these—the tone of complaint prevails. The public realm, as it encroaches on the private, steadily reduces the powers of the individual; but it cannot take away his power to despair, and sometimes he seems to be making the most of that. However, there are several other avenues commonly taken: stoicism, nihilistic anger, and comedy. Stoicism and comedy are sometimes mixed, as in the case of the late German dramatist Bertholt Brecht, but our own contemporary American stoicism comes from Hemingway, and its best American representative at present is John O'Hara.

O'Hara is properly impatient with people who suffer too intensely from themselves. The characters in his latest collection of stories, *The Cape Cod Lighter,* for whom he shows a decided preference, appear to be bluff, natural people, who know how to endure hurt and act with an elementary and realistic sense of honor. When Ernest Pangborn in the story "The Professors" learns that he has misjudged his colleague Jack Veech and understands at last that Veech's behavior has been decent and manly, he is moved to say something to him but does not know what to say.

> A compliment would be rejected, and a word of pity would be unthinkable. Indeed the compliment was being paid to Pangborn; Veech honored him with his confidence and accorded him honor more subtly, more truly, by asking no further assurances of his silence.

The emotion we feel here is made possible by long reticence, by the deep burial of self-proclamation or self-assertion. We recall the pure decencies of schooldays, and the old chivalrous or military origins of these. These, surely, are virtues of silence and passivity. We endure. We are rewarded by a vision of one another's complexities, but there is no possibility of a flourish, or of rhetoric, or anything that would make an undue personal claim.

This is no longer the sovereign Self of the Romantics, but the decent Self of Kipling whose great satisfaction it is to recognize the existence of a great number of others. These numerous others reduce personal significance, and both realism

and dignity require us to accept this reduction. Such stoicism
of separateness is the opposite of sensibility with its large
claims for the development of internal riches.

But the O'Haras are curiously like the Updikes in at least one
respect. They are scrupulous craftsmen and extraordinarily
strict about their writing. Nothing unrealistic, unnatural, or
excessive (as they define these qualities) is suffered to appear. O'Hara insists upon a hard literalness in his language
which reminds one of the simple crystalline code of his characters. There is a roughness in O'Hara which may make the
writer of sensibility feel like a dude. O'Hara's self-identifica-
tion is obviously with the workman, with the average, with
plain people. Or perhaps he feels himself to be a part of the
majority, which is to say, of the crowd. Certainly he does not
merely react against what he judges an incorrect definition of
the individual; he hates it violently. And conceivably he hates
it in himself. His view of sensibility or of an intricate and
conceivably self-indulgent privacy is, like Hemingway's (in
The Sun Also Rises, for instance), entirely negative. He sees
the romantic Self with the eyes of the crowd. And the crowd
is a leveler. The average it seeks is anything but Whitman's
divine average.

The absolute individualism of the Enlightenment has fallen.
Contemporary writers like Brecht, or Beckett, or the Beats,
and recently and most atrociously William Burroughs in his
Naked Lunch, have repudiated it in a spirit of violence. Some
have been violently comic at its expense, others ruthlessly nihilistic and vengeful. Among them there are some who gather
unto themselves more and more and more power only to release it destructively on this already discredited and fallen individualism. In this they seem at times to imitate the great
modern consolidations of power, to follow the example of
parties and states and their scientific or military instruments.
They act, in short, like those who hold the real power in society, the masters of the Leviathan. But this is only an imitation
of the real power. Through this imitation they hope perhaps
to show that they are not inferior to those who lead the modern world. Joint Chiefs or Pentagons have power to do as they
will to huge populations. But there are writers who will not
reckon themselves among these subordinate masses and who
aim to demonstrate an independent power equal to the greatest. They therefore strike one sometimes as being extraordi-

narily eager to release their strength and violence against an enemy, and that enemy is the false conception of Self created by Christianity and by Christianity's successors in the Enlightenment. Modern literature is not satisfied simply to dismiss a romantic, outmoded conception of the Self. In a spirit of deepest vengefulness it curses it. It hates it. It rends it, annihilates it. It would rather have the maddest chaos it can invoke than a conception of life it has found false. But after this destruction, what?

I have spoken of complaint, stoicism, sensibility, and nihilistic rage, and I would like to touch now on recent American writers who have turned to comedy. It is obvious that modern comedy has to do with the disintegrating outline of the worthy and humane Self, the bourgeois hero of an earlier age. That sober, prudent person, the bourgeois, although he did much for the development of modern civilization, built factories and railroads, dug canals, created sewage systems, and went colonizing, was indicted for his shallowness and his ignoble and hypocritical ways. The Christian writer (see Dostoevsky's portrait of Luzhin in *Crime and Punishment*) and the revolutionary (see Mangan in Shaw's *Heartbreak House*) repudiated him and all his works. The First World War dealt a blow to his prestige from which it never recovered. Dada and surrealism raised a storm of laughter against him. In the movies René Clair and Charlie Chaplin found him out. He became the respectable little person, the gentlemanly tramp. Poets of the deepest subversive tendencies came on like bank clerks in ironic masquerade.

The trick is still good as J. P. Donleavy has lately shown in his novel *The Ginger Man*. His hero, Sebastian Dangerfield, a freewheeling rascal and chaser, presents himself with wickedly comic effect as an ultrarespectable citizen with an excellent credit rating, one who doesn't know what it is to hock other people's property for the price of a drink, the gentlemanly sack-artist.

The private and inner life which was the subject of serious books until very recently now begins to have an antique and funny look. The earnestness of a Proust toward himself would seem old-fashioned today. Indeed, Italo Svevo, a contemporary of Proust, in *The Confessions of Zeno*, made introspection, hypochondria, and self-knowledge the subjects of his comedy. *My* welfare, *my* development, *my* advancement, *my* earnestness, *my* adjustment, *my* marriage, *my* family—all will make the modern reader laugh heartily. Writers may not wholly agree with Bertrand Russell that "I" is no more than a grammatical expression, but they do consider certain claims of the "I" to be definitely funny. Already in the 19th century Stendhal became bored with the persistent "I-I-I" and denounced it in characteristic terms.

Perhaps the change that has occurred can be clearly illustrated by a comparison of Thomas Mann's *Death in Venice* with Nabokov's *Lolita*. In both stories an older man is overcome by sexual desire for a younger person. With Mann, however, this sad occurrence involves Apollo and Dionysus. Gustave von Aschenbach, an overly civilized man, an individual estranged from his instincts which unexpectedly claim their revenge, has gone too far, has entered the realm of sickness and perversity, and is carried away by the plague. This is a typically Nietzschean theme. But in *Lolita* the internal life of Humbert Humbert has become a joke. Far from being an Aschenbach, a great figure of European literature, he is a fourth- or fifth-rate man of the world and is unable to be entirely serious about his passion. As for Lolita's mother, the poor thing only makes him laugh when she falls in love with him—a banal woman. To a very considerable extent Humbert's judgment of her is based on the low level of her culture. Her banality makes her a proper victim. If her words about love and desire had not come out of a bin in which the great American public finds suitable expressions to describe its psychological and personal needs, she might have been taken more seriously. The earnestness of Mann about love and death might be centuries old. The same subject is sadly and maliciously comical in *Lolita*. Clare Quilty cannot be made to take even his own death seriously and while he is being murdered by Humbert, ridicules his own situation and Humbert's as well, losing at last a life that was not worth having anyway. The contemporary Aschenbach does not deny his desires, but then he is without the dignity of the old fellow and is always on the verge of absurdity. Wright Morris in his new novel *What a Way to Go* explicitly makes comedy of the *Death in Venice* theme. His American professors in Venice, discussing *Death in Venice* all the while, seem to feel that there is small hope for them. They decline to view themselves with full seriousness. They believe their day is over. They are unfit, and dismiss themselves with a joke.

We must carefully remind ourselves that, if so many people today exist to enjoy or deplore an individual life, it is because prodigious public organizations, scientific, industrial, and political, support huge populations of new individuals. These organizations both elicit and curtail private development. I myself am not convinced that there is less "selfhood" in the modern world. I am not sure anyone knows how to put the matter properly. I am simply recording the attitudes of modern writers, including contemporary Americans, who are convinced that the jig of the Self is up.

What is the modern Self in T. S. Eliot's *Waste Land*? It is the many, crossing the bridge in the great modern city, who do not know that death has already undone them; it is the "clerk carbuncular" taking sexual liberties of brief duration with the "lovely lady" who, after she has stooped to folly, puts a record on the gramophone. What is the Self for French novelists of the first postwar era like Louis Ferdinand Céline, or for writers like Curzio Malaparte or Albert Camus in the second postwar era? Man, in a book like *The Stranger,* is a creature neither fully primitive nor fully civilized, a Self devoid of depths. We have come a long way from Montaigne and his belief in a self-perfecting, self-knowing character.

Recent American comic novels like *Lolita,* or *The Ginger Man,* or Burt Blechman's *How Much?,* or Bruce Friedman's first novel *Stern* examine the private life. It is as if they were testing the saying of Socrates, that the unexamined life was not worth living. Apparently they find the examined life funny too. Some cannot find the life they are going to examine. The power of public life has become so vast and threatening that private life cannot maintain a pretense of its importance. Our condition of destructibility is ever-present in everyone's mind. Our submission seems required by public ugliness in our cities, by the public nonsense of television which threatens to turn our brains to farina within our heads, by even such trifling things as Muzak broadcasts in the elevators of public buildings. The Self is asked to prepare itself for sacrifice, and this is the situation reflected in contemporary American fiction.

As for the future, it cannot possibly shock us since we have already done everything possible to scandalize ourselves. We have so completely debunked the old idea of the Self that we can hardly continue in the same way. Perhaps some power within us will tell us what we are, now that old misconceptions have been laid low. Undeniably the human being is not what he commonly thought a century ago. The question nevertheless remains. He is something. What is he?

And this question, it seems to me, modern writers have answered poorly. They have told us, indignantly or nihilistically or comically, how great our error is, but for the rest they have offered us thin fare. The fact is that modern writers sin when they suppose that they *know,* as they conceive that physics *knows* or that history *knows*. The subject of the novelist is not knowable in any such way. The mystery increases, it does not grow less as types of literature wear out. It is, however, Symbolism or Realism or Sensibility wearing out, and not the mystery of mankind.

1963

PART THREE

||||||||||||||||||||||||||||||||

The underground

The barbarian is at the gates

LAWRENCE LIPTON

WHAT is taking place in the literature of the Holy Barbarians is something more profound than the emergence of a new school. It is a change in the literary use of language itself.

What is better than reading Vergil or memorizing Goethe (*Aalles Vergängliche ist nur ein Gleichnis, etc.*)? Why, eating outdoors under an awning for eight francs at Issy-les-Moulineaux. *Pourtant je suis à Sèvres*. No matter. I have been thinking lately of writing a *Journal d'un Fou* which I imagine to have found at Issy-les-Moulineaux. And since that *fou* is largely myself I am not eating at Sèvres, but at Issy-les-Moulineaux. And what does the *fou* say when the waitress comes with the big canette of beer? *Don't worry about errors when you're writing. The biographers will explain all errors.* I am thinking of my friend Carl who has spent the last four days getting started on a description of the woman he's writing about. "I can't do it! I can't do it!" he says. Very well, says the *fou*, let *me* do it for you. *Begin!* That's the principal thing. Supposing her nose is not aquiline? Supposing it's a celestial nose? What difference? When a portrait commences badly it's because you're not describing the woman you have in mind; you are thinking more about those who are going to look at the portrait than about the woman who is sitting for you. Take Van Norden—he's another case. He has been trying for two months to get started with his novel. Each time I meet him he has a new opening for his book. It never gets beyond the opening. Yesterday he said: "You see what my problem's like. It isn't just a question of how to begin: the first line decides the cast of the whole book. Now here's a start I made the other day: Dante wrote a poem about a place called H———. H-dash, because I don't want any trouble with censors."

Think of a book opening with H-dash! A little private hell which mustn't offend the censors! I notice that when Whitman starts a poem he writes:—"I, Walt, in my 37th year and in perfect health! . . . I am afoot with my vision . . . I dote on myself . . . Walt Whitman, a kosmos, of Manhattan the son, turbulent, fleshy, sensual, eating, drinking and breeding . . . Unscrew the locks from the doors! Unscrew the doors themselves from their jambs . . . Here or henceforward it is all the same to me . . . I exist as I am, that is enough . . ."

With Walt it is always Saturday afternoon . . .[1]

Note in how many particulars Henry Miller writing in the mid-thirties, and Whitman whom he cites, anticipated the beat generation: the insistence on the spontaneous, the improvised, the importance of living in the present moment, the sensuality, naturalness, contempt for censorship, the sense of holiness, the openness—even to leaving doors unlocked, a common practice among the beat. What is more pertinent at this point, however, is Henry Miller's use of language. And his approach to the problem of the written word. It is not an approach to the written word at all, in fact. It is the spoken word committed to writing. It is oral in structure.

"Oral languages," says Edmund Carpenter, "tended to be polysynthetic, composed of great tight conglomerates, like twisted knots, within which images were juxtaposed, inseparably fused; written communications consisted of little words chronologically ordered. Subject became distinct from verb, adjective from noun, separating actor from action, essence from form. Where preliterate man imposed form diffidently, temporarily—for such transitory forms lived but temporarily on the tip of his tongue, in the living situation—the printed word was inflexible, permanent, in touch with eternity: it embalmed truth for posterity.

"This embalming process froze language, eliminated the art

[1] Henry Miller, *Black Spring* (Obelisk Press, Paris).

of ambiguity, made puns 'the lowest form of wit,' destroyed word linkages. The word became a static symbol, applicable to and separate from that which it symbolized. It now belonged to the objective world; it could be seen. . . . Writing didn't record oral language; it was a new language, which the spoken word came to imitate. . . . Gutenberg finished the process." [2]

The written word, written in speech forms imitative of the written word, reached its *reductio ad absurdum* in the Victorian novels. When Thackeray satirized writers like Disraeli and Bulwer-Lytton, he was satirizing not only the genteelism of the middle class but the bookishness of their Geneva code language, a style that by the 1890's had begun to burlesque *itself*, unconsciously. Human speech is oral and nonlinear as Carpenter and his associate Marshall McLuhan have demonstrated in their experiments with communications media at the University of Toronto. When it is set down in writing it is merely being recorded for playback. Playback may be by eye and, where the reader is capable of it, by the "audio-imagination," as Eliot calls it, or "the inner ear," Marianne Moore's name for it, but it does not come fully alive again until it is played back by the human voice box. A poem can be mastered, that is, it can be understood on every level of meaning; it can be "explicated" in the manner of the New Criticism, all its allusions traced to their sources and identified, its metrics scanned, its grammar and syntax unscrambled, all of its ambiguities ferreted out and classified according to William Empson, and the act of communication will still be incomplete unless the sound is played back to the listening ear. The inner ear is not enough, no matter how much audio-imagination the poet has or the listener possesses. The printed poem is not the poem. It is only the "score" of the poem, just as in music the score is not the music. It has to be *played back*.

If it is written in the Geneva code, it will sound stilted when it is read aloud, no matter how well it "reads" on the printed page. It will sound like the printed page would sound if it could speak: clipped, precise, evenly spaced, no word lighter or darker than any other word, in short, a good job of printing. If it is written as oral language, it will play back naturally and convincingly. The same thing is true of prose. Try reading the following passage from Jack Kerouac's *The Subterraneans* silently, then read it aloud and the difference becomes immediately apparent.

It's too much. Beginning, as I say with the pushcart incident—the night we drank red wine at Dante's and were in a drinking mood now both of us so disgusted— Yuri came with us, Ross Wallenstein was in there and maybe to show off to Mardou Yuri acted like a kid all night and kept hitting Wallenstein on the back of his head with little finger taps like goofing in a bar but Wallenstein (who's always being beaten up by hoodlums because of this) turned around a stiff death's-head gaze with big eyes glaring behind glasses, his Christlike blue unshaven cheeks, staring rigidly as tho the stare itself will floor Yuri, not speaking for a long time, finally saying, "Man, don't bug me," and turning back to his conversation with friends and Yuri does it again and Ross turns again the same pitiless awful subterranean sort of non-violent Indian Mahatma Ghandi defense of some kind (which I'd suspected that first time he talked to me saying, "Are you a fag you talk like a fag," a remark coming from him so absurd because so inflammable and me 170 pounds to his 130 or 120 for God's sake. . . .)[3]

J. D. Salinger had already broken that literary ground, of course, in the middle forties:

I was surrounded by jerks. I'm not kidding. At this other tiny table, right to my left, practically on *top* of me, there was this funny-looking guy and this funny-looking girl. They were around my age, or maybe just a little older. It was funny. You could see they were being careful as hell not to drink up the minimum too fast. I listened to their conversation for a while, because I didn't have anything else to do. He was telling her about some pro football game he'd seen that afternoon. He gave her every single goddam play in the whole game—I'm not kidding. He was the most boring guy I ever listened to. And you could tell his date wasn't even interested in the goddam game, but she was even funnier-looking than *he* was, so I guess she *had* to listen. Real ugly girls have it tough. I feel so sorry for them sometimes. Sometimes I

[3] Jack Kerouac, *The Subterraneans* (Grove Press, New York).

can't even look at them, especially if they're with some dopey guy that's telling them all about a goddam football game. On my right, the conversation was even worse, though. On my right there was this very Joe Yale-looking guy, in a gray flannel suit and one of those flitty-looking Tattersall vests. All those Ivy League bastards look alike. My father wants me to go to Yale, or maybe Princeton, but I swear, I wouldn't go to one of those Ivy League colleges if I was *dying,* for God's sake. . . .[4]

Catcher in the Rye, the book from which this excerpt is taken, is to be found everywhere on the bookshelves of the beat. Reading aloud, both poetry and prose, is a common practice in the pads. It is not difficult for the beat generation youth to identify itself with the book's hero, Holden Caulfield. He not only *sounds* right to them but the things he says are often the things they say:

If he'd had to shoot anybody, he wouldn't've known which direction to shoot in. He said the Army was practically as full of bastards as the Nazis were.

I swear if there's another war, they better stick me in front of a firing squad. I wouldn't object.

The people who applauded the show-offy, tricky stuff of the night club entertainers were the same morons that laugh like hyenas in the movies at stuff that isn't funny.

George Mandel is another writer who possesses an oral style and is popular in beat generation circles for what he says as well as for the way he says it. Here are some examples from his book *Flee the Angry Strangers:*

Those culture perverts from uptown. *Any*one from uptown. And downtown. Everywhere I go. I tell you our society is at the bottom of its spiral.

The whole commercial scene is animal against animal . . . everybody's mouth going with words like priests and kings and congressmen with words and no understanding . . . You can keep reality. Work is for slaves; I'm free.

The so-called spiritual leaders who are all spirit and no brains, all sky and no earth . . . the jerks with the electric word of officialdom who do nothing but separate people.

[4] J. D. Salinger, *The Catcher in the Rye* (Little, Brown & Co., Boston).

A whole nation of people suspending consciousness in whatever way they could: in churches and movie houses, before television sets, in barrooms and in books. . . . The whole world (seeking) hard for its narcosis. . . . Dope fiends and philosophers, prostitutes and poets, artists and hoods, darlings, dreamers, derelicts and every American variety of displaced persons. . . . Whether praying step by step up tottering towers toward some illusion of heaven, or playing notch by notch down any available avenue of escape, from a stupid movie to a charge of heroin—the whole world is hooked.[5]

One thing is already evident, that if the holy barbarians have their way with the national culture the new American literary tradition, now in the making, is not going to be in the England-via-New England line of descent. The schools and the reputation-making organs are still in the hands of teachers, critics, and editors in the England-via-New England tradition, but defections from their own ranks have become increasingly common in the last few years and newcomers into the schools, magazines, and publishing houses are changing the picture continually. Where print is still closed to them, they either start publishing ventures of their own or take to the oral medium of records. For it is really the oral elements from foreign cultures in which those elements have never completely died out that are being transfused by the holy barbarians into the bloodstream of American culture.

The best way to approach the literature of the beat generation is through its antecedents. If you ask the poets, they will name Whitman, Mallarmé, Poe, Baudelaire, Rimbaud, Verlaine, Yeats, Eliot, Pound; there will be talk in some quarters of looking into Swinburne again (didn't he introduce Baudelaire to the English-reading world?); Shelley will be quoted, Marlowe rather than Shakespeare (though I have heard *The Phoenix and the Turtle,* attributed to the Bard, praised as "a far-out swinging poem"); Blake's philosophical poems are being eyed speculatively again as they were in the booming twenties when there was something like a Blake boom, even though it was never listed on the big board. These new poets will go on to name Robinson Jeffers, Hart Crane, William Carlos Williams, Kenneth Rexroth, Kenneth Patchen, Dylan Thomas, Edward Dahlberg, E. E. Cummings, Kenneth Fear-

[5] George Mandel, *Flee the Angry Strangers* (The Bobbs-Merrill Company, Inc., Indianapolis).

ing, and Louis Zukofsky and, judging from the letters I receive and from the behavior of some of my youngest visitors, I, too, am sometimes included as among their literary "ancestors." This is a wide range of taste, but if you look closely at the list, you may notice that nearly all of them have one thing in common: they are not patricians of belle-lettres in the royal roster of the Academy. If they have "made it" with English Lit at all—and some of them have, if they've been dead long enough (literally or literarily)—they made it the hard way, the long way round.

Most of the same people will be named by the prose writers of the beat generation, too. The line between poetry and prose is very thinly drawn in these circles. Many insist there is no line at all. Asked to name their prose ancestors, however, they will usually come up with James Joyce, Henry Miller, F. Scott Fitzgerald, Ernest Hemingway (his early short stories in particular), Sherwood Anderson, Louis-Ferdinand Céline, William Faulkner, André Gide, Franz Kafka, D. H. Lawrence (his poetry as well as his prose), Thomas Wolfe; and some of the older, more political-minded among the prose writers of the beat generation would add Theodore Dreiser and John Dos Passos to this list. All of them have heard of B. Traven but, except for *The Death Ship*, his work is not widely read in beat circles anymore.

Admittedly, neither list is complete, but it is representative, I think. Conspicuously missing are such titans of the twenties as James Branch Cabell, Louis Hergesheimer, Carl Van Vechten, and earlier writers who were widely read by the writers of the twenties (and their readers) such as Jack London, Guy de Maupassant, Anatole France, and Sigrid Undset. John Steinbeck and Richard Wright lead a kind of twilight existence in the literary experience of the beat generation writers, but Nelson Algren is very vivid, very much in the foreground. If I did not mention him among the "influences" and ancestors, it is because he is regarded as a contemporary, along with Salinger and Mailer and Mandel. Dostoevski is, as I have noted earlier, an all-pervading influence that, for this very reason, no one thinks of mentioning. Recently, owing to new reprints or new translations, Nikolai Gogol and Isaac Babel are being read. Gorki is still read in some circles but Tolstoy, Andreiev, Turgenev, and Lermontov are known only by name. Chekhov is still read by the short story writers among the beat with pleasure and profit. Thomas Mann and

Marcel Proust are honored and unread classics. William Saroyan's early short stories are sought out in yellowing paperbacks, and in some quarters he is listed as an "influence" among beat writers. Henry James is tough going for them, despite the lively press agent job that has been done on him in recent years. Sinclair Lewis has joined Henry James as "schoolbook stuff," so the younger writers tell me—an uneasy twosome! Mikhail Sholokhov's *And Quiet Flows the Don* has joined Erich Maria Remarque's *All Quiet on the Western Front* as "one of those war books" that one must get around to reading one of these days just to see what all the shootin' was about. Fashions like reading Stendhal or Trollope may make a stir in English classes and among the exurbanites but not in beat writer circles. The same is true of the occasional *succès de scandals*, like Vladimir Nabokov's *Lolita* or Boris Pasternak's *Doctor Zhivago*. They are read by beat writers but, being translations, they can have little effect on style or content in their own writing. Nabokov's *Lolita,* for all the praise that many critics lavished on its style, is still a foreign language to beat writers, and its shock value is nil, if not actually incomprehensible, in the pads.

The same thing is true of passing fashions in poet-revivals. Somebody writes a critical essay in one of the university quarterlies or in the *Saturday Review* about Robert Frost and the English majors go rushing to the undergraduate library to snatch everything catalogued under Frost, R. off the shelves. Or Carl Sandburg is seen on television once again and the public library has a small run on Sandburg, C. But the beat poets are unmoved by such flurries of interest in writers they have read exhaustively at college or in the public library five or ten years ago and found unrewarding as far as language or the tricks of their craft are concerned! They can learn more from one page of Charles Olson or even a good translation of Zen poems.

Polish, in the classroom sense of "good writing," is no more important to them in a poem or a piece of prose than it is on their shoes. That is one reason why the university-bred poets of the forties have had virtually no influence on the poetry of the beat generation. Of the fifteen poets anthologized by John Ciardi in his *Mid-Century American Poets,* all were college bred and twelve had taught or were teaching in colleges and universities, but none of them has been able to achieve anything like the freedom of style or content that rings a bell with the beat. It is not their college meal ticket or their learning that is held against them—some of the best-educated men and women in the history of American literature are numbered among them. It is just that they can't swing with that beat because they are too conscious of every word they put on paper: you can't dance freely if you have to watch your step. The security of the academic life can become as addictive as heroin and harder to kick. Besides, there are too many eyes looking in at the mating with the Muse, cramping the creative act. In time the built-in censorship becomes familial, like a loved, benevolent monster who provides everything, everything except the freedom to be a clown or a fool. You can be the court jester on a university payroll but you can't be the all-out, truth-telling bard and still hold the Chair of Poetry. You can't even be an honest critic of literature, lest you fall into the trap of being guilty of association with the truth-telling writer.

For the same plus a few additional reasons, the Robert Penn Warren-Allen Tate-John Crowe Ransom Axis is "nowhere" as far as the holy barbarians are concerned, and the feeling seems to be mutual. Like the Poll Tax Dixiecrats in Congress who hold all the key chairmanships, this Confederate Bund has bottled up everything that comes out of the beat writing camp and, in the publications they control, nothing of the kind is ever reported out of committee.

Yet the holy barbarians respect learning wherever they find it, on campus or off, but on this point the feeling is *not* mutual. "They never *read* anything," one college English teacher charged during a symposium on the beat generation in which I participated. He himself was a Rhodes scholar, had been "named" by the un-American committee and "was allowed to resign." Since then he had made the rounds of the pads in Venice West and San Francisco and seen the bookshelves and attended the readings and yet, when it came to making a public statement about it, he reverted to an intramural position, defending the academic gates against the barbarians. Besides, as a Leftist in politics, disaffiliation is defeatism to him, and poverty, voluntary or involuntary, is a crime against the Cause. Rightists and Leftists stand shoulder to shoulder at the gates when it comes to required courses, credentials, and degrees.

1959

Underground writing, 1960

PAUL GOODMAN

THE history of literature is the adding on of new themes and scenes, along with new techniques, styles, and author attitudes. Nevertheless, a special problem is raised by our present tendency to write up, as if in one feverish cooperative effort, everything that is underground and hitherto unmentioned. We apparently want to break down in principle any barrier between underworld and public world, and between what is kept silent and what is literature. Why do we publicize the underworld, why don't we let it remain under?

As with every other spontaneous act in our unsatisfactory era, this effort commences either as a reaction of despair or as a generous gesture of reform; but with astonishing rapidity it is corrupted to the style and effect of the global Thing it means to attack. Because the writers are themselves inwardly betrayed, their frankness rapidly becomes lewd and their impulse to direct action often turns into punk fascism.

To get our bearings, let us recall that in other times the underworld was kept under not necessarily because it was base or shameful. For instance, the ancient Mysteries seem to have been the important community religion of the Greek folk, far more than was the vastly written-up cult of Olympus. Yet they were by no means for publication, so we have few texts from which to learn much about them. From antiquity through the Middle Ages, even in so verbal a subject as philosophy, the highest tradition of certain sects was passed on secretly from the master only to the disciple who had the right character. And of course in less verbal disciplines, apprentices did not learn from books, and there were no books. Socrates and Plato were dubious about writing things down, and in the Chinese tradition, Lao-tse and Confucius, disagreeing on everything else, agreed on this: "We do not speak about the divine."

In most societies there has been silence or reticence also about much of the middle part of life. Concerning Periclean Athens, for example, I should dearly love to have some direct vital statistics, *e.g.*, what were the free and slave populations? At what age (barring plague) did men die? People simply took such affairs for granted and did not write them up. And of course throughout history nothing is said about happy sex or happy married life, although romantic love, sexual failure, and marital failure have been literary topics par excellence. This reticence does not necessarily mean that sex was considered private or that the societies were antisexual. No such conceptions exist in antiquity, not to speak of many more primitive societies. But what is there to write? It is the kind of thing that you *do*. Romantic sexuality is written up precisely because it touches on what you can't do; it is a kind of completing of unfinished situations. (Insofar as sex is an art, however, there is a place for speech and writing and even for how-to-do-it manuals; we have some charming ancient ones. But unfortunately, just where instinct is most distorted, there is the strongest drive for "proving" and impersonal technique rather than for culture and art, and I suppose that our own manuals, at least, often cater to this drive.)

At the bottom of the ladder, finally, throughout most of history, illegal low life has, prudently, not courted publicity. It would have been considered a point not of prestige, as with us, but of simple idiocy, for the secrets of a thieves' or addicts' gang to be exposed and written up. One did not blab. The exceptions are remarkable and force us to speculate. There is evidence that Villon wrote his jargon poems for the *coquillards*, the gang, themselves, as if they were a proper community; yet the poems are published and courtly in form, and they merge harmoniously with his lamentations of low life in proper French and with his standard poems about the general human condition. In his own life, we know, he bestrode the two worlds; the fact that he also did so in writing makes us think of the breakdown of medieval culture, the upsurge of the vernaculars, the disasters of the Hundred Years' War. Villon is an interesting contrast to our Genêt, an artist of equivalent stature. Villon surveys the scene of his low life from the point of view of universal humanity; Genêt finds animation only in his low life and struggles to find in it some universal humanity. Another obvious example is Defoe, in the seamy age of Walpole. Here we seem to get something more like "modern" reporting.

So we return to our own disposition to write up the unutterable, the unmentionable, and the underworld. I want to explore three different general motives for this, so I won't mention any names, since every writer should be treated fairly as an individual.

TWO

First, of course, this underground reporting is simply part of our wretched universal reporting and spectatoritis. On the one hand, it is technological. "Objective" reporting of "scientific" data makes no distinction in what it surveys, any more than a camera shies away. In the past history of literature and painting, a new scene, like a new technique, was painfully won to meet a new expressive need; but mechanical reporting eats up every scene omnivorously, and the great presses print off anything that has the format of objective reporting and might sell. The same occurs with the "scientific method" of so-called sociology; any kind of problem "area" is given the works, and the result has no relevance to solving the problem.

Also, we verbalize a lot in this way because active life does not come off for us. It is an easy way of being on the scene without being involved—just as the sociologists can sharpen their tools and work the area without doing any agriculture. In this respect, *Contact* or *Kulchur* or *Big Table,* with their criminal, underground, or Beat issues, are no better than *Life* or *Look.* We substitute journalism for philosophy, poetry, and politics. We regard our existence as though it were already history or nothing better than fiction; and since the essence of existence, its presentness and challenge, is omitted, we get inaccurate history and weak fiction. Thus, far too much gets written and yet the proper function of letters is neglected or swamped. As part of the popular culture, the scenes of the underworld are like the rest of the chewing gum.

THREE

A second motive for the publication of the underworld is more promising but disappointing in the performance. It is that, since the legitimate world has become lifeless and contemptible, we explore in the illegitimate for vitality. We seem to propose, by affirmation and publication, to make *this* the public world or at least an acceptable part of the public world. The need is pathetic, but beggars aren't choosers. It is no news that, just to live on to tomorrow, many of us have to be illegal. (For instance, I have experienced in a lawyer's office that very few of my friends could appear in court as character witnesses. Though they are fine folk, they could not survive a superficial cross-examination. Certainly I could not.) Thus it is probably a wise course to counterattack ideologically and creatively and get everybody used to the dirty words and the illegal scenes. This is a customary job of advance-guard writing.

We must distinguish two contrasting aspects of our illegitimacy. Given our moronic system of morals and property, it is impossible to live without sinning and trespassing; and in the tight organization of modern society, any spontaneous gesture is a threatening non-conformity. Then to be illegitimate may be simply the continuing defiant affirmation of free love, anarchism, progressive education, and productive work like arts and crafts, that belonged to the bucolic age of Greenwich Village. Our difference is that we have come a further step from bohemianism in honest poverty. It is harder to be decently poor; urbanism and technology are still further out of human scale; civil liberties are harder to defend. The result is that, especially among the unseasoned, a larger number resign from the fight altogether.

But also, given the inhuman pressures and temptations of commercialism, regimentation, and community fragmentation, inevitably there are criminality, flight to the margin, and personality disturbances that are not properly efforts for natural satisfaction in difficult circumstances, but are hostile reaction-formations. Such are the spite, conceit, fantasies of power, and the throwing of tantrums that are the usual tone of hipster letters. The kind of reactive vitality that used to characterize delinquent hoodlums now spreads to middle-class, middle-aged gentlemen who can write books; and naturally it rings bells on Madison Avenue, where there is the same resentment of earnest effort.

Rebellious humanism and reactive hipsterism are by nature incompatible. The positive satisfaction of life; or life striving for satisfaction, being frustrated, and becoming angry—these pay off in a real world of real contacts. There is no need to win "proving" victories, to be one-up in every encounter. Conceit becomes boring and violent methods are rarely constructive. Nevertheless, as the case is *socially*, these two aspects of illegitimacy, humanist and hipster, are lumped together and damned together, and often have to live together. It becomes necessary for a writer to vindicate them together. We who simply want community, productive culture, justice, and pleasure understand that, as Kropotkin said, "So long as one person is in prison, I am not free." Besides, some of us suffer, perhaps neurotically, from a thankless compassion that supports the conceited, wasteful, and violent because they are like sick children.

Unhappily, in the peculiar market of publication, bad writing drives out good. Rebel humanism has an unpopular style; it seems never to pose the "problems" that everybody is talking about—how could it, since the problems are falsely posed? Even muckraking, a proper function of humane letters, *e.g.*, disclosure of police brutality, has a miserable way of becoming sadomasochistic, just as "pacifist" films, on the whole, exacerbate violence. But most fatally, serious humanistic writing really *is* old-fashioned and out of touch. Consider, simply, that a man who for years has accurately understood the worth of Hollywood, the networks, and their related world—which soon includes the whole apparent world —and who has treated them appropriately, that is, with contempt and neglect, such a man will finally have little to say to an audience for whom, perforce, those things have been the *only* world, even though known to be a phony world. One cannot understand, for instance, why Nathanael West is admired, for oneself signed off from California with Aldous Huxley. But the young people must regard that world as important, since it is the only one they have experienced, and it seems that West teaches them a possible attitude to survive by.

The mass public, of course, takes to its heart just that aspect of the illegitimate which is reactive to its own official ideology and mores and which, inevitably, shares the same psychology of power, sensation, and success. The seamy scene of hip literature is an attractive forepleasure, and the acting out of every office clerk's conceit and castration complex provides a relevant thrill. This reportage serves the same function for the philosophy of the mass audience as the bathos of Tennessee Williams does for its sexuality. The poet caters to the tender pornographic side, combining lust with punishment; and the hipster prose writer caters to the conceited power side, combining know-how with putting down. This is utterly boring.

In my opinion, there is something dishonorable and exploiting, queasy-making, about hipster writing—and, similarly, much of the school of Sartre. Life strategies that are brutal necessities for folk who are in clear and present danger, and that precisely would not be written up, are toyed with by intellectuals who evoke fantasy dangers so that they can thrill to extreme situations; and indeed thereby they create unnecessary real dangers, as if life weren't hard enough. It sounds as though they were calling up the underground for spite, as a psychological reaction to blocked creativity—not otherwise than the resentful Stalinists of the thirties. The rhythm becomes jabbing and the tone shrill; the fantasy is for the cool to seize power, even via Jack Kennedy. But our real need is otherwise. The case is that our society is in a chronic low-grade emergency. To alleviate this, so that outgoing life can revive, requires patience, fortitude, and music; curtly rejecting anything phony but having faith in abiding goods and powers. Instead, these writers, lacking the stamina of natural strength, cop out and plunge into the pointless brawl.

FOUR

Let me suggest another motive for writing up the underworld that I think is more reasonable. By making all scenes equal, by writing one's situation as it is, whatever it is, writers might hope to get rid of "standards" altogether and perhaps of "writing" altogether. (Unfortunately, the writers who seem to have this motive, *e.g.*, some of the Beats, are both so ignorant and so hopped up that they don't know what they're after and sell themselves short.)

This is to revive old-fashioned nihilism, to clear the decks. In the nineteenth century, in a scarcity economy, the nihilism was more politically revolutionary and religiously Christian;

in the "affluent society" it consists of quitting and being religiously Taoist and pacifist. The aim is certainly not to substitute the underground as a new power, but to form a new community from scratch. I have shown elsewhere that this is a happy direction for an advance-guard.

A nihilist program is a beautifully democratic approach to literature. It seems designed for the millions of the inarticulate who say, "If I could only write, I have a story to tell!" All of the faithful are encouraged to be creative, a very different thing from making whole art-works, the products of a complicated culture. One is permitted to be fragmentary; by learning the trick of spontaneous association, one can achieve exciting poetic moments; by employing the primitive rhetorical devices of repetition, incantation, and crescendo, it is possible to read a scattered page aloud as if one had made a whole poem; and of course by writing "wd" and "cd" and using the slash mark on the typewriter, one is in the swim. Music (bongo) and painting are also Everyman's.

A critic cannot help being bemused, for indeed this Beat art is a remarkable historical product. Consider how the most exquisite efforts of modern art to break free of convention and get back to the elements of expression—one could mention Mallarmé's symbolism, Rimbaud's vision, Pound's and Eliot's fragmentation and pastiche, Apollinaire's and Cummings' ideograms and typography, W. C. Williams' neo-Wordworthianism, Viennese atonality, Webern's pointillism, Stravinski's and Varèse's percussion, Bártok's rhythm, polyrhythms from Bali and New Orleans, Picasso's abstraction and collage, Matisse's fauvism, Kandinsky's nonobjectivism, Mondrian's and Albers' elementarism, Pollock's action and Kline's gesture—how all of these intensely cultivated sources have met up with the deliberately programmatic realism of Sherwood Anderson, Joyce, Lawrence, Céline, and others, to give a lingua franca to amateur boys. They have a means of esthetically expressing how they are. None of their art is inventive, little of it is any good, yet there is in it a valuable contribution, its very communitarianism, and supported by the sense of a community—the very opposite of the dueling of the hipsters—literature is cultivated as an action on the audience, to increase the community. When they have read their poems at one another, they can barge in for bed and board like Samoans.

Culturally they, and we, are not up to this nihilism. Those who abdicate from the economy and university of the big society become a sect rather than a universal solvent. The "scene" soon becomes a stereotyped subject matter, with monotonous repetition of jejune experiences and standard props, rather than a modest account of just where one happens to be thrown, with its materiality and wonder. Public readings become boringly drunken rituals. And to one's astonishment, the creative community spits with envy at proper writers. The situation is bitterly ironical: on the one hand, we who are cultivated artists and realize how little that's worth (though let me speak no ill of the Creator Spirit) would gladly see our culture relapse into the human community; yet every youth feels thwarted by his writer's block and spiteful because he doesn't know anything.

To sum up: the resigned beatnik publicizes his scene as the only world; the impotent hipster calls up the underworld to put down everybody else; and the technological popular culture makes an amalgam of underworld and public world that is as nourishing as chewing gum. Yet I don't think it is at present possible to return to a classical silence. Our literary task must be to get rid of distinctions altogether and recognize only the human beings as existing.

FIVE

What are the "human beings"? When there are dominant groups and minorities, legal and underworld groups, the minorities and the underworld are necessarily "in the right," for they exist as a repressed potentiality within the dominating majority, and there is nothing to do with such a repression but undo it. If they did not symbolize something within the preponderant group, there would be no "Negroes," "homosexuals," or "Jews," but only varieties of people; and the underworld would be either citizens or frank outlaws at war with us. Once they emerge into notice as "problems," the minorities and the underworld are a lively revolutionary force.

It is an inner boundary that creates dominant groups and minorities, and the success of a revolution is to eradicate the boundary, to liquidate the problems. It is not to give equal justice to different classes—though justice is always indispensable; it is surely not to transform the downs into ups, which would be simply a compulsive acting-out of the repressed resentment and rebellion. To give an actual social example: for the whites the "Negro problem" is their own psychological problem, to be psychiatrically treated. (For the Negroes, of course, it is also a problem of personal dignity and social justice, to be solved by resisting and fighting.) Now the bother with much underground writings at present is that it is a fetishism of the underground—it does not eradicate the boundary. Base or noble properties are assigned to addicts and addiction, or to breathless violence, or to queer society. This is not different from socialist realism or the religion of Catholic writers. But no behavior or ideology is in fact such a big deal; for only the human beings exist. The literary problem is not to present the scene but to show the man destroyed, fulfilled, or chastened in the scene. Also, unless this is done, we do not even get the scene but only its props, for there is no exploration of causes and ideals. Some writers, sensing this superficiality, treat the scene as symbolic of "real life"; but this gambit is bound to be boring, for it requires extraordinary spirituality to write allegory, and the "real life" of these authors is very thin gruel.

To one with any memory or history, it is evident that the need for prejudice, for inner boundaries, goes deeper than the particular content people are prejudiced against at any time. Right-thinking people were just as upset by tobacco as they are now by marijuana. Reading in popular novels of 1880, one eerily senses the same dismay about marriage across class lines that is now felt about marriage across color lines; and, especially among Jews, marriage across religious lines used to be mourned like death. It is as if people cannot feel they exist except by affirming, with a shudder, that they are different from something that they are against.

But to be rid of it, we must *indeed* do without the boundaries. This might mean, for instance, taking it for granted that a chap (like young Freud), busy with God's work and touchingly in love with a well-bred girl, is also sending himself on cocaine, and that's just how it is; or to give a common example, that a splendid teacher is naturally queer for his students. As might be expected, it is just this matter-of-fact attitude that is shocking to the audience and unacceptable to the publishers, whereas any kind of "underground" writing has become perfectly acceptable. The problem for modern writing is not treating some "underground" property, but simply coping with the facts of life with reason, compassion, learning, and imagination.

This brings me, finally, to the dilemma that, in my opinion, is the most serious that faces an earnest writer at present.

This is the fact, which I mentioned above, that especially for younger readers the dominant scene in our society—of role-playing, front personalities, and phony achievement—is the only culture and manners that they think they have experienced, it is the "real world," even though they dissent from it. This simulacrum of life is not worth criticizing in detail, and since literature is the criticism of life, there is no function for literature. With regard to this dominant scene, the only possible literary tone is the apocalyptic one, which of course some writers have hit on.

But the case is not so desperate, for the dominant scene only seems to occupy the world. This phony world stays in existence precisely by the tension of an inner boundary: people conform against their better impulse because they are afraid to be different and excluded; and they compel others to the same behavior in order to protect the image they have invested their lives in. It is a structure of conceit made by the polarity of proving and success versus failure and shame; and its characteristic feelings, if they can be called so, are face-saving and embarrassment. In *Growing Up Absurd* I pictured this world as a Closed Room with a Rat Race as the center of fascination, powerfully energized by the fear of being outcaste. If this is so, the underground writing we have been getting is only one more expression of the same world. But contrariwise, if, as I urge, our writers refuse to take seriously the boundaries, the distinctions between respectable and outcaste, and begin to consider only the human beings as real, then even the younger readers must recognize that they too have had a different experience than they thought.

This idea gives a curious literature—I myself essayed it in *The Empire City*—about a kind of real persons living in an illusory system, with such comic and dreadful adventures as then befall them. They are sane; their behavior seems crazy, but it is society that is crazy; but they bitterly suffer, for one lives in the only society that there is. Or imagine this theme in a more elementary work, say, a film about children: we would show nothing but shots of children, laughing children, jumping children, children bawling beat by mamas in the park, children playing ball, children whose hands are slapped because they touch their genitals, children crying themselves to sleep, children in disgrace because they have pissed in their pants in school, children twisting the arms of other children.

1960

The novel of outrage

a minority voice in
postwar american fiction

IHAB HASSAN

OUTRAGE, which is my theme and hopefully my metaphor, is thought both fashionable and tedious nowadays. This is because we are inclined to deprecate an idea in two ways: we either dismiss it as faddish or else we ignore it as antique. Indeed, a few of us manage to have it both ways. Perhaps I should begin with some effort to reclaim the idea of outrage from our distaste.

Fashions rightly dismay us; they repel our sense of permanence and truth. It is sad to see men, who admittedly cannot bear too much reality, settle for less reality than they can encompass; it is sad to see the unctuous veil of fashion drawn across radical perplexity or pain. Still, we can judge fashions too harshly. If they are a conspicuous mode of spiritual consumption, favored by modern men in search of a chic soul, they also serve as Perseus' shield, reflecting the Medusa face of our time. Fashions sometimes reflect and deflect what men cannot behold directly.

But in the long view reaching back to prehistory, outrage seems less fashionable than antique. Recent studies of African anthropologists, popularized by Robert Ardrey, claim that man is not a tool- but a weapon-wielding animal; as Ardrey baldly states: "Civilization is a compulsory consequence of our killing imperative." Historians are also fond of reminding us that terror and injustice are nothing new; the atrocities of the Thirty Years' War put the atrocities of our century in perspective. I cannot accept the implications of such statements; nor do I believe that the struggle against brutality can be tempered by the knowledge that in the corridors of history there are many torture houses.

I should like to suggest that the idea of modern outrage—and by outrage I really mean a radical threat to man's nature—is best viewed as a dangerous part of our experience, manifest in literature and outside of it. That such an idea may be inherent to our response to art is acknowledged by many artists, primitives and precisionists alike. "Is art always an outrage—must it by its very nature be an outrage?" Lawrence Durrell asks. Durrell does not develop his question, although it is clear from the context that he has the art of Henry Miller foremost in his mind. Now whatever we may think of Henry Miller, we can agree that he holds no patent on anguish in contemporary letters. Samuel Beckett, who stands at the other pole from Miller in avant-garde literature, shares with him the feeling of human violation, a violation silent and deep. In any case, we come closer to the meaning of outrage, as it makes itself available to the literary imagination, when we ponder Lionel Trilling's notion that modern literature puts the very being of man on dark trial. Outrage is indeed the final threat to being, the enforced dissolution of the human form; it is *both* the threat and the response to it.

Such may be the final meaning of our term; its more immediate sense can be found in any dictionary. The word implies excess, the passing beyond all bounds; it signifies disorder, extravagance, fury, insolence; it refers to violent injury and gross and wanton offense. Outrage is rage without measure, but its secret rhythm is one of assault and protest, force and counterforce. The demonic and the absurd pervade this rhythm. Outrage, then, as I propose to use the term, is an irrational dialectic of violence threatening the human form, the very nature of man. In this dialectic, action and reaction are compressed, beyond time, in a form of terrible unity.

This is probably too abstract, whereas literature cries for concreteness. Consider Ivan Karamazov. His case is infamous; it remained for Camus to bestow on him the ravaged dignity of modern man. To Ivan the whole of creation is a botch. " 'I don't want harmony,' " Ivan says to Alyosha.

" 'From love of humanity I don't want it. I would rather be left with unavenged suffering. . . . And so I hasten to give back my entrance ticket. . . . It's not God that I don't accept, Alyosha, only I most respectfully return him the ticket.' 'That's rebellion,' murmured Alyosha, looking down." It is indeed metaphysical rebellion. Ivan gives back to God his entrance ticket to this life. Why? Because the life God gave to man is perpetually unjust. Ivan's sad conclusion is, "Everything is permitted." The conclusion leads him to madness, as it leads his lesser shadow, the surly Smerdyakov, first to parricide, then to suicide. The case of Ivan suggests that the response to outrage is a delayed outrage, madness or suicide, the denial of being. "To be nothing—" Camus writes, "that is the cry of the mind exhausted by its own rebellion."

Consider another case. Ivan, we saw, ends mad; Ahab in all likelihood is mad from the start. Ahab does not merely decline his part in creation; he strikes at the heart of it. The passage is well known. Let me quote from it:

> All visible objects, man, are but as pasteboard masks. . . . If man will strike, strike through the mask! How can the prisoner reach outside except by thrusting through the wall? To me, the white whale is that wall, shoved near to me. . . . He tasks me; he heaps me; I see in him outrageous strength, with an inscrutable malice sinewing it. That inscrutable thing is chiefly what I hate. . . . Talk not to me of blasphemy, man; I'd strike the sun if it insulted me. For could the sun do that, then could I do the other . . .

If the sun can commit outrage, so can Ahab. This is the pure logic of violence stated in the voice of berserk pride. Here is the point Melville makes for us: in outrage there is no clear action and reaction, force and response; there is identity and terrible union. Dismembered Ahab strikes, and striking Ahab ends lashed to the body of his archantagonist, the mutilated whale.

In their moment of trial, then, Ivan and Ahab show us how far metaphysical rebellion can go, and show us too how protest can turn back against the protestant. Ivan and Ahab reveal that true outrage is identity in an awful realm of being; that demonic action and demented passion, becoming one, define a different condition of existence, a new void beyond existence. Outrage, then, unites opposites as a metaphor does; it *is* a kind of existential metaphor. It is a metaphor producing monstrous metamorphoses; in that surreal document of violence, Lautréamont's *The Songs of Maldoror,* we recall that the shark which Maldoror violates and the spider which violates him are both transformations of himself. And it is a metaphor producing an inhuman space.

This last point can be clarified by further attention to the nature of violence in the novel. Violence may be temporal; it may act on fictional characters in time. In his definition of "the novel of violence," W. M. Frohock notes: "Their characters tend to be passive victims who change and evolve according to the will of time . . . the real agent, the active force, is time itself." Frohock has in mind the work of American writers of the twenties and thirties: Faulkner, Hemingway, Dos Passos, Wolfe, Farrell, and others. The writers who concern me, however, are of a later generation; their use of violence, although it has something in common with earlier uses, shows a different emphasis. The violence I associate with contemporary fiction is not temporal but spatial; it is not historical but ontological; it is an inescapable part of a barren landscape. For force has a withering touch; it turns men into things. Simone Weil understood this, and knew how to interpret both our experience and the experience of Homer's Achaeans in the lurid light of might. Force in the contemporary world, however, is unmediated by ritual and ceremony; it is stark as nothing human or perhaps divine can be. In *The Mortal No,* Frederick J. Hoffman describes five stages in the dehumanization of modern violence. The assailant, the agent of force, is identified first as a person, the author of a *crime passionel;* second as ideological instrument; third as mob; fourth as machine; and last as landscape. The "assailant as landscape" suggests to Hoffman "a total withdrawal of the humanly familiar from both the assailant and the victim. Moreover, the assailant and the victim are both a part of the landscape." This metaphor of violence in a landscape or inscape stripped of everything human is the extreme definition of outrage that my discussion assumes.

Such an idea of violence seems to presage only our nullity, our doom. It is certainly at odds with traditional forms of violence, say, the heroic and purposeful violence of Georges Sorel's revolutionary syndicalism. Yet one is still moved to wonder: if outrage is our metaphor of absence and void, may it not also serve, as Sartre's image of the hole does, as *an appeal to being?* Can we allow ourselves to see in it new intimations of an apocalypse? And may not outrage also contain within it the possibilities of rebirth? These are not questions we can glibly answer. Sartre, for that matter, offers us no comfort. "Thus the passion of man is the reverse of that of Christ," Sartre judges, "for man loses himself as man in order that God may be born. But the idea of God is contradictory and we lose ourselves in vain. Man is a useless passion."

Sartre's judgment, however, is not entirely corroborated by the contemporary American novel. The latter, I think, provides us with dramatic images that give a richer sense of my theme. What I have done so far is merely to propose an abstract idea of outrage. Such an idea defines a genre of recent fiction mainly by defining its outer limits. This is to say that in the nearer reaches of terror or violence, the old novel of protest and the new novel of outrage are not always sharply distinct. It is only when we approach a starker horizon that the genre gains some clarity. My intention is to move gradually toward that point, using nine novels as my example.

I begin with an ambiguous novel of outrage, one that also happens to be artistically flawed. William Styron's *Set This House on Fire* (1960) treats, in distraught and melodramatic fashion, the regeneration of Cass Kinsolving. The regeneration of Cass, bumbling, guilt-ridden drunkard that he is, dates from his murder of a degenerate rapist, Mason Flagg. We move in a foggy world which the narrator describes as "a grotesque fantasy of events lacking sequence and order . . ." We are witness to the degradation of Cass at the hands of Flagg who forces him to paint pornographic pictures, to perform before an audience as a seal, and to sing bawdy songs on all fours. Flagg violates Cass's dignity, and to make doubly sure, he rapes Cass's beloved Francesca. Violence, however, begets violence; Cass breaks open Flagg's skull with a stone. But the murder, although it may be of questionable justice, proves to be a redemptive act; victim and assailant do not become one. By concealing the murder, Luigi, the police corporal, forces Cass on his own resources; he robs him of the luxury of self-recrimination, the ease of guilt. In his darkest hour Cass mutters: "And as I sat there . . . I knew that I had come to the end of the road and had found nothing at all. There was nothing. . . . I thought of being. I thought of nothingness. I put my head into my hands, and for a moment the sharp horror of *being* seemed so enormous as to make the horror of nothingness less than nothing by its side . . ." This is the brief moment of outrage for Cass, brief because he ends by accepting the burdens of freedom. But *Set This House on Fire* remains a flawed book by a very gifted writer, and one of its moral flaws is that while it brings us artificially close to the facts of violence, it ends by evading them.

The same criticism could be made of James Baldwin's *Another Country* (1962). The novel, although marred by a certain triviality of incident and feeling, is ambitious. Baldwin, as we know, is not used to viewing the racial question discretely; he sees it in an apocalyptic light. "God gave Noah the rainbow sign: No more water, the fire next time!" Hence the sulphurous title of his latest tract for our time. It is a time overcast by heavy clouds: "there seemed to be no way whatever to remove this cloud that stood between them [the friends of Baldwin's youth] and the sun, between them and love and life and power . . ." This sentiment, which finds its source in the condition of outrage, permeates *Another Country*. But the far country that Ida and Rufus, Vivaldo and Eric, Cass and Richard inhabit can be blacker than a Negro's skin; it is the country of *love*. For Baldwin recognizes that the problem of race is at bottom a hunger of flesh and heart; he sees that it is as chaotic in its infinite inversions as the plight of love. The metaphor of outrage in *Another Country* is an erotic metaphor which attempts to embrace victims and tormentors as lovers embrace in bed. Whatever threatens the characters is both absent and ubiquitous. Jowly policemen with baleful eyes, scowling on the streetcorners of Harlem, stand there merely to reflect that invisible threat. The visible tormentors in the book are both Negroes: Rufus, who destroys Leona before taking his own life, and his implacable sister, Ida, who preys on Ellis, the man she despises, and on Vivaldo, the man she loves. Vivaldo is willing to shed his white skin for Ida; but Ida knows the limits of her affections. "Our being together doesn't change the world, Vivaldo," she cries. Nothing is really changed because fear corrupts every act. Fear of what? Vivaldo's momentary terror in the discovery of homosexual love, and Ida's ancient terror in the knowledge that her blackness must forever color her love, are finally the same terror of chaos. *Another Country* identifies outrage with chaos, which it mitigates with the rhetoric of protest and the poetry of love. It is a pity that the novel sometimes lapses into a sentimental doggerel of sex.

The landscape of chaos fills the vaster spaces of Ralph Ellison's *Invisible Man* (1952). It is not in love, however, but in irony and in art that Ellison's hero finds his refuge. "Step

outside the narrow borders of what men call reality and you
step into chaos . . . or imagination," the narrator warns.
Scene after surreal scene of the novel proves his warning
true. The hero's quest moves not like an arrow but a boomer-
ang, and the search for clarity and light ends underground. "I
have been boomeranged across my head so much that I now
can see the darkness of lightness," the hero ironically says.
"And I love light. Perhaps you'll think it strange that an invisible man should need light, desire light, love light. But
maybe it is exactly because I *am* invisible." Light is not
white; light, Ellison makes clear, is being, and the invisibility
of the hero, who puns desperately on *yam* (I am), is the symbol of his absence. But, once again, the logic of violence asserts itself. The robbers of the hero's identity possess a paler
identity than his own. The mad doctor is after all right; addressing the hero, he says: "Behold! a walking zombie! . . .
He's invisible, a walking personification of the Negative. . . .
The mechanical man!" These words better describe the white
philanthropist, Norton, who stands by the invisible man's side
as a mirror image of invisibility. Ellison's novel diffracts the
light of all colors and shows that the true color of outrage is
colorlessness. Such characters as do have a sense of their own
being, Clifton or Mary, leave no biography behind; the rest
flit about in space like shadows. But the hero at least comes to
understand that where blindness prevails, human identity becomes a matter of vision and not of visibility.

Of this first triad of novels, Ellison's probably shows the
clearest authority. Like the other novels, however, it marks
an initial stage in the fiction of outrage. For outrage in these
works is finally mediated by a residual faith in man's will, in
man's dignity or mind. The assault on the human form is
partial; the assailant, although not easily identifiable, appears
in some socially recognizable guise. The characters move in a
field of violence, but violence has not become total or demonic yet. The characters manage, therefore, to preserve a
measure of their humanity; they are men and women we can
still accept.

We approach a grimmer phase of outrage in Paul Bowles's
The Sheltering Sky (1949). The novel has a certain hardness
and clarity, like quartz, and has the senselessness of stone. Its
characters make no conscious decisions, show no recognizable motives; they are subject to a dumb fatality. Three
Americans, Kit and Port Moresby, and Tunner, have turned
their backs on the United States and have plunged into the

most barbarous part of North Africa. Their journey, flight or search, can only be understood as a given fact like Port's nihilism, like Kit's passivity, like the frozen love between them. Port, of course, longs for the state of consciousness represented by the vast, reciprocal blankness of the African desert and sky; he has taught himself to "deny all purpose to the phenomenon of existence—it was more expedient and comforting." His absurd death from typhoid is therefore apt. So is the fate of Kit. Driven by Port's death into some corner of her childhood, she walks like a somnambulist into the desert, is raped by two nomads, serves as a concubine in a mud-walled cubicle, and finally disappears in the Casbah, utterly mad. The face of negation is revealed against a pitiless landscape; civilization is stripped of all its masks, and the sheltering sky, ironically, fails to shelter the Moresbys from what lies behind it: "Just Darkness. Absolute Night." Yet Bowles, unlike Camus with whom he invites facile comparisons, does not endow the nihilism of the novel with any moral significance. (This also happens to be true of Bowles's second novel, *Let It Come Down*, which fails to convince us that the murder Dyar commits confers on him a particular status in existence.) What Bowles manages to create, through the detached violence of man and nature, is a gaunt metaphor of man's primal hunger for being, a hunger, Bowles suggests, which can only be satisfied by a surrendering of the Western ego.

Such a metaphor carries a faint religious aura. The aura is more palpable in James Purdy's novella, "63: Dream Palace." Fenton Riddleway, nineteen, and his younger brother, Claire, recently orphaned, take refuge in a deserted house, in a strange city. They are entirely alone with the smell of rotting wood and the sound of rats' feet; the few people they see move about them like "shades in hell." Fenton, although he fiercely denies God and slaps Claire when the latter speaks of Him, has an apocalyptic sense of doom; for him, it is "the latest time in the world." His blind need is for rebirth, for the resurrection that the lurid signs of the Negro revivalist churches proclaim. His need for rebirth, however, finds tawdry expressions; it is associated with the love and riches promised by the greatwoman, Grainger. Between him and this dream stands Claire; for Claire is the weight of history and the heaviness of love, "so now he wanted Claire to be dead, and despite the fact that the only two people in the world he had loved were Mama and Claire." Fenton, hopped up on some drug, ends by wringing Claire's neck, and after leaving his brother's body to putrefy, he returns to bury him in the attic by match light. The overpowering stench hardly troubles him. "For part of the night he found that he had fallen asleep over Claire's body, and at the very end before he carried him upstairs and deposited him, he forced himself to kiss the dead stained lips he had stopped, and said 'Up we go then, motherfucker.' " Lovelessness, even more than godlessness, Purdy seems to say, is the center of our nonbeing; for even love, in an age of perversity, declares itself as an outrage, binding brothers in a ghoulish pact. Purdy, we see, enacts the violence that a writer like Kafka usually holds in a state of abeyance—it is interesting to compare Purdy's *Malcolm* with Kafka's *Amerika*—and therefore Purdy misses the universality of the latter. He also ends by softening religious terror, deflecting it toward childish desires.

This is scarcely true of the late Flannery O'Connor. Living as a Catholic in the Baptist South, she saw theology run wild, and saw heresy and worship become indistinguishable. Her first novel, *Wise Blood* (1952), may be labeled a study of religious fervor in the grotesque manner; yet we must heed her words when she says, "I am interested in the lines that create spiritual motion. It never occurred to me that my novel was grotesque until I read it in the papers." The hero of the novel, Hazel Motes, is a young man with a pure and demonic heart. The descendant of revivalist preachers, he is himself a preacher of the Church Without Christ. Motes brooks no compromises with spiritual hypocrisy; in fact, he murders a fake prophet employed by a rival preacher to deceive the credulous. "No truth behind all truths is what I and this church preach!" Motes cries to the people from the top of a broken-down car. Is this dementia, or is the spectacle of godlessness about Motes enough to convert protest into outrage and prayer into blasphemy? We know that his demonic purity drives him to blind his eyes with quicklime, wear barbed wire next to his chest, and walk with broken glass in his shoes. Yet is not the fate of Motes, inhuman as it may seem, still brighter than the dehumanized fate of Enoch Emery who makes the stuffed body of a savage his "jesus," and who puts on a gorilla suit to commune with his fellow men? Motes responds to nihilism with fierce negation, reacts to spiritual death with murder and blasphemy; but he also ends by offering himself as a ritual sacrifice. The perpetrator of outrage is at the same time its primary victim. When Motes is found nearly dead in a ditch, and his body is taken to his rapacious landlady, even she can recognize that his violence had struck a "pinpoint of light" in the town's darkness; Motes, she thinks, may be wending his way "back to Bethlehem." (Outrage is even more clearly a prelude to prophecy in Miss O'Connor's later novel, *The Violent Bear It Away* [1960].)

In our second triad of novels the human form is viciously assaulted while the true nature of the assailant remains unidentified. The characters use no buffers against outrage; they are not socially but metaphysically condemned. Their fate, in this world at least, seems immitigable. Yet they still subsist in a realm where violence, although demonic, serves a sacrificial purpose; it carries them, beyond death or madness, to a deeper consummation of their destiny. It is as if outrage, taking them beyond the common pale of humanity, could substitute for religious experience.

The last three novels I want to mention are neither religious nor religiose. Mailer's first work—and it is a mistake to define Mailer's achievement by that work—is surely a profane book. In *The Naked and the Dead* (1948), the primary realities are fear and power; the eternal fact is death. The stench of a dead Japanese soldier fills the nose of Red Valsen, who wonders, "Is there really anything special about man?" The sense of futility that emanates from the novel is even larger; the campaign of Anopopei, which Mailer wants us to consider as a focus of History, develops as grim and mechanical exercise in absurdity. Who or what remains human? Even the lives of the characters before the war are represented through the agency of an inexorable "Time Machine": "They were still on the treadmill; the misery, the ennui, the dislocated horror. . . . Things would happen and time would pass, but there was no hope, no anticipation." But the distinctive terror of the novel is not temporal; it is spatial, filling the very air the soldiers breathe with hate or fear. The exercise of power transforms men into objects; this is precisely what happens to Lieutenant Hearn when he is forced by General Cummings to pick up a cigarette butt off the floor. The only two men who exhibit an independent energy of being are demonic, and both fail their demonic dream. General Cummings, sadistic and impotent, does not really win the campaign; victory is the result of a bloody order issued by a bungling aide. And Sergeant Croft, efficient maniac and murderer, fails to climb the mountain against which he pits himself. Both men nurture an idea of their manifest destiny as gods; both are finally driven back to the broken humanity they have helped to break. Mailer shows that outrage is not only a product of military dehumanization; nor is it simply a matter of historical judgment: "I tell you nearly all of humanity is dead, merely waiting to be disinterred," Cummings declares. True outrage, Mailer implies, attends man's dream of omnipotence. For in a universe without value or purpose, the human need for being forces men to assert their godhead, which is a way of asserting meaning as an extension of the self. "I hate everything which is not in myself," Croft believes, and thereby permits himself everything.

In *The Cannibal* (1949) war provides John Hawkes with a still more cunning occasion of outrage. Malice is part of Hawkes's comic and poetic art. "If the true purpose of the novel is to assume a significant shape and to objectify the terrifying similarity between the unconscious desires of the solitary man and the disruptive needs of the visible world, then the satiric writer, running maliciously as the head of the mob and creating the shape of his meaningful psychic paradox as he goes, will serve best the novel's purpose," Hawkes states. But if Hawkes is a satirist, his barbs are coldly forged in ancestral fears, and his target is nature which leers at the jocular antics of evil men. Everything in *The Cannibal* is blighted; time is frozen, leaving the history of three wars congealed in a single nightmare. The mayor of Spitzen is too blind to tend his chronicles; the undertaker has run out of fluid for his corpses; all the banners are in the mud. "Rotting sandbags killed the weeds, filled the air with the must of burlap, and when they fell to nothing, left white blotches over the ground." We are placed in a world drained of life and energy, except for the atavistic power of revenge, the corrupt force of illusion. On this scene four events take place; all are murders. An American colonel orders Pastor Miller to be shot; Zizendorf, in revenge, kills two "collaborators"; Zizendorf also plots and accomplishes the murder of Leevey, the lone Jewish American soldier who patrols one third of occupied Germany on a motorcycle; and the mad Duke, who has been stalking Jutta's little boy throughout the novel, finally catches his quarry, kills and eats him. The cycle of retribution, we see, ends by identifying victim and victimizer; the cunning metaphor of outrage is cannibalism, that archaic mode of assault by incorporation. When the novel ends, we are back at the beginning. Violence rules the rotting landscape; the inmates of an insane asylum are at large; and the history of German romantic politics finds on a rutted road the deed that reenacts a universal fantasy of man. Hawkes succeeds, as few others do, in convincing us that terror is not merely a political force; it is also the sick dream of men in search of their own aboriginal self. In the end, the main characters of *The Cannibal* "shut their eyes against the sun."

The characters in William Burroughs' trilogy, which includes *Naked Lunch* (1959), *The Soft Machine* (1961) and *The Ticket that Exploded* (1962), are not even conscious of the sun. The characters are somewhat peculiar; insect people and sentient ooze, bloodless signs in a relentless equation of human need, jerky caricatures of a science fiction, engaged in a galactic war. "I offer you nothing. I am not a politician," Burroughs says. He offers a deposition against the human race, a testimony of outrage in the metallic voice of a subtracting machine. His universe is a satiric nightmare, the kind of nightmare machines dream when they dream of culture or of history. A deadly bitterness pervades Burroughs' work: sex is usually perversion or violation, the erotic correlative of deceit; junk is the perfect expression of the Negative, a biological correlative of death; and money is the counter of control and the price of need, a social correlative of exploitation. The politics of Burroughs are elemental: sex, junk, and money are all instruments of Authority, and Authority itself is an Infernal Machine. Against Authority, Burroughs proposes Obscenity as a provisional measure and Silence as an ultimate weapon. For Language itself is the final control of the Nova Criminals. To speak, therefore, is to lie; to speak is to surrender. "RUB OUT THE WORD FOREVER." Or if you cannot, adopt at least the "Cut Up Method of Brion Gysin." In *Naked Lunch* the cut up method is used sparingly; Burroughs relies more heavily on the literary techniques of metamorphosis and of hallucination. Both serve to destroy the objective reality of the world, the separate identity of things. This is in keeping with Burroughs' vision of chaos and disintegration. But the technique also serves to emphasize the parasitic nature of his universe: "Larval entities waiting for a Live One." The universe of death is insatiate; there is never enough life to quell its need. Hence Burroughs' outrage, which attempts to redeem creation by abolishing it, abolishing both Word and Flesh. "All right, so you sewed up a planet—now unsew it—. . .Reverse all your gimmicks—. . .Reverse and dismantle your machine . . ." It is hard to decide whether this jocose apocalypse is a consummation of Western nihilism, a rediscovery of Oriental nirvana, or simply a pathological cry against the world.

William Burroughs might have defined for us the extreme limit of outrage had his statement been more subtle or credible. His work, nonetheless, portrays a total assault on the human form and a response equally total. Action and reaction merge in that apocalyptic destruction of creation that is the complete metaphor of outrage. Mailer and Hawkes do not go quite so far; but they share with Burroughs his refusal to find a usable content in terror. Their vision of the demonic is like Burroughs': in all these novels, we are truly at a dead end.

We may have now reached the far end of outrage; we have not necessarily reached the artistic apogee of postwar fiction. Obviously, I have limited my view severely. I have not mentioned such writers as Saul Bellow and J. D. Salinger, who exert a wide influence on the contemporary imagination. Nor have I discussed parallel genres of fiction, full of roguish laughter and anarchic exuberance, which reveal a brighter facet of our age.

The novel of outrage remains the voice of a minority. It seeks, nonetheless, to find emblems of our art, rage and mortality. Sometimes it succeeds in creating a genuine metaphor of the terror we live by ignoring. Its artistic resources are conceived in opposition to the idea of culture and to the sense of history. And its literary aim is to evolve a spatial structure, denying time which is, in the words of Joseph Frank, "the very condition of that flux and change which . . . man wishes to escape when he is in a relation of disequilibrium with the cosmos . . ." Yet in this endeavor the novelists of outrage distinguish themselves from earlier masters, from Proust and Joyce, Eliot and Mann. For it is not myth that provides them with the basis of a spatial form; it is terror; it is the threat of nothingness. This is probably owing to their perception that man is not only "in disequilibrium with the cosmos"; he is also in a state of ontological jeopardy. In the literary uses they make of this perception, the novelists of outrage become part of what I consider the avant-garde movement in current literature, exploiting a fictional genre that may find its origins, as Leslie Fiedler believes, not in the writings of Richardson but of Sade. The movement in America has not yet found a figure of authority comparable to

Beckett. Mailer might emerge as such a figure when his "tale of heroes and villains, murderers and suicides, orgy-masters, perverts, and passionate lovers," his tale of "lust to capture Time," sees the light of day; and Burroughs might still persuade us that he is the man. Meanwhile, John Hawkes remains our most accomplished author in the genre; and new writers like Hubert Selby, in *Last Exit to Brooklyn,* and Burt Blechman, in *Stations,* make new bids.

Artistic judgments, however, are not the most serious judgments a critic nowadays can make. At a time when literature finds ways to deny, subvert, or transcend its own peculiar powers, the critic should court the deeper dangers of his profession. These dangers are revealed mainly in his capacity to judge himself. It might be possible for him then to entertain the possibility that criticism may be futile and that art may be finally irrelevant. The literature of outrage encourages us to take this view. It does so, I think, by its appeal for profound changes in man's condition, its intimations of apocalypse. For if the threat of outrage is indeed an absence of being, can we still hope to dispel the void in humanity by the magic of the Word? And if terror indeed acts as a space machine, turning Flesh into dust, can we still hope to find surcease in the play of consciousness? I propose no answers to these questions that the academic mind usually finds spurious. But neither can I ignore their lurking presence in current literature. Perhaps our task is more modest than these heavy questions seem to require. Perhaps our task is still to make outrage and not literature superfluous, not to kill the Word but to bring the Flesh back to life. Do we need an apocalypse of consciousness to achieve that end? I am certain of one thing only: that the New Sophistication which threatens nowadays to shape our intellectual judgments in such matters will leave us witty, fearful and arid. Perhaps the most serious threat to the life of the spirit in our days comes from those who fear overmuch the terrible excesses of spirit; perhaps the enemy of being is *l'homme moyen intellectuel!*

1965

Dirty words?

BENJAMIN DeMOTT

WHAT'S fresh? what's hot? what swings with the writing mob? Shhh, baby, not so *loud*. Home and away, among artists and hacks, stillness is In: the move is toward muteness: *silence* is the boffo new literary word.

Every man for himself, of course, in manipulating this Word. In England and West Germany the antilanguage line is episte-logico-semantical. The most fashionable English lady novelist of the moment began her career by creating a genius called "The Silencer," a chap who insists that:

> Only the greatest men can speak and still be truthful. . . .
> Only the strongest can rise against [the] weight [of theory]. For most of us, for almost all of us, truth can be attained, if at all, only in silence. [Iris Murdoch, *Under the Net*]

And the coming young German poet, Helmut Heissenbüttel, asks himself:

> —*does to distinguish mean to distinguish what from what and someone*
> *from someone or simply that it depends and how does one distinguish . . . ?*

Whereas in France and America you work the vein by coming on hard against orators. Henri Michaux, who for years has been cultivating a mystique of the inaudible, holds that the clearest mark of meanness and stupidity is adeptness at public speech. In *Light Through Darkness* this writer defends hashish on the ground that the hashishee is a fast man at spotting oratorical sin:

> One day when during one of these [hashish] moments I was looking at a study in a review having a very limited, almost secret circulation, the study by an erudite young philosopher, I heard something that sounded like the murmur of crowds gathered to listen to these words. Well, Well! The sentence, even when later I read it cold, philosophic though it appeared, was . . . a sentence that could never come from the pen of one who had not caressed the idea of appearing . . . on a platform.

And J. D. Salinger, zenning against words here at home, lays it down about the Gettysburg Address that if Lincoln had been "absolutely honest," he would "simply have come forward and shaken his fist at his audience" and walked away without uttering a word.

But while national differences exist, they are not so pronounced as to threaten the fundamental unity of the language-baiters—or to inhibit criticism from celebrating the emergence of a new international literary theme. American partisans of romantic-existential-apocalyptic fiction have, in the course of their celebrations, gone so far as to discover a "tradition" of holy silence-mongering in modern literature. Some among them even declare that language-baiting nowadays reflects "nothing less than the desire to redeem Western values." [1]

The latter opinion hasn't yet won universal assent, partly because people who back it produce charts of literary "influence," and pairings of literary men, that add up to chaos (Thomas Mann and William Burroughs, for example, or Coleridge and Joseph Heller). Yet this school of critics is by no means insignificant. It has sacred texts—Nietzsche, *Civiliza-*

---

[1] The phrase occurs in an *American Scholar* essay (Summer 1963) by Ihab Hassan about "the growing distrust of language as a medium of expression, and [the] distrust of form, which has impelled certain modern writers to cultivate chance and disorder. . . ." Hassan discusses a wide range of writers—French Symbolists, Absurd Playwrights, new-wave novelists, Corso-Kerouac, and Salinger himself. Warmly appreciative of the word-baiters, he remarks that "in this strident era of overcommunication . . . we are more likely to perish by the word than by the sword, and least of all to perish by a loving silence."

tion and Its Discontents, and Norman O. Brown. It offers an uncomplicated version of the genesis and meaning of the attack on public language. (The claim is that the attack can only be understood as a selfless, life-renewing protest against repressive abstraction and order.) And the figures and ideas honored by the school are difficult to dislodge from privileged status. Novelists who pontificate about matters other than the limits of language sooner or later have to face the standard critical queries. How does the story earn the statement? what allowance has been made for experience that contradicts the generalization? But the writer who takes up the theme of silence as glory (or speechmaking as sin) enjoys cosy immunity from the start. Words are the one means of justifying the contention that language is the foe of honesty and reality: how then can you expect a word-hater to explain his hatred?

There are, however, limits to this immunity—or, rather, there ought to be limits to it. No secular literary theme, international or otherwise, benefits from credulous assessment; when literary motives are sanctified or buried beneath fan-letter cant about the "desire to redeem Western values," they become that much more difficult not only for readers but for writers themselves to understand. The need of the moment is for a start toward a historical account of how the word-baiters and silence-mongers came to be what they are, a survey of the cultural facts underlying bookish assertions that human speech is valueless. Only when this information is in hand will there be much to stop critics turned campaign biographers from transforming authorship into a confidence game.

Where would such an account begin? With politics, social change, and the sociology of writing, of course. Needless to say, a good number of the passionate near-mutes in romantic literature have quasireligious significance. Symbols like Eliot's "still point"—or Wordsworth's Leechgatherer, or Keats's Urn, or Poe's Raven—illustrate the connection between the imagination of a wordlessness and the longing for transcendence. And there are great novelists—Lawrence, Conrad, Tolstoy—whose reflections upon the inadequacies of language stand as footnotes to a large-scale argument against rationalism. (One lesson of *Anna Karenina* is that a man must learn not to define, not to attach words to his feelings, not to state the terms of ideal experience. "What am I about?" Levin asks at the end. "Knowledge, sure, unattainable by reason, has been revealed to me, to my heart, and here am I obstinately trying to express that knowledge in words. . . .")

But while it is clear that the impulse to deprecate language can sometimes be traced to religious hunger for meaning inexpressible in abstractions, it is equally clear that attacks upon the word often have direct social and political reference. Their focus is the lower-class man who has learned to speak up, learned to make himself felt despite the poverty of his birth, education, and training. Flaubert crowded his pages with such men; nowhere in the *Sentimental Education* does his irony carry more contempt than in the descriptions of the citizen-orators of 1848. Zola was interested in the type (in *Germinal* Etienne's virtue is smutched when he shifts from the role of silent witness of suffering to that of the platform agitator). And in the Grand Inquisitor, Dostoevsky brought the character of the wordy usurper to the summit of its development. The Inquisitor's denunciation of Jesus pours on, a furious tide of intellectual passion, for thousands of words; the Listener does not speak. When it is over the Inquisitor sees that:

> The Prisoner had been listening intently to him all the time, looking gently into his face and evidently not wishing to say anything in reply. The old man would have liked him to say something, however bitter and terrible. But he suddenly approached the old man and kissed him gently on his bloodless aged lips. That was all his answer.

The writer thus announces that true virtue is wordless. And, through the Inquisitor's speech, he establishes that in men of power, eloquence is the outward sign of a monstrous inner sin of selfishness.

Why would a writer choose to make this point? In part because of the conviction that, in the postrevolutionary era, eloquence has become a means rather than an end, a gimmick for "improper advancement" rather than a decent symbol of constituted authority (like the mace and robe). The counterpart of this conviction is the belief that in the new world those who manipulate the word are climbing, unentitled, essentially inferior ranters—men who cannot win the authority they covet except by stimulating the lowest self of a mass audience. But it would be a mistake to pretend that either conviction is born of a wholly disinterested, objective contemplation of the run of historical events. Novelists and poets attempt to persuade their audiences to share these convictions not only because the latter are "correct" but because public acceptance of them will advance the literary interest in a vital power struggle.

That the literary interest has been in grave need of advancement for a long while is a commonplace among students of changes in the relation between men of power and men of words. In prerevolutionary societies of mass illiteracy possession of the word was a strong guarantee of power. The writer could support his sense of his "difference" not merely by consulting his muse or by pointing at his books but by reflecting on the quality of his relation to power and on his position in the social hierarchy. The difference was, in fact, less immediately psychological than socioeconomic. Only the elite manipulated symbols: governors and wordmen were, in relative terms, at one.

But the word belonged to everyman after the flood, as already observed. (A half-hour session of Flaubert's "Club of Intellect" includes orations from adolescents, printers, lunatic professors, farmer-priests, shopmen, wine salesmen, and masons—not to mention passing drunks and bums.) And, harassed by the "competition" of people who only a generation before hadn't dared even to think, much less to talk or write, writers intent upon maintaining a place were badly placed. One alternative was to search out, from among a muddle of possible constituencies, some comparatively inarticulate group that might still be considered "in need of a voice." The other was to offer a representation of the world of universal talk that established *silence*, the eschewal of words, as the defining characteristic of the natural aristocrat.

More than one major novelist of the century refused to be trapped into an irrevocable choice between these options. Dickens speaks for a group he imagines to be inarticulate ("Dead, your Majesty. Dead, my lords and gentlemen . . . "), as though resigned to a position away from the center of power. But many of his symbols and comic inventions express longing for the obliteration of the racketing voices which, in the new civilization, diffuse the power of the word. Conrad takes as a theme the emptiness of the rhetoric of "Christian imperialism," but simultaneously makes himself a spokesman for an undiscovered, uncounted constituency: the exploited pagan horde.

In the long sweep of postrevolutionary time, however, it

grew increasingly difficult even for the most gifted and self-as-
sured artist to keep his poise in the face of endlessly multi-
plying scribblers and oratorical fantasts. And the well-known
result was that writers in great numbers gave up the search for
constituencies, and rejected the notion that the attention of a
man of power was worth striving for.

That this choice did not mean a total loss of audience isn't
mysterious. Postrevolutionary events both intellectual and social helped to create a climate favorable to mockery of the
pretensions of magistrates and governors. Late-nineteenth-cen-
tury ideas of culture, class, and consciousness weakened faith
in governors as men of another order of being. (*All* men are
bound by myth, repression, and economic interest.) And the
governors themselves spent little effort in maintaining the social forms which, even after a revolution, might have lent special authority to their words. Their slobbish behavior practically enforced upon all ascendant democrats a view of balanced sentences and elevated speech as dress-up. And the prevalence of this view in turn guaranteed that the displaced
writer who leered at speechmakers (he'll be loosening that
collar later on, why not now?) would run no risk of offending
his audience.

But to be in contact with such an audience—climbers, out-
siders, and other ordinary folk who read with their lips—was
small satisfaction for literary men. So long as a novelist
merely teased managerial or legislative chatterers and rhetori-
cians, after the fashion of Mark Twain, he functioned as the
voice of the democratic wave that had swamped him; by hint-
ing that leaders were just folks, he reassured citizens that no
word and no power could be higher than theirs. To clear a
way toward a place of distinction comparable to the one he
had lost, the writer needed first of all to dissociate himself
completely from barroom-barbershop opinionators, Rotary
ranters, and letters-to-the-editor men on the one hand, and
from the ghostwritten culture of the false elite on the other.
He could take a step toward this end by adopting tones of detached generalizing contempt, and by dramatizing the powerlessness of the new officeholders. (The dominant theme of the
nineteenth-century political novel is that of the unmanageabil-
ity of events, military, diplomatic, economic.) But the direct
course was to find means of effecting a redistribution of property—language itself—whose reality as power was most palpable to him as literary man.

Just here lay the usefulness of the theme of silence, and of the new polarity of abstraction versus existence. The invention of a super- or anti- language about language (one that devalued the mass-owned word) could not be expected to refurbish the old alliance of governors and littérateurs, or to reopen old lines of communication. The terms of the superlanguage were magical, exempt from the "limits of words," incapable of being blended into debate in the great chamber of "lies" inhabited by managers of public affairs. But the new language could bring about the collapse of distinctions between the false elite and the masses; it enabled the writer to stand before his audience as a priest before a congregation of identical human beings, all of whom were inferior to him by virtue of the inadequacies of their language and their unawareness thereof. And this was, for literary men, an essential turn of events. As long as the high public estimate of the value of public words ("free speech") went uncontested, he couldn't raise his voice, hence could not rise. But when that estimate was cast in doubt, a dozen possibilities emerged. In the act of calling for an end to abstraction he could set taboos on the language of the mighty as well as of the base. By directing his fury at the sin of "hypostatization" he could shame the world for having failed to give him its word. And by creating silence as the only conceivable redeemer for nonliterary man, he might well restore the uniqueness stripped from him by egalitarians at the hour of the socialization of the word.

Every reader will think of his own examples of work touched by these motives and themes. Eliot's *Coriolan*, read as a political rather than religious poem, is a perfect paradigm of the politics of silence: a voiceless true leader is set in absolute opposition to a quacking vox populi. Powerless orators and masscult monologuists are prime objects of mockery in Joyce's *Ulysses:* one function of myth in this book is to dramatize differences between the world as it was when the elite owned the word and as it is when every shopgirl has a "literary imagination" (Nausicaa against Gerty McDowell). And the shape of Joyce's career betrays a determination to exact public acknowledgment that his language is remote from that of governors and proles. But the most telling evidence of the reality of the themes in question is that serious books have actually taken as their subject the writer's need for a unique "line" about language that will deliver him from impotence.

Consider for example the novel of Iris Murdoch's that was

quoted earlier. The chief figures of *Under the Net* are, by name, Jake Donaghue and Hugo Belfounder; the relation between them is described by the narrator as "the central theme of [the] book." At the opening of the tale Donaghue is a talented but feckless mooching hack and translator, penniless, homeless, unlucky in love; Belfounder, on the other hand, is a powerful manager, blessed with a "unique intellectual and moral quality," lucky in love, and wealthy (he has made successive fortunes in the armament and motion-picture industries, because he inspires "universal confidence" and has "an iron nerve"). Jake Donaghue's friends attribute his failure to develop his literary gifts to laziness, but, as the course of the story makes clear, that explanation is too easy. The fact is that early in his writing life Jake became acquainted with Belfounder, and was dazzled by what seemed an overwhelmingly original and persuasive set of ideas about language. Belfounder's ideas are the staple stuff of the language-baiter: words are but a veil, "all stories [are] lies," "*actions* [alone] don't lie," "truth can be attained . . . only in silence." But they have a paralyzing effect upon Jake Donaghue. He cannot discount them as products of writerly bitterness about mass-age men of action who cynically cut themselves in on the power of the word. Belfounder isn't a writer but a man of action: he not only possesses power *and* the word but even, as it appears, the girl Jake loves: he inspires terror, not analysis. Jake does, in the early sequel, flee in fear from Belfounder; he avoids appointments with him, eventually changes his domicile in order to escape the man's eye. But the flight that counts, as an expression of terror, is the retreat from a career: Jake disowns his ambition and lapses into relative silence.

Viewed as a dramatization of deficiencies of modern literary power, this novelistic situation presents no severe problems of interpretation. Miss Murdoch's story is about the theft of the muse by the manager—a flat reversal, as it were, of Camus's dictum that "we must make . . . our poets into captains of industry"; its one bold trick is the identification of the muse with the theme of silence itself. The latter theme is, to repeat, both shield and weapon for the postrevolutionary writer; by deprecating the word he (in fantasy) seizes a place above the word-owning masses, and above the false elite (managers, men of action) as well. And therefore the expropriation of the theme by a manager is a double frustration for a writer—an event out of which much dramatic capital can be made. The capital is not wasted in *Under the Net*. Time and again the

novelist brings into sight a character or event eligible for the
irony of a word-baiter (mass-age political oratory is ridiculed
in a chaotic scene presenting a labor union leader incompe-
tently addressing a crowd of workers on a movie set—from a
prop Roman chariot). And time and again Jake Donaghue
the writer witnesses the event, or observes the character, in
the company of the word-baiting man of power—and suffers
accordingly, since such occasions deprive him even of an illusion that his responses are unique.

But *Under the Net* is about recovery as well as about theft.
Absorbed at the start with Donaghue's frustrations, the book
subsequently recounts his progress toward a renewal of faith.
And, as might be expected, the moment of crisis in the progress occurs when Jake recovers silence as a theme of his own
creation.

The novelist works with some ingenuity to prepare for this
moment. She assigns the position of narrator to her hero, the
writer, thereby freeing herself from the obligation to explain
fully his mistakes of perception. The scenes in which the man
of power seems, to Jake's mind, to be developing his subtle
views about the limits of language are done largely in indirect
discourse. These views are at length made known to the
reader through excerpts from a book of dialogues called *The
Silencer* that Jake himself has composed, in theory as a representation of Belfounder's thinking. By a careful manipulation
of events the revelation of Belfounder's reaction to this document is postponed to the end of the tale. And before that moment occurs the reader has been offered several hints that
Jake Donaghue is a self-deceived character who perversely at-
tributes to the man of action ideas that are in fact his own.

But despite the elaborate preparations, the turnabout encounter between writer and manager in which the manager insists that the ideas about language in *The Silencer* actually belong to the writer, not to him, is awkward and unconvincing.
The once self-sufficient man of power becomes, too suddenly,
a figure ridden with envy of the literary artist. ("Wherever did
you get all those ideas from? . . . Your thing [*The Silencer*]
was so clear. I learnt an awful lot from it.") The explanation
of Jake's original awe is lame. (" 'The trouble with you,
Jake,' said [Belfounder], 'is that you're far too impressed by
people. You were far too impressed by me. . . . You can
. . . create things. . . . I never made a thing in my life.' ")
And the reversal of positions—Belfounder humiliated, the
writer elevated—is melodramatic in execution. (The manager

gives up his power and goes off to a job in the provinces as a watchmaker, and the writer returns to *The Silencer* and his other manuscripts, aware at last that the themes expressed in these works are not only his own but, potentially, the substance of significant works of art.)

The likelihood is that the author of *Under the Net* was clear neither about her ideas nor about the best means of embodying them in believable sequences of human action. The ambiguity of the arguments "for and against language" is one visible sign of unease; Miss Murdoch is far more comfortable when dealing with linguistic issues as part of intellectual history (see her criticism), than when confronting them as determinants of human behavior. Other signs are the contrived quality of the denouement, and the frenzied injection of brawls and high jinks (the book is filled with what became, in the Angry novelists, the standard junk of mid-twentieth-century picaresque). But the question of the quality of the book is for the moment irrelevant. What matters is that *Under the Net* is, demonstrably, a narrative based on the assumption that possessiveness about the word and resentment of the expropriation of language by nonwriters are genuine facts of feeling for the modern writer. And the action of the work is ruled from beginning to end by a conception of the theme of silence as both strategy and therapy—the one means by which writers can effect the emasculation of their oppressors and the restoration of their own potency.

The same uses of the theme are visible in the fiction of J. D. Salinger. The case of Seymour Glass is, to be sure, superficially dissimilar to that of Jake Donaghue. Seymour's creator presents himself as a man concerned not primarily about writers but about the common fate of sensitive men. And as a consequence his manner of articulating the theme of literary power-through-silence is more oblique than Iris Murdoch's. Yet, as everyone knows, Salinger is not in the habit of keeping distance between himself and his sensitive protagonists; their agonies become his, the torments of a writer caged in the modern world. And his stories insist that the least tolerable of these agonies is the endless, meaningless, hopelessly barren yammering of the figures who conceive themselves to be the practical managers of this world.

Few things are plainer in Salinger's fiction than his desire that his complaint against nonliterary or pseudoliterary wordmongers be understood as a religious gesture, a protest against selfishness and for organic existence. The Glass family stories are decorated with a score of epigraphs, excerpts from fables, and aphorisms whose burden is the incommensurateness of language to life; Seymour himself insists that "the human voice conspires to desecrate everything on earth." And enthusiasts of Salinger have made much of these decorations even arguing that the work they adorn develops a "sacramental notion of silence." But while there is no denying the intensity of the writer's feeling for silence as a value, neither is there reason to doubt that this value, as expressed in a Salinger story, is a strategy as well as a sacrament. The world of these stories is composed of two camps: people of apparent power, people of apparent powerlessness. The villainous wordmongers—brisk, manipulative, self-confident, exactly rendered managers—are characters of apparent power. The sensitive word-baiting protagonists—writers all in essence (whether by profession or in embryo)—are people of apparent powerlessness, helpless types whom the yakking managers ceaselessly harry into and out of classrooms, rest rooms, hotels, bathtubs, marriages, careers. . . . And it is in the context of this seeming imbalance of power that both the human and political dimensions of Salinger's protest against the word appear. The aim of the protest isn't only to lay on the record an impersonal plea for nonabstract existence; it is also to recover magical potencies for literary man—by devaluing the chatter of the Lane Coutells of the world, figures of phony authority and competence.

Nor is the protest limited to canting undergraduates or dirty-word scribblers or efficient Moms—witness the ruminations about Lincoln and Gettysburg mentioned above. These diary entries of Seymour's have bearings at once broader and subtler than those of the ordinary paradox of purity (we are all murderers, none of us is innocent enough to speak). When Seymour envisions absolute honesty at Gettysburg as incapable of more than a fist-shaking gesture, one of his effects is to characterize the honest *political* leader as a man unutterably remote, separated both from the people he leads and from the events that occur during his tenure. For Salinger's audience the fruit of this invention is a release. To understand the Presidency as powerless whenever decent is to banish the idea of responsibility and wash everyman's hand of the Whole Thing. If authority cannot be virtuous, or if virtue become a head of state can only turn on the nation and chide it for its actions, then chaos and corruption are natural laws, and no individual citizen needs to concern himself with the national events that occur in his lifetime. But for the writer there is a release of a different order—release from the wearing pressure of belief that the chatterers, the figures of apparent strength (whether "great orators" or bathroom barkers), in truth possess any power whatever. I, the mute but revealed Honest Seymour-Abe, started nothing, managed nothing, finished nothing: things happened "out there," stupidity in the mass drove them on, authority was never more than helpless, there are no men at the top. The writer asserts through his hero that if he as writer cannot be competent and responsible, if he as writer cannot be a man of power, then power does not exist: the word-mongering false elite should admit its futility and subside.

Inherent in this logic is an ideal of political virtue impossible enough, perhaps, to be described as religious. But examination of the conflicts elsewhere in Salinger's fiction indicates that the writer's vision of honesty stems only in part from torment about the gap between reality and the ideal. Its ultimate spring may well be *ressentiment* itself, a motive of revenge—a will to strike back at the nonwriters of the immediate circle, and through them at doltish pseudoleaderly millions of others who, sure of their own tongue, have dismissed the literary imagination as a superfluity.

Parallels to the situations and conflicts just discussed can be located in a great number of contemporary writers—but a multiplication of instances would be evasive. And the same can be said of efforts to decide whether word-baiting is one more special "sickness" of the age.[2] The plain case is that not for a century or more has adoption of a "healthy" attitude toward language been a living alternative for literary man. The modern writer who damns the word, the modern technician or scientist who trusts it "within limits," are both conditioned by gen-

[2] For the record it may as well be noted, though, that freedom from voices that talk judgmentally back out of the air is a deep longing of the paranoiac; the latter uses his own speech as a means of silencing other speakers whose words threaten his being. In the chapters on the madness of D. P. Schreber which conclude his *Crowds and Power*, Elias Canetti has a valuable commentary on the subject. Culling evidence from the memoirs of Schreber, who was Senatspräsident of the Dresden Court of Appeals until his illness, Canetti observes that "the thing most important to [this madman] was the safety of words. To him all sounds were voices, the universe was full of words: railways, birds and paddle-steamers spoke. When he was not uttering words himself they immediately came from others. *Between* words there was nothing. The peace he spoke of and longed for would have been a *freedom from words*. But this was not to be found."

eral history and by the history of literacy itself. For the technician, a man without precedents who understands that he has
everything to gain, the response cannot be unfavorable. For
the writer, a man whose gift can never again be an indisputable mark of command, the response cannot be favorable. The
latter isn't alone in his sense of loss; other men of mind in his
age are engaged in efforts to recover mastery of language as
the defining property of the elite. It is by no means fanciful to
hold that most of the new academic enterprises of the humanities in this century—analytical philosophy, linguistics, semantics, the new techniques of literary criticism, the very emergence of literature as a study—owe their inception in part to
the desire of the clerk to repossess himself of mystery, to take
language out of the public domain, to give just deserts to an
age in which everyman believes he owns and understands the
word. But solidarity with these inquirers promises nothing to
the writer: they too are competitors, violators of literary
power. Far from offering him a restorative community, they
deepen his depression, sharpen his conviction that silence
must be his theme.

It is one thing, however, to grant the inevitability of this
theme, the total absence of alternatives (healthy, convalescent, or whatever), and another to stand abashed in its presence. The reader who dismisses the theme of silence as a rare
paranoiac infection misreads the past: in the twentieth century there is no way for the writer to meet his need for self-
trust save by deprecating the word of others. The reader who
argues that the attack upon the word is propelled only by a
sensible desire to dramatize scientific discoveries—as, for example, that language is no mirror, and the thingy world is a
dream—scores a debater's point (while oversimplifying the relation between art and the history of ideas). But the reader
who claims that a novelistic sermon on the inadequacies of
language, or a passage of abuse of the Gettysburg Address, or
an advertisement of a writer's availability as a candidate for
the Presidency, is in its pure and single essence a reaction to
repressive modern civilization is a sentimentalist. Because he
refuses to allow for the effect of feelings of powerlessness
upon any man's attitude toward power, this reader confuses
acts of self-interest with acts of self-renunciation.

And there is, to repeat, only one way out of the confusion.
The new clichés must earn their keep or lose it in face-to-face
encounter with the contention that their roots lie in narrowly

private interest. To confront them in the stance of the ready-made convert is to turn mindlessness itself into a value.

The significance of this conclusion can of course be enlarged. For there is at least a possibility that the fury directed at other appurtenances of postrevolutionary civilization besides language may also be subject to analysis as a mode of revenge. Critics who deny this possibility, stoutly maintaining that the ideal reader of modern literature can only be a convert, run no risk of the charge of inhumanity; they prove their openness to literary assault by rising bewildered and disturbed from apocalyptic texts. (The example of Professor Trilling comes to mind.) And the same cannot always be said of those who are eager to shrug off literary damnation of the age: their common conclusion, namely that at the present moment every educated citizen is wiser as well as stupider than the wisest writer, because freer of the past, is too often proclaimed as a triumph.

But rivalries for the crown of Sensibility shouldn't be allowed to obscure the truth that the lesson implicit in the writings of word-baiters does have substantial weight of its own. Accepting the silent saint as a wholly disinterested, self-renouncing redeemer not only means being oblivious to a subtle power grab, a sly act of aggression. It also requires a pretense that alienation never deflects, never embitters, never blinds, the mind that suffers it. And this pretense, whether cruel or generous to those who believe with Seymour-Abe that no one but the writer "*has* to speak," does severe damage to the largest human causes that literature is presumed to serve. "If one starts deploring the inadequacy of language to reality," Sartre once remarked, "one makes oneself an accomplice of the enemy, that is, of propaganda." The struggle to hold free of such complicity is, as the remark implies, a struggle for the survival of means of compelling rulers as well as rhymers to give their open word. Everywhere the century testifies that this struggle is neither abstract nor "existentially" corrupt. Everywhere the century testifies that in its defeat casualties heavier by millions than at Gettysburg go down, poets and proles inseparable in the mass.

1965

Anatomy of black humor

BURTON FELDMAN

IF some critics are right, Black Humor may be the only new or important development in American fiction since World War II. The important writers are John Barth, William Burroughs, and Thomas Pynchon—but also James Purdy, Joseph Heller, J. P. Donleavy, Bruce Friedman, John Hawkes, and Terry Southern (according to really ambitious critics, there is even a Grand Tradition which includes everybody good from Andy Warhol and Voltaire back to Aristophanes).

The label fits some of these writers poorly, but generally they do share a new mood and manner. Their view of life is audaciously "black"—subversive, enraged, even apocalyptic. The stage groans with the wreckage of bewildered innocents and sinister megalomaniacs, cannibals, and intellectual rapists. But the Black Humor manner short-circuits any strong response to this. The novels stay coolly "humorous," murderously farcical, coldly zany, cosmically slapsticky. Black Humor likes nutty plots, mischievous messages, and an acrobatic style. Barth invents a wondrous echo-chamber that no longer needs a human voice; Purdy portrays the most intense events with a calculated deadness that stalemates his subject; and Burroughs gets more detached as his prose gets more chaotic.

What results from this hot-and-cold douche is an enigma. Instead of much blackness or humor, there is a nightmarish neutrality and grotesque deadpan, an elaborate novelistic impasse to feeling and judgment. But the strangest result is this:

Reprinted from *Dissent* (March-April 1968) by permission.

the effect of all this savage gesture and cold comedy is disappointingly mild, even harmlessly "literary."

This is odd because Black Humor scarcely wishes to be so mild or merely "literary." On the contrary; this writing would like to disavow and destroy any moral or sympathetic bond between itself and the reader. It wants to be utterly remorseless toward all the pieties and proprieties. Reading the perfect Black Humor novel would be like driving on ice. And the Black Humorist hopes to be that passenger beside you who helpfully fondles an ice pick while telling unnerving stories. In short, Black Humor would like to be a pitiless comedy. But something seems to be going wrong.

Such a complaint about Black Humor springs neither from outraged liberal idealism nor from an old-fashioned preference for uplifting literature. The truth is that Black Humor disappoints because it is not as pitilessly black or comic as it pretends to be. Given the wretchedness and folly of our century, a genuinely scathing black-comic view would be a welcome purgative. If we can't have tragic poets, we could certainly use some Swifts. Far from being too audacious, Black Humor isn't audacious enough for a world like ours. So the reader may be pardoned if he casts aside literary gentility and gets a little remorseless himself. The ordinary reader will find that he can trump the nihilism or apocalypse of these novels in a twinkling. There is always Auschwitz, or King Leopold in the Congo, or Hiroshima. Such a reader can only be agreed with if he concludes that the world is surely worse than Black Humor is telling him.

But it may be as irrelevant to talk about Black Humor in terms of Auschwitz as to compare Barth or Pynchon to a Russian satirist like Sinyavsky. Auschwitz is after all an unmistakable horror; Sinyavsky satirizes an unmistakably powerful and dangerous political regime. These issues are clear. Black Humor instead seems to be wrestling with something subtler, more insidiously shapeless—American culture in all its permissive restrictions and glossy emptiness. Indeed, the grand theme of Black Humor is nothing else than fraud. The iciest novel in American literature, Melville's *The Confidence Man*, is itself a "comically" uncanny and savage assault on national and cosmic fraud. But to mention Melville is only to emphasize how tame Black Humor seems. Melville's later and bitter obscurity may provide a clue here, as may Sinyavsky's recent imprisonment for "subversion." Neither Melville nor Sinyavsky demeans his themes. The power of their work springs in part from their ability to make us feel the really formidable stature of the enemy. They convince us that to oppose cosmic fraud or political repression will cost heavily —and that such opposition can thus ennoble and even give joy. By contrast, the saddest side of Black Humor is that it can find no compliments to pay its enemy. For all the violence of its assault on American culture, Black Humor gives no sense that this enemy is worth attacking. It is only there, a vast middle-class moonscape; and then Black Humor slips off into fantasy and parody.

As its reliance on parody shows, Black Humor does not unmask the illness hidden under our bland surface; it merely mimics the violence in front of the scene. Melville's ferocity could convey awesome energy because it was an active force. But Black Humor's violence, though tiresomely inflated, is passive. It is violence stylized, theatricalized, overblown—but static.

This does not mean that Black Humor intends its violence to be decorative. There is something of the terrorist in the Black Humorist. Like the classic terrorist, he nurses contempt for the middle class, and seeks a shortcut solution to the problems of complacency and hypocrisy. Disdainful and ruthless, from his impregnable aesthetic fortress, he strikes out at fraud. But Black Humor has one great advantage over the real terrorist—as over a Melville or Sinyavsky: it risks nothing.

For Black Humor's literary terrorism is mated to affluence. Perhaps "Black Humor" never was a good coinage—this kind of writing might better be called "Affluent Terrorism." It wishes to reform but also to indulge us; to scourge us and yet leave us comfortably what we were, neutralized. This ambivalence shows up again in Black Humor's obsession with violence. It is only playing, one knows that. No one will get hurt. If there seem to be pain or degradation or death on the page, the effect will be made incongruous with the fact, sidetracked into a gag, hammed up, parodied away.

The real terrorist was often a man of resentment, dispossessed and declassed; feeling cheated, he could turn into a deadly enemy of his society. Black Humor, however, springs from affluence, not deprivation. It foments no revolutions but only literary disdain for its perplexed and perplexing culture. Needless to say, any American novel of worth has resisted the same cultural corruptions. Black Humor does not differ in its rejection of affluence, but only in rejecting it affluently. It can afford to be zany or inhumanly aloof, out of it, punitive with impunity.

For the first time, we may have an intelligentsia at work in the American novel. Rigid European parallels are again misleading: a better comparison is with the "older" American novel. Black Humor novelists are "educated" as American novelists never were before. The point is not sheer learning, but the attitude held toward learning. Melville was genuinely erudite, and the rest were scarcely ignoramuses. But the older American novelist typically is self-educated; his independence of insight as well as parochialism of judgment rise from this. Black Humor is our most knowing and sophisticated novel. But no new age of American urbanity is predicted. Talking plain American, it is more like a shift from buying to spending. One might say that the older American novelist—so self-educated, so distrustful of the Academy—got used to earning what he had to know and wanted to know. He did this painfully, stubbornly, badly, and often went broke (no second acts in American literature). The Black Humorist spends learning, rather than earning it. Black Humor novels burn knowledge with abandon, as gaily and irresponsibly as the millionaire lighting his cigar with a $1000 bill. Nothing personal is intended. It is a generation of college graduates, with higher education assumed at birth. The older American novelist is often described as antiintellectual, when in fact he is usually antiacademic. The Black Humorist is sometimes said to be a new intellectual, when in fact he is merely academic.

One can call Black Humor a literature of the academy even while admitting that it takes up the American novel's homely themes of sex, money, loneliness, and the rat-race. To all these temptations, however, Black Humor stays cool. The old-fashioned novelist is rarely indifferent to sex or power: they pull at him ferociously. Sometimes, as in Fitzgerald or Mailer, he even has the imagination and nerve to want to conquer and enjoy them. It may seem paradoxical that Black Humor is at once so detached and yet so existentially drenched in these American realities. It is no paradox. Black Humor is existential in an academic way.

All these novels are inconceivable without the hoary themes behind them of absurdity, alienation, nihilism, and the exhaustion of an age. Black Humor stands to existentialism as the American social novel of the thirties stood to European left-wing thought and revolution. In Hemingway and Dos Passos, European Marxism got transmuted into a peculiarly American kind of compassionate anarchism. In turn, Black Humor Americanizes existentialism into a merciless anarchism. For Black Humor has little or nothing to do with what lies behind existentialism as nourishing and steadying forces—Kierkegaard's Christianity, Nietzsche's aspirations to greatness, or Sartre's and Camus' experience during the Resistance. Black Humor exploits the existential style without the substance. Nihilism becomes a mere literary convention. It has no kinship with the novels of Sartre or Camus, where absurdity earned its right to speak amid the painful actualities of politics and history.

Existentialism has always spoken for commitment. By comparison, Black Humor makes such commitment—unspecific as it is—seem like the Ten Commandments. Committed only to detachment, Black Humor can never be betrayed or duped or ever be wrong. That would be an enviable position, but the suspicion grows that such detachment connives with the middle class rather than opposes it. In this joyless literary burlesque house the stripteasers and blue comedians will do anything but really enrage or satisfy the customers; make them a little excited and then frustrated, yes. It becomes clear that one genuinely new aspect of Black Humor is its appearance in the novel. One suddenly realizes how the American-English novel, like Anglo-American philosophy and political thinking, has always been a moral agent as well as a realistic image. It may be good-bye to all that. The novel used to teach us to resist social pressures. We may now have to learn sobriety and plainness so we can resist at least some of our novels.

1968

The higher sentimentality

LESLIE FIEDLER

PRIMITIVISM is the large generic name for the Higher Masculine Sentimentality, a passionate commitment to inverting Christian-Humanist values, out of a conviction that the Indian's way of life is preferable. From this follows the belief that if one is an Indian he ought, despite missionaries and school boards, to remain Indian; and if one is White, he should do his best, despite all pressures of the historical past, to go Native. Ever since the oft-quoted observation of Crèvecoeur that there must be something superior in Indian society since "thousands of Europeans are Indians, and we have no example of even one of those aborigines having from choice become Europeans . . . ," White men in America have continued to echo that primitivist hyperbole, whose truth cannot be diminished merely by disproving Crèvecoeur's facts.

Crèvecoeur's own *Letters from an American Farmer* ends with a declaration that he is about to pack up his family and head out for a wigwam in the forest, a resolution which, once he had written it down, he felt quite free not to live. But this seems irrelevant; for, in theory at least, the rejection of Our Side and the identification with Theirs involved in purely literary renegadism ought to be as disturbingly real as the act, say, of Simon Girty going over to the redskin enemy.

Yet, in fact, most of the literature written by literary renegades affords us only the easy pleasure and secondhand self-righteousness once derived by Victorians from reading about the tribulations of the poor. Even a symbolic desertion to the Indians should seem an outrage, a blasphemy—certainly not just another pious gesture, one more Good Work. But precisely this sense of do-gooding mars for me the would-be primitivism of certain authors who, in addition to loving Indians and propagandizing on their behalf, lived with them and knew them intimately: Oliver La Farge, for instance, whose *Laughing Boy* was once taken very seriously indeed, and Frank Waters, whose *The Man Who Killed the Deer* is once again in print twenty-five years after its first appearance.

The pretense of writing from within the consciousness of Indians intrinsic to such fiction leaves me always with the sense of having confronted an act of impersonation rather than one of identification, a suspicion of having been deceived; and this is reinforced when the presumable wisdom of the alien Red Man turns out to be some quite familiar cliché of our own culture—as when toward the end of Waters' novel, Byers, his surrogate and spokesman, thinks:

We are all caught in the tide of perpetual change. These pueblos, these reservations must sometime pass away, and the red flow out into the engulfing white. . . . So both must sometime pass: the Indian with his simple fundamental premise untranslated into modern terms, and finally the white with his monstrous materiality.
But perhaps there would still be time, thought Byers, to learn from these people before they pass from this earth which was theirs and is now all men's—the simple and monstrous truth of mankind's solidarity with all that breathes and does not breathe . . .

The book ends not on this relatively somber note, however, but with a temporary Happy Ending, the postponement of the Vanishing American's vanishing for one more generation, as the Sacred Lake is saved for the tribe, and yet one more boy adopted into a kiva to be initiated into the old ways.

Despite such concessions to Hollywood taste, however, Waters' book has a continuing appeal to the young, whose disaffection from a life dedicated to work and success makes them susceptible to even the *kitsch*iest evocations of the Indian alternatives. It would be hard to understand otherwise how such a conventional example of slick fiction as William Eastlake's "Portrait of an Artist With 26 Horses" (about an Indian who gives up living in the white man's world, believing this involves giving up his wife and son, only to discover that they are waiting for him, having learned on their own such bits of esoteric wisdom as "money isn't everything" and "it won't buy happiness") was included in a recent collection made by Donald Allen and Robert Creeley, calling itself *New American Story*.

A more considerable and impressive try at the same sort of thing is Peter Matthiessen's *At Play in the Fields of the Lord*, which recounts at its center the story of a college-educated, brainwashed North American Indian called Lewis Meriwether Moon by a romantic father who had loved the memory of that doomed explorer for having crossed the continent without—he had been convinced—killing a single Indian. Moon, a mercenary soldier with a patched-up plane as his stock-in-trade and a Jewish hipster for a partner, finds himself among still primitive South American tribesmen; appalled at the emptiness of his own life, the lovelessness of his own world, he makes it back to nakedness and mindlessness in the jungle mud.

There is much in Matthiessen's book that is palpably false (his hippy Jew from the Bronx is incredible, his white missionaries stereotypes out of Somerset Maugham); but he renders with real convincingness the downward progress of Moon: first detaching himself by will from one way of life, then falling by necessity out of another, until, in utter loneliness, he recapitulates the beginning or invents the end of man. And at that extreme moment he mourns the passing of his people, even before he bewails himself:

> . . . a well of sadness for things irredeemable and gone flowed over him. The Indian nation had grown old; he knelt down like a penitent and wept. He wept for Aeore and the doomed people of the jungle, and he wept for the last old leatherfaces of the plains. . . .
>
> He felt bereft, though of what he did not know. He was neither white nor Indian, man nor animal. . . .
>
> He thought, Am I the first man on the earth; am I the last?

Finally, such works depend upon a pathos too simple, a world-view too naive, to sustain a major literary effort, however adequate they may seem to the living needs of the young. I, at any rate, have never been as much moved by any of the fictions derived from nostalgic primitivism as by a letter written me just after the death of Hemingway and my own published responses to it. Composed by a young Montanan who had just attended a meeting of the Native American Church, an Indian peyote cult with fundamentalist Christian trimmings, it is a deliberate nonliterary, even antiliterary document; and maybe this is part of the real point, since a novel in praise of the analphabetic past stirs more ironies than it can ever resolve. "I hope you will pardon this midsummer madness," the letter begins, and "madness" is the keynote, my correspondent continuing a little later:

> Since attending an all night prayer meeting with . . . the Cheyenne I am also mad on Indians. I expected to have hallucinations, I did not expect to encounter truths. . . . What one sees, and this has no meaning (I suppose) until one has seen it, is one's mirror image, the image everyone (especially Hemingway) is secretly searching for, the answer to the question "What am I *really* like?" . . .

If Hemingway obsesses the writer, it is because Hemingway seems to him what he in fact was—except in the facetious talking-in-his-sleep of *Torrents of Spring*—the inventor for our time of the False Western. Hemingway (along with books and the movies) lies; the Indians (along with drumbeating and peyote) tell the truth: this is the simpleminded thesis.

> The mental mirror of the conqueror cannot be found in the culture of the conqueror. The mental mirror of the conqueror can only be found in the eyes of the conquered, those people who do not read or write or leave histories or legends, but simply live and die unremembered. It took hours of fire watching and drum-beating and chanting and meditation before that deepest of liberal prejudices, that underneath the skin we are all alike, finally wore off. . . . We are bred and inculcated from childhood in the doctrines and belief of winners. We are conquerors, upmen, all of us, collectively and individually. (The Jews, being a traditionally conquered people, get off more easily, but only in a relative way.)

Perhaps the parenthetical comment suggests one reason why Jews have played so large a role in creating the New or anti-"Upman" Western Novel; though, as a matter of fact, they did not begin to do so until, in America and especially in the field of the arts, they began to move rapidly into the establishment, *i.e.*, to go "up."

I cannot think of a single Hemingway hero, who was not, in one way or another, a conqueror's hero. Brave, stoic, modest, essentially unanalytic, never grasping, dedicated to honor in the face of events which made honor meaningless. . . . We conquerors heroize Gary Cooper and Natty Bumppo, because by pretending that they are really like us, we are able to create a mirror image of ourselves that is pleasing. . . .

The mirror image that the American public has loved to find for itself in the Hemingway novels is the opposite of the true mirror image of the American public. Those of us who have come close to the pioneers in Montana know . . . those great heroes of the west, eulogized Monday through Friday on TV, were the most selfish, ruthless, cunning, conniving, grasping bastards in the history of the World. And to cover this up . . . they imitated, mimicked, mocked and claimed for themselves the nature of the person they tortured and murdered, the American Indian. No wonder the only good Indian is a dead Indian. They give the lie to the frontier myth. . . . The frontier heroes were mock Indians. . . .

At this point, my correspondent might well have sat down to write just such a satire of the Old West as David Markson produced in *The Ballad of Dingus Magee*. But, remembering Hemingway, he turns in another direction:

Anyway, the thesis which I never got to is that Hemingway is the colossal literary upman, playing the winner's game all the way. Like all good Nazis (racial upmen) he went nuts at the end. The Indians are colossal downmen (they are too lazy to write). While we have been playing checkers they have been playing give away. As a result they have nothing but poverty, anonymity, happiness, lack of neuroses, wonderful children and a way of life that is free, democratic and in complete fulfillment of the American dream, the one Hemingway longed for.

And as a final note, an obvious afterthought, he adds (thus emboldening me to use his text as I have):

I personally have joined the Cheyenne and am never going to use this thesis. I'm playing give away.

Madness, drugs, caricature, and abuse: many of the essentials of the New Western are already present here; but the setting will not do, for finally the Reservation (half island in time, half ghetto in space) is as inadequate a West in the latter half of the twentieth century as the remembered forests of Barth and Cohen, or the remote ones of Matthiessen. La Farge and Waters and Eastlake and even my friend fresh from firewatching in Montana are seeking the West in a past which is not less lapsed because it has been preserved in a few enclaves, flanked by motels and souvenir shops, and connected by superhighways. If there still exists for us a Wilderness and a Place-out-of-Time appropriate for renewal rather than nostalgia, rebirth rather than recreation, that place must be in the Future, not the Past: that Future toward which we have been pointed ever since the Super-Guy comic books and the novels of science fiction shifted the orientation of Pop Art by one hundred and eighty degrees.

But the real opposite of nostalgic is psychedelic, the reverse of remembering is hallucinating, which means that, insofar as the New Western is truly New, it, too, must be psychedelic.

The term is embarrassingly fashionable and disconcertingly broad in application, including, in the field of fiction alone, examples as varied as science fiction itself, both in its classic form, and in such extensions as Burrough's *Nova Express,* Harry Matthew's *Tlooth,* and Anthony Burgess' *A Clockwork Orange;* metapolitical fables, emerging out of the wreck of Marxist ideology, like the story behind that astonishing movie, *Morgan;* and even such High Church Christian allegories, pretending to be fairy tales, as J. R. R. Tolkien's *The Lord of the Rings.* But no other name fits as well the New Western, which, like the Old Western at its most authentic, deals precisely with the alteration of consciousness.

Besides, many of the so-called "psychedelics" themselves, those hallucinogenic drugs, at least, found in nature rather than synthesized in the laboratory (marijuana, peyote, the Mexican Mushroom, Ayahuasca, etc.), are our bridge to— even as they are gifts from—the world of the Indian: the world not of an historical past, but of the eternally archaic one. And so, too, are those other once-magical plants, now long socialized and deprived of power, *yerba maté,* coffee, cacao, and, especially, tobacco, on which Shamans once saw visions—and which somehow still threatens us Whites, as our Big Medicine, whiskey ("The White Man's Milk," the Indians called it), still threatens the Indian. It is easy to forget how those first hippies of the Western World, Raleigh, Marlowe, and company, cultivated a life-style based on homosexuality, a contempt for Established Religion, and "drinking" tobacco; for all that survives of the first Indian-inspired Drug Cult are a handful of lyrics, apt to strike us as much more amusing than dangerous:

> The Indian weed withered quite,
> Green at morn, cut down at night,
>   Shows thy decay;
>   All flesh is hay;
> Thus think, then drink Tobacco.

Nothing in the seventeenth century compares in scope and avowed seriousness even with the literature of the nineteenth century Drug Cult (centered around opiates, and therefore implicated in the myth of an Absolute East rather than a Polar West), from Poe and Coleridge and DeQuincy to Baudelaire—much less with the prose and verse being composed now on, or in the name of, "pot." Certainly it is hard to identify a tobacco-style, as one can an opium-style, and even a marijuana (or, as we come to synthesize a Super-West of our own, an LSD) one.

In Cohen's *Beautiful Losers*, for instance, the sort of vision evoked by psychedelics, or bred by the madness toward which their users aspire, is rendered in a kind of prose appropriate to that vision—a prose hallucinated and even, it seems to me, hallucinogenic: a style by which it is possible to be actually turned on, though only perhaps (judging by the critical resistance to Cohen's book) if one is already tuned in to the times. Yet even he felt a need for an allegiance to the past as well as the future, to memory as well as madness—or perhaps more accurately a need to transmute memory into madness, dead legend into living hallucination; and for him the myth of Catherine Tekakwitha served that purpose.

For us, however, on the other side of a border that is religious as well as political, mythological as well as historical, her story will not work; and what we demand in its place is the archetypal account of no analogous girl (for us women make satisfactory devils, but inadequate saints), but the old, old fable of the White outcast and the noble Red Man joined together against home and mother, against the female world of civilization. This time, however, we require a new setting, at once present and archaic—a setting which Ken Kesey discovered in the madhouse: *our* kind of madhouse, which is to say, one located in the American West, so that the Indian can make his reappearance in its midst with some probability, as well as real authenticity.

Perhaps it was necessary for Kesey to come himself out of Oregon, one of our last actual Wests (just as it was necessary for him to have been involved with one of the first experiments with the controlled use of LSD), since for most Americans after Mark Twain, the legendary colored companion of the white fugitive had been turned from Red to Black. Even on the most naive levels, the Negro has replaced the Indian as the natural enemy of Woman; as in the recent film *The Fortune Cookie,* for instance, the last scene of which fades out on a paleface *schlemiel* (delivered at last from his treacherous whore of a white wife) tossing a football back and forth with his Negro buddy in a deserted football stadium. Similarly, in such sophisticated fiction as James Purdy's *Cabot Wright Begins,* the color scheme demanded by the exigencies of current events is observed, though in this case, the relationship has become overtly and explicitly homosexual:

. . . His dark-skinned prey seated himself under the street-lamp and Bernie, more desperate by the moment, seated himself next to him, then almost immediately introduced himself.

His new friend accepted the introduction in the manner in which it was meant. They exchanged the necessary information about themselves, Bernie learning that his chance acquaintance was Winters Hart, from a town in the Congo. . . . Taking Winters Hart's left hand in his, Bernie held his friend's dark fingers on which he wore a wedding-ring, and pressed the finger and the hand.

Far from being annoyed at this liberty, Winters Hart was, to tell the truth, relieved and pleased. Isolation in a racial democracy, as he was to tell Bernie later that night, as they lay in Bernie's bed together, isolation, no thank you.

The title of the chapter from Purdy's book from which this passage comes is "One Flew East, One Flew West"—referring, I suppose, to the two sexual choices open to men; but it reminds us of the title of Kesey's archetypal Western, *One Flew Over the Cuckoo's Nest,* which represents a third possibility of White transcendence: madness itself.

A myth in which the non-White partner for whom the European American yearns is Black rather than Red, we tend to interpret as a parable of an attempt to extend our sexuality, to recover our lost *libido;* while one in which the White Man longs for an Indian, we are likely to read as signifying a desire to breach the limits of reason, to extend our consciousness. Mark Twain tried valiantly to reverse this in his two books involving Huck Finn, making Injun Joe rather than Nigger Jim the threat to white womanhood; but trying in *Pudd'nhead Wilson* to imagine the only really sexually desirable woman in all his works, he felt obliged to make her minimally and by legal definition Black. Moreover, future Jims all the way down to Purdy's Winters Hart have tended to become ever more frankly the objects of *eros.* And this is fair enough, since in the language of archetype the Negro stands for alien passion, and the Indian for alien perception. (Or perhaps this is only another way of saying that at the level of deep imagination the Indian is male and the Negro female; the former Yang, the latter Yin.)

In no case does the longing for a Negro companion represent in the male a temptation to escape society once and for all by the final expedient of going out of one's head. Ike McCaslin in Faulkner's "The Bear," seems at first glance an exception; but the Sam Fathers who initiates him into lifelong isolation remains quite ambiguous, being Negro and Indian at the same time, maybe more Indian than Negro in the heart of the wilderness, where the crisis of the tale is enacted. In Faulkner's later work, his boy-heroes are humanized by their Negro mentors, saved for society rather than persuaded to abandon it by those bland, resilient post-Uncle Toms like Lucas Beauchamp. To be sure, an occasional female in Faulkner may have her madness compounded by the Negro upon whom she projects it, like Joanna Burden in *Light in August,* infuriated rather than satiated by the sexuality of Joe Christmas, who may, indeed, be less a Negro than a pretender to Negro-ness.

Even the most nearly lunatic of Faulkner's projections of his youthful self, Quentin Compson, is pushed over the brink not by finding a Negro Companion, but by failing to find one. His suicide on the verge of manhood may have been precipitated in part by a lifelong obsession with the impurity of White women, symbolized for him by his sister Caddy's soiled underpants; but it is more immediately occasioned by the absence in Cambridge of anything closer to a true Uncle Tom than Deacon, who blasphemously camps the role. Finally, Faulkner can imagine no America without the Negro

—and when he tries to imagine someone like himself imagining it, he conceives of him wigging out of that world completely. But his Indians (the old Ikemotubbe, for instance, of his short stories) are vanishing by definition, disappearing as fast as the forests of the American past.

Not so with Ken Kesey, whose novel opens with an obviously psychotic "I" reflecting on his guards, one of whom identifies him almost immediately, speaking in a Negro voice: "Here's the Chief. The *soo*-pah Chief, fellas. Ol' Chief Broom. Here you go, Chief Broom. . . ." Chief Bromden is his real name, this immense schizophrenic, pretending he is deaf-and-dumb to baffle "the Combine," which he believes controls the world: "Look at him: a giant janitor. There's your Vanishing American, a six-foot-six sweeping machine, scared of its own shadow. . . ." Or rather Bromden is the name he has inherited from his white mother, who subdued the full-blooded Chief who sired him and was called "The-Pine-That-Stands-Tallest-on-the-Mountain." "He fought it a long time," the half-breed son comments at one point, "till my mother made him too little to fight any more and he gave up."

Chief Bromden believes he is little, too, what was left in him of fight and stature subdued by a second mother, who presides over the ward in which he is confined ("She may be a mother, but she's big as a damn barn and tough as knife metal . . .") and, at one point, had given him two hundred successive shock treatments. Not only is Mother II big, however, especially in the breasts; she is even more essentially *white:* "Her face is smooth, calculated, and precision-made, like an expensive baby doll, skin like flesh-colored enamel, blend of white and cream and baby-blue eyes . . ." and her opulent body is bound tight in a starched white uniform. To understand her in her full mythological significance, we must recall that seventeenth century first White Mother of Us All, Hannah Duston, and her struggle against the Indians who tried to master her.

Hannah has represented from the start those forces in the American community—soon identified chiefly with the female and maternal—which resist all incursions of savagery, no matter what their course. But only in the full twentieth century is the nature of Hannah's assault made quite clear, first in Freudian terms and then in psychedelic ones. "No, buddy," Kesey's white hero, Randle Patrick McMurphy, comments on the Big Nurse. "She ain't pecking at your *eyes.*

That's not what she's peckin' at." And when someone, who really knows but wants to hear spoken aloud what he is too castrated to say, asks at *what,* then, R. P. McMurphy answers, "At your balls, buddy, at your everlovin' *balls.*" Yet toward the close of the book, McMurphy has to be told by the very man who questioned him earlier the meaning of his own impending lobotomy at the hands of the Big Nurse ("Yes, chopping away the brain. Frontal-lobe castration. I guess if she can't cut below the belt she'll do it above the eyes"), though by this time he understands why he, as well as the Indian (only victim of the original Hannah's blade), has become the enemy of the White Woman.

In his own view, McMurphy may be a swinger, and in the eyes of his Indian buddy an ultimate Westerner, the New American Man: "He walked with long steps, too long, and he had his thumbs hooked in his pockets again. The iron in his boot heels cracked lightning out of the tile. He was the logger again, the swaggering gambler . . . the cowboy out of the TV set walking down the middle of the street to meet a dare."

But to Big Nurse—and the whole staff of the asylum whom, White or Black, male or female, she has cowed—he is only a "psychopath," not less sick for having chosen the nuthouse in which he finds himself to the work-farm to which his society had sentenced him. And she sees the purpose of the asylum as being precisely to persuade men like him to accept and function in the world of rewards and punishments which he has rejected and fled.

To do this, however, she must persuade him like the rest that he is only a "bad boy," *her* bad boy, quite like, say Huckleberry Finn. But where Huck's substitute mothers demanded that he give up smoking, wear shoes, go to school, she asks (it is the last desperate version of "sivilisation") that he be sane: "All he has to do is *admit* he was wrong, to indicate, *demonstrate* rational contact and the treatment would be cancelled this time."

The choice is simple: either sanity abjectly accepted, or sanity imposed by tranquilizers, shock treatments, finally lobotomy itself. But McMurphy chooses instead if not madness, at least aggravated psychopathy and an alliance with his half-erased, totally schizophrenic Indian comrade—an alliance with all that his world calls unreason, quite like that which bound Henry to Wawatam, Natty Bumppo to Chingachgook, even Ishmael to Queequeg (that versatile Polynesian, who, at the moment of betrothal, whips out a tomahawk pipe, quite as if he were a real Red Man). And this time, the alliance is not merely explicitly, but quite overtly directed against the White Woman, which is to say, Hannah Duston fallen out of her own legend into that of Henry and Wawatam.

For a while the result seems utter disaster, since McMurphy, driven to attempt the rape of his tormentor, is hauled off her and duly lobotomized, left little more than a vegetable with "a face milk-white except for the heavy purple bruises around the eyes." Whiter than the White Woman who undid him, white as mother's milk: this is McMurphy at the end, except that Chief Bromden will not let it be the end, will not let "something like that sit there in the day room with his name tacked on it for twenty or thirty years so the Big Nurse could use it as an example of what can happen if you buck the system. . . ."

Therefore in the hush of the first night after the lobotomy, he creeps into the bed of his friend for what turns out to be an embrace—for only in a caricature of the act of love can he manage to kill him: "The big, hard body had a tough grip on life. . . . I finally had to lie full length on top of it and scissor the kicking legs with mine. . . . I lay there on top of the body for what seemed like days. . . . Until it was still a while and had shuddered once and was still again."

It is the first real *Liebestod* in our long literature of love between white men and colored, and the first time, surely, that the Indian partner in such a pair has outlived his White brother. Typically, Chingachgook had predeceased Natty, and Queequeg, Ishmael; typically, Huck had been younger than Jim, Ike than Sam Fathers. Everyone who has lived at the heart of our dearest myth knows that it is the white boyman who survives, as the old Indian, addressing the Great Spirit, prepares to vanish. Even so recent a novel as Berger's *Little Big Man* has continued to play it straight, closing on the traditional dying fall, as Old Lodge Skins subsides after a final prayer, and his white foster son says:

> He laid down then on the damp rocks and died right away. I descended to the treeline, fetched back some poles, and built him a scaffold. Wrapped him in the red blanket and laid him thereon. Then after a while I started down the mountain in the fading light.

But on the last page of *One Flew Over the Cuckoo's Nest*,

Chief Bromden is on his way back to the remnants of his tribe who "have took to building their old ramshackle wood scaffolding all over the big million-dollar . . . spillway." And his very last words are: "I have been away a long time."

It is, then, the "Indian" in Kesey himself, the undischarged refugee from a madhouse, the AWOL Savage, who is left to boast: *And I only am escaped alone to tell thee.* But the "Indian" does not write books; and insofar as Kesey's fable can be read as telling the truth about himself as well as about all of us, it prophesies silence for him, a silence into which he has, in fact, lapsed, though not until he had tried one more Gutenberg-trip in *Sometimes a Great Notion.*

It is a book which seems to me not so much a second novel as a first novel written (or, perhaps, only published) second: a more literary, conventionally ambitious, and therefore *strained* effort—for all its occasional successes, somehow an error. *One Flew Over the Cuckoo's Nest* works better to the degree that it is dreamed or hallucinated rather than merely written—which is to say, to the degree that it, like its great prototype *The Leatherstocking Tales,* is Pop Art rather than *belles lettres*—the dream once dreamed in the woods, and now redreamed on pot and acid.

Its very sentimentality, good-guys bad-guys melodrama, occasional obviousness and thinness of texture, I find—like the analogous things in Cooper—not incidental flaws, but part of the essential method of its madness. There is a phrase which reflects on Kesey's own style quite early in the book, defining it aptly, though it pretends only to represent Chief Bromden's vision of the world around him: "Like a cartoon world, where the figures are flat and outlined in black, jerking through some kind of goofy story that might be real funny if it weren't for the cartoon figures being real guys. . . ."

Everywhere in Kesey, as a matter of fact, the influence of comics and, especially, comic books is clearly perceptible, in the mythology as well as in the style; for like those of many younger writers of the moment, the images and archetypal stories which underlie his fables are not the legends of Greece and Rome, not the fairy tales of Grimm, but the adventures of Captain Marvel and Captain Marvel, Jr., those new-style Supermen who, sometime just after World War II, took over the fantasy of the young. What Western elements persist in Kesey are, as it were, first translated back into comic-strip form, then turned once more into words on the conventional book page. One might, indeed, have imagined Kesey ending up as a comic book writer, but since the false second start of *Sometimes a Great Notion,* he has preferred to live his comic strip rather than write or even draw it.

The adventures of Psychedelic Superman as Kesey had dreamed and acted them, however—his negotiations with Hell's Angels, his being busted for the possession of marijuana, his consequent experiences in court and, as a refugee from the law, in Mexico—all this, like the yellow bus in which he used to move up and down the land taking an endless, formless movie, belongs to hearsay and journalism rather than to literary criticism, challenging conventional approaches to literature even as it challenges literature itself. But *One Flew Over the Cuckoo's Nest* survives the experiments and rejections which followed it; and looking back five years after its initial appearance, it seems clear that in it for the first time the New West was clearly defined: the West of Here and Now, rather than There and Then—the West of Madness.

The Westering impulse which Europe had begun by regarding as blasphemous (as, for instance, in Dante's description of Ulysses sailing through the Pillars of Hercules toward "the world without people"), it learned soon to think of as crazy, mocking Columbus and his dream of a passage to India, and condemning as further folly each further venture into a further West after the presence of America had been established (think, for example, of Cabeza de Vaca walking into the vast unknown and becoming, on his impossible adventure, a god to those savages whose world he penetrated).

It is only a step from thinking of the West as madness to regarding madness as the true West, but it took the long years between the end of the fifteenth century and the middle of the twentieth to learn to take that step. There is scarcely a New Western among those I have discussed which does not in some way flirt with the notion of madness as essential to the New World; but only in Leonard Cohen (though Thomas Berger comes close) and in Kesey is the final identification made, and in Kesey at last combined with the archetype of the love that binds the lonely white man to his Indian comrade—to his *mad* Indian comrade, perhaps even to the *madness* of his Indian comrade, as Kesey amends the old tale.

We have come to accept the notion that there is still a territory unconquered and uninhabited by palefaces, the bearers of "civilization," the cadres of imperialist reason; and we have been learning that into this territory certain psychotics, a handful of "schizophrenics," have moved on ahead of the rest of us—unrecognized Natty Bumppos or Huck Finns, interested not in claiming the New World for any Old God, King, or Country, but in becoming New Men, members of just such a New Race as D. H. Lawrence foresaw. (How fascinating, then, that R. D. Laing, leading exponent among contemporary psychiatrists of the theory that some schizophrenics have "broken through" rather than "broken down," should, despite the fact that he is an Englishman, have turned to our world and its discovery in search of an analogy; he suggests that Columbus's stumbling upon America and his first garbled accounts of it provided an illuminating parallel to the ventures of certain madmen into the regions of extended or altered consciousness, and to their confused version, once they are outside of it, of the strange realm in which they have been.)

Obviously, not everyone is now prepared, and few of us ever will be, to make a final and total commitment to the Newest West via psychosis; but a kind of tourism into insanity is already possible for those of us not yet ready or able to migrate permanently from the world of reason. We can take, as the New Westerns suggest, what is already popularly called —in the aptest of metaphors—a "trip," an excursion into the unknown with the aid of drugs. The West has seemed to us for a long time a place of recreation as well as of risk; and this is finally fair enough, for all the ironies implicit in turning a wilderness into a park. After all, the West remains always in some sense true to itself, as long as the Indian, no matter how subdued, penned off, or costumed for the tourist trade, survives—as long as we can confront there a creature radically different from the old self we seek to recreate in two weeks' vacation.

And while the West endures, the Western demands to be written—that form which represents a traditional and continuing dialogue between whatever old selves we transport out of whatever East, and the radically different other whom we confront in whatever West we attain. That other is the Indian still, as from the beginning, though only vestigially, nostalgically now; and also, with special novelty and poignancy, the insane.

If a myth of America is to exist in the future, it is incumbent on our writers, no matter how square and scared they may be in their deepest hearts, to conduct with the mad just such a dialogue as their predecessors learned long ago to conduct with the aboriginal dwellers in the actual Western Wilderness. It is easy to forget, but essential to remember, that the shadowy creatures living scarcely imaginable lives in the forests of Virginia once seemed as threatening to all that good Europeans believed as the acid-head or the borderline schizophrenic on the Lower East Side now seems to all that good Americans have come to believe in its place.

1968

PART FOUR

||||||||||||||||||||||||||||

Shapes and language

of the novel

Notes on the wild goose chase

JOHN HAWKES

IN Rex Warner's novel *The Wild Goose Chase*, a fiction of unusual climate, there are two men—the hero, George, and his companion of lesser capabilities, Bob—who have traveled "far on bicycles." These two are trying to gain entrance to The City, the place beyond the horizons of our imagination, by way of an academy called The Convent, where they are expectantly awaited by the headmaster. Their road is barred, however, by a Captain of Police and his foreign patrol. Without a moment's pause, the captain subjects the travelers to the special examination prescribed for all who seek entrance into the academy:

> George looked at the piece of paper on which was written: Candidates are requested to write their answers legibly and in as few words as possible. Every question should be attempted.
>
> OPTICS
> 1. What is meant by "Optics"?
> ZOOLOGY
> 1. Name two, or at the most three, animals.
> ECONOMICS
> 1. (Need not be attempted.)
> PERSONAL
> 1. What is your sex?
> 2. Are you fair-haired, blue-eyed, Conservative, Communist, tinker, tailor, interested in the drama, a wearer of spectacles, aviator, a drunkard, religious, musical, able to ride a push-bicycle? (Cross out inappropriate words or phrases.)

Reprinted by permission of Harold Ober Associates Incorporated.
Copyright © 1962 by The Massachusetts Review Inc.

IMBECILITY TEST
1. What material goes into the construction of a
   wall built entirely of brick?
2. A snail is walking up a post. In every half hour it
   advances 1¼ inches. How long will it take to
   reach the top?

"What's the game?" said George, when he had read
the examination paper.

All those still seeking the high mysterious flights of the
Wild Goose, or concerned with that place into which the
creative arts have fled, or who find the examinations stiffer as
they grow older, must also ask the fair question, "What's the
game!" Bob, for one, could not pass this test until the Captain allowed him to copy George's answers.

I think the poet is better equipped to respond *resonantly* to
such a questionnaire than the prose writer; the poet, to my
mind, comes more easily to the spirit of the human test.
Poets, for instance, thinking of the snail, can write: "I shaped
out of bread a little animal, a sort of mouse. Just as I was
completing her third paw, why look, she began to run. . . .
She fled away under cover of the night." [1] Or

> The eager note on my door said, "Call me,
> call when you get in!" So I quickly threw
> a few tangerines into my overnight bag,
> straightened my eyelids and shoulders, and
>
> headed straight for the door. It was autumn
> by the time I got around the corner, oh all
> unwilling to be either pertinent or bemused, but
> the leaves were brighter than grass on the sidewalk! [2]

To me the poem—the eager note on the door—is the experimental effort in a short form. And when the experiment
is the youthful practice of old men, when it no longer arises
merely from the genuine need of the young but becomes the
zealous vision in the older and brightly roving eye, then the
effort is a firm, scandalous, and exciting thing. These are the

[1] Henri Michaux, "Enigmas," *Selected Writings*, translated by Richard Ellman (New York, 1951).

[2] Frank O'Hara, "Poem," *New World Writing: 1* (New York, 1952).

poets who have no other purpose than to presume upon the peculiar unorthodoxy of their authorship; they sing the game. But there are also fiction writers who sing, who have private purposes, who hope for more in the novel than trying to build brick walls of brick.

Between poetry and the "longer form" of experimental fiction there exists a kinship, a seedling intemperate spirit, within which may be found the climate of the imaginative process. The climate is cold; the process is arbitrary, single-minded, a formalizing of our deepest urgencies. Like the poet, the experimental fiction writer is prompted to his narrative only by the vision which exclaims above him, or is driven to it from below; like the poet he enters his created world—loosening the shivers of his energy or restraining them—with something more than confidence and something less than concern over the presence of worms in the mouth. Like the poem, the experimental fiction is an exclamation of psychic materials which come to the writer all readily distorted, prefigured in that nightly inner schism between the rational and the absurd. And the relationship between the sprightly destructive poem and the experimental novel is not an alliance but merely the sharing of a birthmark: they come from the same place and are equally disfigured at the start. A comic sense of the dream, the presumption of a newly envisioned world, absolute fastness, firmness, insistence upon the creation of that other landscape where the moon hangs like a sac loaded with water or the devil wears "a lavendar shirt and thin black suit and a panama hat" [3]—this unchallengeable elevation of impulse and sudden poetic outspokenness drifts also through the climate of what we may still think of as "avant-garde" prose. As in Djuna Barnes's short novel *Nightwood:*

. . . every movement will reduce to an image of a forgotten experience; a mirage of an eternal wedding cast on the racial memory; as insupportable a joy as would be the vision of an eland coming down an aisle of trees, chapleted with orange blossoms and bridal veil, a hoof raised in the economy of fear, stepping in the trepidation of flesh that will become myth; as the unicorn is neither man nor beast deprived, but human hunger pressing its

[3] Flannery O'Connor, *The Violent Bear It Away* (New York, 1960).

breast to its prey. Such a woman is the infected carrier of the past. . . .

Recently *Time* magazine, pernicious as ever, dismissed the *Selected Writings* of Djuna Barnes by saying that the best of her work, *Nightwood,* offered little more than "the mysterioso effect that hides no mystery," and even Leslie Fiedler has described Djuna Barnes's vision of evil as effete. Yet all her myth and fear are mightily to be envied. Surely there is unpardonable distinction in this kind of writing, a certain incorrigible assumption of a prophetic role in reverse, when the most baffling of unsympathetic attitudes is turned upon the grudges, guilts, and renunciations harbored in the tangled seepage of our earliest recollections and originations. It is like quarreling at the moment of temptation. Or it is like working a few tangerines on a speedily driven lathe. Djuna Barnes is one of the "old poets," and there is no denying the certain balance of this "infected carrier" upon the high wire of the present. She has moved; she has gone out on a limb of light and indefinite sexuality and there remains unshakeable. She has free-wheeled the push bicycle into the cool air.

Djuna Barnes, Flannery O'Connor, Nathanael West—at least these three disparate American writers may be said to come together in that rare climate of pure and immoral *creation*—are very nearly alone in their uses of wit, their comic treatments of violence and their extreme detachment. If the true purpose of the novel is to assume a significant shape and to objectify the terrifying similarity between the unconscious desires of the solitary man and the disruptive needs of the visible world, then the satiric writer, running maliciously at the head of the mob and creating the shape of his meaningful psychic paradox as he goes, will serve best the novel's purpose. Love, for Djuna Barnes, is a heart twitching on a plate like the "lopped leg of a frog"; for Flannery O'Connor it is a thirty-year-old idiot girl riding in an old car and tearing the artificial cherries from her hat and throwing them out the window; for Nathanael West, love is a quail's feather dragged to earth by a heart-shaped drop of blood on its tip, or the sight of a young girl's buttocks looking like an inverted valentine. Each of these writers finds both wit and blackness in the pit, each claims a new and downward sweeping sight and pierces the pretension of the sweet spring of E. E. Cummings. Detachment, then, is at the center of the novelist's experiment, and detachment allows us our "answer to what our

grandmothers were told love was, what it never came to be";
or detachment allows us, quoting again from *Nightwood,* to
see that "When a long lie comes up, sometimes it is a beauty;
when it drops into dissolution, into drugs and drink, into disease and death, it has a singular and terrible attraction." But
mere malice is nothing in itself, of course, and the product of
extreme fictive detachment is extreme fictive sympathy. The
writer who maintains most successfully a consistent cold detachment toward physical violence (as West does, for instance, when he describes the plump quail being snipped
apart with tin shears, or describes the dwarf Abe Kusich
being beaten against a wall like a rabbit) is likely to generate
the deepest novelistic sympathy of all, a sympathy which is a
humbling before the terrible and a quickening in the presence
of degradation.

I think that we *are* unwilling to be either pertinent or bemused. But I too believe in fiction—hard, ruthless, comic—
and I myself believe very much in the sack of the past slung
around our necks, in all the recurrent ancestral fears and
abortive births we find in dreams as well as literature. The
constructed vision, the excitement of the undersea life of the
inner man, a language appropriate to the delicate malicious
knowledge of us all as poor, forked, corruptible, the feeling
of pleasure and pain that comes when something pure and
contemptible lodges in the imagination—I believe in the "singular and terrible attraction" of all this.

For me the writer should always serve as his own angle-
worm—and the sharper the barb with which he fishes himself
out of the blackness, the better.

1962

Notes on the new style

WILLIAM PHILLIPS

IT'S all anti these days: anti-literature, anti-art, anti-morality, anti-society, anti-ideology, anti-matter. Some people, mostly those with one foot in the past, are *for* something, but the young, and those who have jumped on the bandwagon of youth, are busy inventing new forms of rejection and secession. It's called cooling it or copping out—depending on whether you're in or out.

This is the new sensibility. Usually a new sensibility is a new literary style which reflects a new life style. At present the life style is so strong that it has taken over the functions of art. Perhaps the new attitudes are too dramatic and un-compromising or have not settled sufficiently to support works of literature, or perhaps the new writing still is not able to stand on its own. Anyway, new fiction has been itself part of the scene, which explains why it is so sprawling and why it is so difficult to fit it into the old frames. Burroughs, Genêt, even Beckett, to some extent Mailer, do not have their niche in the history of the novel the way, for example, Faulkner, or Bellow, or Flannery O'Connor, or Nathanael West do —a situation obviously confusing to those teachers and critics who would like to keep up with new beliefs by holding on to their old ones.

Some of the new fiction must then be seen as a break with the past. There was an earlier break with tradition that brought the literary exile back into the fold. Both these changes have been played down, however, because literary history, which takes to similarities more than differences,

Reprinted from *The Nation* by permission of the author and publisher.

tends to flatten out the past. Even criticism, which should know better, has done the same thing, because the kind of criticism that goes in for theory and historical connections usually abhors discontinuity and has a weakness for traditions which have been academically certified. For some critics, to question the lines of tradition is as unthinkable as to question the idea of heredity or history. Hence the common version of what happened to the novel fails to explain why the figures of what might be called the Golden Era—Proust, Mann, Joyce, even Kafka, who falls outside most schemes—seemed to mark the end of a line.

These novelists, who dominated the early part of the century, were sustained by two beliefs: that society had a certain shape and direction; and that, though they were outside it, in some mysterious, often perverse, way they represented its ideals and its possibilities. They were in and out but comfortably so, nestled in the tradition, going back to the Romantics, of an intellectual aristocracy that acted as both rebel and prophet. When Joyce made his famous pledge "to encounter . . . the reality of experience and to forge the uncreated conscience of my race," he was not so far out as he seemed at the time. Earwicker, after all, was Everyman. Nor was Mann way out when he created the artist-bourgeois hero, who had it both ways. Kafka, I think, broke out of this essentially aesthetic view of society, because he was impelled more by his own morbid experience and his own feelings than by the myths of belonging and not belonging. In his indifference to society and hence to conventional motivations, Kafka was closer to the current sensibility than some of his more explicitly avant-garde contemporaries. But even Kafka was not free of the bruised humanism behind the panoramic and allegorical fiction of Joyce, Mann and Proust. The Waste Land tradition in the novel seemed to require these big, suggestive themes, roaming through time and space, for only on such a scale could the agonies of the hero be blown up to represent man's fate.

As we know, this culture-hero has had a long literary career. He began as an English Romantic, as an angel who doubled as a devil. Nietzsche and Dostoevsky played up his morbid and diabolical side. He appeared in some movements as the alienated man. He turned up at one time or another as a symbolist, a dadaist, an exile. He was also a political rebel, sometimes a revolutionary. On the whole he was nourished on the idea that the forces making for a better society were to be found in society itself. Hence he opposed the values it practiced, not the values it professed.

In the following period, the novel came down to earth. It took its place in society, but without a theory of society, or of art. It lost its ambition. The novel became smaller, less symbolic, less self-conscious, more like the ordinary idea of ordinary experience. Not only was the tradition of the big brooding novel played out; more important was the fact there was no longer a main tradition. Instead, there were many little traditions that lost their power over new writing and broke down into vague conventions and influences. The novel took off in many directions. Thus we got genre novels, regional novels, novels of manners, exotic novels, academic novels. The shift could be seen in the early Hemingway and Faulkner, for whom the narrative was more important than the theme. But even more typical of the new era were figures like Kingsley Amis, Iris Murdoch, Katherine Anne Porter, Mary McCarthy, Bernard Malamud, Saul Bellow. They were all novelists of manners—social, moral, and sexual manners —all committed to a genre in which the writer stakes out his claim in a society that is taken for granted. They were not morbid, or apocalyptic, or angry. The cold war between the writer and his society was over.

The most representative novelist of the period is Saul Bellow, perhaps because he is one of the most gifted and self-conscious writers today. His first novel, *Dangling Man,* which seems to have been forgotten because it falls outside the pattern of the later work, comes out of the tradition of the heroic antihero. In its scale and its conception *Dangling Man* reflected the new adjustments to more modest views of the world. But he was still a marginal man, an artist-intellectual set apart by his values and his anxieties. In fact, reviewers who did not believe in alienation were quite hostile to Bellow's novel, despite the fact that the dangling man had both feet on the ground.

Obviously, the young Bellow was, if not an alienated man, an alienated writer. But his later writing shows a steady de-alienation. *The Victim,* a novel about anti-Semitism, seems to be a transitional work, for the transformation of the Jew from the alienated man to the victim of injustice meant that the conflict was now situated in social conventions and institutions. But the two later, more expansive novels are more explicit. Augie March still had a little of the old freewheeling, self-assertive, and self-pitying quality of the dangling man. This could be a self-portrait, a mixture, as in most writers, of what Bellow feels and what he thinks he should feel. But Augie's drifting was no longer on the metaphysical edges of society; he was a wanderer on the inside, a borer-from-within. As Augie made his way into the experiences of the average man, with his charm, his wit, and the jauntiness of his sufferings, he grew into a picaresque hero. Augie became a Tom Jones of contemporary America: a little less roguish, a little more self-conscious, still an adventurer within his own time and country—an American.

The outsider was now the insider. But it took more than ideology to make this reversal; it was accomplished, as it always is in fiction, by bringing what one saw together with what one looked at. It took a certain literary insight to connect the peculiar footloose, sharp-eyed quality of American life with the legendary traits of the alienated man; and no doubt much of Bellow's appeal comes from his domestication of the wanderer to fit in with the new sense of America.

Herzog completes the process of dealienation, though the dangling man seems to be here again. But he returns through the back door, through sex, which makes him a case rather than a symbol. Like all the earlier heroes, Herzog sighs and sags, but this time he reaches the end of his rope and not the end of existence. He can't make it because he has lost his grip and because he has bad luck with his women. This is a story of maladjustment, not the allegory of a dropout. Clearly, Herzog has the inside track to understanding as well as to suffering, and if he has trouble—who hasn't? The end is ambiguous because Bellow recognizes that ambiguity is the most certain form of reality, at least in fiction. Still, one is left with the feeling that Herzog will probably make it. And if he does, it is because he exemplifies the optimism, made more explicit in various essays and reviews, that Bellow apparently needs to overcome his doubts. Otherwise, you would get only the whining of the dangling man, who makes us feel sorry for him because he thinks he is smaller than his fate and larger than his lot. The letters Herzog writes to famous men and to the world at large provide the clue: they are nutty and absurd and full of the folklorish wisdom of people who have nothing to do with practical things, but they are the letters of someone who is always playing the game.

Bellow's fiction also shows a formal break with the earlier

tradition. It is relaxed, discursive, almost like a throwback to the beginnings of the novel, when the plot hung on the meanderings and fortunes of the hero. Yet Bellow did not invent the style. It was in fact the prevailing one, though it naturally took a different form in such different temperaments as Mary McCarthy, who has an eye for cant and social immorality, or Bernard Malamud, whose civilized passions are those of a Jewish epicure, or Henry Miller, who confuses his dreams with his frustrations. Most of the novels of the period were worldly in tone as well as in theme and situated in a particular locale. In this respect, Mary McCarthy was perhaps most typical: her concern with the observable world fit right in with the breakup of the big novel, while her sophistication kept her away from naturalism.

But maybe more important than individual temperament was the national temperament. The new turn was largely American, and the reason, I think, was the native bias against monolithic traditions. It was much more American to believe in the present than in the past, and in geography rather than history. If there was a dominant myth it was that America existed in its constant rediscovery of itself. In the period after the war this antimyth took the form of feeling that big ideas were played out, that the novelist now had the job simply of writing about the things he saw and felt.

The very diversity of American life made for a diversity of fiction. But a similar mood existed abroad and European writers were quite receptive to American influence. In England, where the native bent for empiricism and urbanity had usually kept the novel from becoming too inflated, a rash of easygoing, talky, comic novels by writers like Henry Green, Kingsley Amis, John Braine appeared after the war. And even more socially-minded writers, such as Doris Lessing or Alan Sillitoe, were more concerned with recording than with generalizing their observations. In France, the national weakness for the rhetoric of ideas naturally persisted. But for the leading figures of the period, for Camus and Sartre, for example, the novel was mostly a comment on contemporary life.

After almost a century of philosophical speculation and literary experiment, the novel had come back to more homely subjects and the novelist no longer thought of himself as the moral conscience in exile.

Nothing lasts very long these days, and now the tide is all the other way. The new sensibility is a swing away from civilization, a kind of decivilization, and not in the name of some higher civilization. The key figures are Burroughs and Genêt, supported, as any new style must be, by lesser writers like Selby, Rechy, and Blechman.

But the transition to the extremes of writing today was made by Norman Mailer, whose first novel was a documentary of his observations, and whose latest was a documentary of his dreams. It has been pointed out that Mailer reversed the usual development of novelists, transforming himself from a conventional and popular novelist to a dissident one. Only recently, however, has the extent to which Mailer has gone back on his past been recognized, and mostly by his critics, who have been ranting against the new immorality. The accusation is not original: it was made against Joyce and Lawrence, as it always has been made against any innovators in sex or morals. And the answer to such indictments, as Leavis said, is that the business of literature is to raise moral questions, not to answer them. If Lawrence broke the rules, it was because he was interested less in sexual conventions than in fulfillment. The same obviously can be said for Mailer. But what concerns us here is that Mailer, in stretching the limits of experience, has come close to the antiworld of Burroughs or Genêt. I say he has come close, because even in so wilful and self-indulgent a book as *An American Dream* Mailer shows he cannot give up the established liberal world with its old-fashioned concepts of power and justice and heterosexual love. Even in his sexual forays, the messianic Rojack, who is out to save women from civilization, is himself trapped in the traditional opposition between work and play, fulfillment and frustration.

In *An American Dream* Mailer's inability to accept or reject all of society is resolved partly by psychosis, a common form of adjustment by people half-in, half-out. The explanation—that escaped most reviewers—for much of Rojack's inexplicable behavior lies in his failure to connect with what he expects of the other characters or what they expect of him. The murder itself, the odd behavior of the police, the foxy calculations of Rojack, all add up to a fantasy as consistent and illogical as psychosis. But the psychotic character in the novel cannot be thought of simply as deranged. The use of psychosis is a means of creating a new system of motivation that would not work in ordinary life, but does in a novel. Such a self-contained system of motivation was used, for example, by Gide in *The Counterfeiters*. In fact, motives in fiction are never real motives, since an imagined character has no existence outside the story, and there is no "person" to which his actions can be related. For this reason, extreme behavior can be given a literary form resembling psychosis. In the past, this was done to make murderers or sex criminals plausible—for example, Stavrogin, Lafcadio or Merseult. Lately, however, dreams and dissociations that border on the psychotic have become a staple of the new sensibility.

Mailer's efforts to flagellate himself into more extreme positions showed up earlier in his essays, though one tended to think of them as shock waves to neutralize the opposition and not to take them too seriously. "The White Negro," the articles on Kennedy and Goldwater, and the self-advertisements all show Mailer constantly straining to get beyond the conventions even of advanced thinking into a cooler, more neutral state of being. In this kind of world, you do not solve things, you experience them; you step up your personal life while cutting down on your involvement with society. But unlike Burroughs, who doesn't know where he ends and the world beings, Mailer is still preoccupied with politics and social causes, that is, with the idea of humanity which lies behind any belief in change and improvement, even self-improvement. No matter how hard he tries, Mailer cannot attain the state of historical amnesia or total personal detachment required to make one's inner life entirely self-sufficient. But the fact that he can't make it gives him much of his strength as a novelist—at least as far as those who haven't gone overboard for the latest in dissociation are concerned.

The contrast between these two major figures, Bellow and Mailer, is quite suggestive. Bellow, who started out as a loner, a moral prowler, has reached the ripeness, the mellowness, the confidence of the established man of letters. Mailer, on the other hand, after an assured career, now acts like a young writer, cocky, nervous and unpredictable. Bellow is admired as a novelist; Mailer has become, particularly for younger people, a messianic underground figure.

As writers keep outdoing each other in destroying the past, each new breakthrough trumps the last one. Compared with Genêt or Burroughs, Norman Mailer sounds almost normal. He is, it is true, a little perverse. But with the help of Norman O. Brown, and some reinterpreting of Freud, perversity can be assimilated to the idea of normality. What we have in Genêt and Burroughs is something else: it is not the extension of "normal" experience to include what used to be regarded as abnormal experience, but a different kind of life, out there, in which dope, and crime, and sexual experiment are taken for granted.

Genêt is by far the most gifted and interesting figure and for this very reason no longer seems so exceptional or so extreme. As with most outstanding writers, his genius justifies his aberrations, and connects them with more traditional ones, particularly in the plays, where the madness of his associations is made natural and plausible. Still, the life represented by Genêt is not the life most of us live, certainly not the outer life and only in part the inner life. Nor is Genêt saying it is a better or a worse life; it is just his. I am not here concerned with judging Genêt or his values. But, I should say that what we call morality is a constantly shifting and unpredictable combination of old and new values. Nor is there any rule tying us to certain more conventional subjects and putting others beyond the pale. It must be said, too, because of the sudden boom in moralizing criticism, mainly on the part of aging critics, that it is sheer cant to pretend one's real or fantasy life is free of the things that are dismissed as too extreme or immoral.

Nevertheless, the fact remains that Genêt, like Burroughs, is writing about a life we associate with the underworld. And the question naturally arises how the underworld became the basis of the new sensibility, which, after all, is taken to be suggestive of contemporary life in general. The answer, I guess, is in the youth, the advanced youth, not all of it, obviously, just those forceful and flamboyant enough to impose their style on the period, particularly on its writing. But this can't be the whole story. The new sensibility can't be just the style of a new literary generation, saying no not only to the world as it is but also to the idea of changing it. Even the most extreme spokesmen must be reflecting more than their own boredom or their own brand of fun. They must be expressing, the way extreme literature has always expressed what a period means, the fact that we are all in some sense cool and disengaged today. Don't we all play with the notion that the very madness of the world is what holds it together?

The new sensibility gives a purity of form to this type of madness by fantasizing institutions out of existence. Neither in Burroughs, nor in Selby, nor in some of the other ad-

vanced novelists are there any social or moral institutions,
any psychological norms, by which people measure themselves and against which they rebel. In fact, there is no rebelling; only abstaining and resigning. Hence violence becomes
personal and, given a bent in this direction anyway, sexual.
In Burroughs we actually get a kind of sexual cannibalism
that doubles as a homosexual and a social symbol. In this sort
of free-for-all the family naturally disappears, too. In fact,
the only place I know where Marx's prediction of the breakdown of the family is actually fulfilled is in the novels of
Burroughs and Genêt. Generally in the fluid world of the antiworld, in which there are no recognizable boundaries, all
the people act like orphans as well as drifters. As I recall,
there are no sons or fathers in Burroughs, only spacemen on
leave from reality. Hence all relations are incestuous and pat-
ricidal and all distinctions of age or authority tend to disappear. Selby's tough adolescents, too, though always in motion,
do not seem to be coming from or going anywhere.

It is interesting to note that many eighteenth and nineteenth century heroes and heroines were real orphans; one
thinks of Tom Jones, Becky Sharpe, and Jane Eyre. Their
rootlessness, like that of the modern orphan, made for mobility. But this was a device used by the novelist to create characters who were not bound by the stability of society, while
the symbolic orphans of today come out of a sense of instability.

I have talked mainly about the more established and the
more dramatic of the new novelists, because they have set the
tone of the new style. But, of course, there are many others,
quite gifted, though less formed. (I have not discussed John
Rechy, who is very much like Burroughs but not so good.)
One of the most accomplished is Selby, who creates an imaginary violence, mostly sexual, that is made to look real by
means of a stylized naturalism. Perhaps the two most original talents are Pynchon, author of that remarkable novel *V*,
and Susan Sontag, who is better known for her criticism than
her fiction. Miss Sontag, I think, is the most intelligent of the
new writers and, paradoxically, the most traditional, though
she has been taken as a spokesman for the new style.

Some of the writers associated with the new sensibility
have not been able to make a complete break. But in the
more extreme figures decivilization has gone a long way. Fiction, particularly, has gone so far one can't imagine what else
could be coming. The old development of character, which

takes for granted that it is possible to grow up, is out. We now have instant realization and instant destruction. As in science fiction, characters will have to be invented instead of being created.

1965

A true lie-minded man

WILLIAM H. GASS

IT seems a country-headed thing to say; that literature is language, that stories and the places and the people in them are merely made of words as chairs are made of smoothed sticks and sometimes of cloth or metal tubes. Still, we cannot be too simple at the start, since the obvious is often the unobserved. Occasionally we should allow the trite to tease us into thought, for such old friends, the clichés in our life, are the only strangers we can know. It seems incredible, the ease with which we sink through books quite out of sight, pass clamorous pages into soundless dreams. That novels should be made of words, and merely words, is shocking, really. It's as though you had discovered that your wife were made of rubber: the bliss of all those years, the fears . . . from sponge.

Like the mathematician, like the philosopher, the novelist makes things out of concepts. Concepts, consequently, must be his critical concern: not the defects of his person, the crimes on his conscience, other men's morals, or their kindness or cruelty. The painter squeezes space through his pigments. Paint stains his fingers. How can he forget the color he has loaded on his brush or that blank canvas audience before him? Yet the novelist frequently behaves as if his work were all heart, character, and story; he professes to hate abstraction, mathematics, and the pure works of mind. Of course, unlike poetry, and despite its distinguished figures, for a long time now the novel has been an amateur's affair, an open field for anybody's running, and it has drawn the idle,

Reprinted from *The Nation* (October 31, 1966) by permission.

sick, and gossipaceous, the vaguely artistic; prophets, teachers, muckrakers, all the fanatical explainers, those dreamily scientific, and those anally pedantic.

Paint stains the fingers; the sculptor's hair is white with dust; but concepts have no physical properties; they do not permit smell or reflect light; they do not fill space or contain it; they do not age. "Five" is no wider, older, or fatter than "four"; "apple" isn't sweeter than "quince," rounder than "pear," smoother than "peach." To say, then, that literature is language is to say that literature is made of meanings, concepts, ideas, forms (please yourself with the term), and that these are so static and eternal as to shame the stars.

Like the mathematician. For the novelist to be at all, in any way, like a mathematician is shocking. It's worse than discovering your privates are plastic. Because there's no narration among numbers. It is logically impossible. Time's lacking.

When David Hilbert, the great logician, heard that a student had given up mathematics to write novels, he is supposed to have said: "It was just as well; he did not have enough imagination to become a first-rate mathematician."

The yammer of thought, the constant one-after-another of sounds, the shapes of words, the terrible specter of spelling, are each due to this fact that meanings are heavenly bodies which, to our senses, must somehow announce themselves. A word is a concept made flesh, if you like—the eternal presented as noise. When I spell then, let's say, "avoirdupois," I am forming our name for that meaning, but it might just as well be written down "dozzo," or still more at length, with the same lack of logic, "typary," "snoddle," or "willmullynull." "Avoirdupois." An unreasonable body. Nonetheless lovely. "Avoirdupois."

There is a fundamental contradiction in our medium. We work with a marble of flaws. My mind is utterly unlike my body, and unless you're an angel, so, I am certain, is yours. Poor Descartes really wrote on the problems of poets: word sense and word sound, math and mechanics, the mind and its body, can they touch? And how, pray God, can they resemble? In the act of love, as in all the arts, the soul should be felt by the tongue and the fingers, felt in the skin. So should our sounds come to color up the surface of our stories like a blush. This adventitious music is the only sensory quality our books can have. As Frost observed, even the empty sentence has a sound, or rather—I should say—*is* a series of nervous tensions and resolves. No artist dares neglect his own world's body, for *nothing else,* nothing else about his book is physical.

In the hollow of a jaw, the ear, upon the page, concepts now begin to move: they appear, accelerate, they race, they hesitate a moment, slow, turn, break, join, modify, and it becomes reasonable to speak of the problems of narration for the first time. Truly (that is to say, technically), narration is that part of the art of fiction concerned with the coming on and passing off of words—not the familiar arrangement of words in dry strings like so many shriveled worms but their formal direction and rapidity. But this is not what's usually meant.

For most people, fiction is history; fiction is history without tables, graphs, dates, imports, edicts, evidence, laws; history without hiatus—intelligible, simple, smooth. Fiction is sociology freed of statistics, politics, with no real party in the opposition; it's a world where play money buys you cardboard squares of colored country; a world where everyone is obediently psychological, economic, ethnic, geographical; framed in a keyhole and always nude; each figure fashioned from the latest thing in cello-see-through, so we may observe our hero's guts, too, if we choose; ah, they're blue, and squirming like a tickled river. For truth without effort, thought without rigor, feeling without form, existence without commitment: what will you give? for a windup world, a toy life? six bits? for a book with a thicker skin? six bucks? I am a man, myself, intemperately mild, and though it seems to me as much deserved as it's desired, I have no wish to steeple quires of paper passion up so many sad unelevating rears.

Nay, not *seems,* it *is* a stubborn, country-headed thing to say: that there are no events but words in fiction. Words mean things. Thus we use them every day: make love, buy bread, and blow up bridges. But the use of language in fiction only mimics its use in life. A sign like GENTS, for instance, tells me where to pee. It conveys information; it produces feelings of glad relief. I use the sign, but I dare not dawdle under it. It might have read MEN or borne a mustache. This kind of sign passes out of consciousness, is extinguished by its use. In literature, however, the sign remains; it sings; and we return to it again and again.

In contrast, the composer's medium is pure; that is, the tones he uses exist for music, and are made by instruments especially designed. Imagine his feelings, then, if he were forced to employ the meaningful noises of every day: bird calls, sirens, screams, alarm bells, whistles, ticks, and human chatter. He could plead all he liked that his music was pure, but we would know that he'd written down sounds from a play unseen, and we would insist that it told a story. Critics would describe the characters (one wears a goatee) and quarrel over their motives, marriages, or mothers, all their dark genes. Although no one wonders, of a painted peach, whether the tree it grew on was watered properly; we are happily witness, week after week, to further examinations of Hamlet or Madame Bovary, quite as if they were real. And they are so serious, so learned, so certain—so laughable— these ladies and gentlemen. Ah well, it's merely energy which might otherwise elucidate the Trinity.

So the novelist makes his book from boards which say LADIES and GENTS. Every scrap has been worn, every item handled; most of the pieces are dented or split. The writer may choose to be heroic—poets often are—he may strive to purify his diction and achieve an exclusively literary language. He may pretend that every syllable he speaks hasn't been spit, some-time, in someone else's mouth. Such poets scrub, they clean, they smooth, they polish, until we can scarcely recognize their words on the page. *A star glide, a single frantic sullen-ness, a single financial grass greediness,* wrote Gertrude Stein. *Toute Pensée émet un Coup de Dés,* wrote Mallarmé. Most novelists, however (it is one of the things that make them one), try to turn the tattering to account—incorporate it cleverly—as the painter does when he pastes up a collage of newspaper, tin foil, and postage stamps. He will recognize, for example, that stories are wonderful devices for control-ling the speed of the mind, for resting it after hard climbs; they give a reassuring light to a dark place, and help the reader hold, like handsome handles, heavy luggage on long trips.

A dedicated storyteller, though—a true lie-minded man— will serve his history best, and guarantee its popularity, not by imitating nature, since nature's no source of verisimilitude, but by following as closely as he can our simplest, most di-rect, and unaffected forms of daily talk, for we report real things, things which intrigue and worry us, and such resem-bling gossip in a book allows us to believe in figures and events we cannot see, shall never touch, with an assurance of safety which sets our passions free. He will avoid recording consciousness since consciousness is private—we do not normally "take it down"—and because no one really believes in any other feelings than his own.

However, the moment that our writer concentrates on sound, the moment he formalizes his sentences, the moment he puts in a figure of speech or turns a phrase, shifts a tense or alters tone, the moment he carries description, or any account, beyond need, he begins to turn his reader's interest away from the world which lies among his words like a beautiful woman among her slaves, and directs him toward the slaves themselves. This illustrates a basic principle: if I describe my peach too perfectly, it's the poem which will make my mouth water . . . while the real peach rots.

Sculptures take up space and gather dust. Concepts do not. They take up us. They invade us as we read, and they achieve, as our resistance and their forces vary, every conceivable degree of occupation. Imagine a worry or a pain, an obsessive thought, a jealousy or hate so strong it renders you insensible to all else. Then while it lasts, you are that fear, that ache, for consciousness is always smaller than its opportunities, and can contract around a kernel like a nut. A piece of music can drive you out and take your place. The purpose of a literary work is the capture of consciousness, and the consequent creation, in you, of an imagined sensibility, so that while you read you are that patient pool or cataract of concepts which the author has constructed; and though at first it might seem as if the richness of life had been replaced by something less so: senseless noises, abstract meanings, mere shadows of worldly employment; yet the new self which fine fiction and good poetry should provide you is as wide as the mind is, and musicked deep with feeling. While listening to such symbols sounding, the blind perceive; thought seems to grow a body; and the will is at rest amid that moving like a gull asleep on the sea. Perhaps we'll be forgiven, then, if we fret about our words and continue country-headed. It is not a refusal to please. There's no willfulness, disdain, exile . . . no anger. Because a consciousness is electrified by beauty: is that not the aim and emblem and the ending of all finely made love?

Are you afraid?

1966

The literature of exhaustion

JOHN BARTH

I want to discuss three things more or less together: first, some old questions raised by the new intermedia arts; second, some aspects of the Argentine writer Jorge Luis Borges, whom I greatly admire; third, some professional concerns of my own, related to these other matters and having to do with what I'm calling "the literature of exhausted possibility"—or, more chicly, "the literature of exhaustion."

By "exhaustion" I don't mean anything so tired as the subject of physical, moral, or intellectual decadence, only the used-upness of certain forms or exhaustion of certain possibilities—by no means necessarily a cause for despair. That a great many Western artists for a great many years have quarreled with received definitions of artistic media, genres, and forms goes without saying: pop art, dramatic and musical "happenings," the whole range of "intermedia" or "mixed-means" art, bear recentest witness to the tradition of rebelling against Tradition. A catalogue I received some time ago in the mail, for example, advertises such items as Robert Filliou's *Ample Food for Stupid Thought,* a box full of postcards on which are inscribed "apparently meaningless questions," to be mailed to whomever the purchaser judges them suited for; Ray Johnson's *Paper Snake,* a collection of whimsical writings, "often pointed," once mailed to various friends (what the catalogue describes as The New York Correspondence School of Literature); and Daniel Spoerri's *Anecdoted Typography of Chance,* "on the surface" a description of all

the objects that happen to be on the author's parlor table—
"in fact, however . . . a cosmology of Spoerri's existence."

"On the surface," at least, the document listing these items
is a catalogue of The Something Else Press, a swinging outfit.
"In fact, however," it may be one of their offerings, for all I
know: The New York Direct-Mail Advertising School of Literature. In any case, their wares are lively to read about, and
make for interesting conversation in fiction-writing classes,
for example, where we discuss Somebody-or-other's unbound,
unpaginated, randomly assembled novel-in-a-box and the de-
sirability of printing *Finnegans Wake* on a very long roller-
towel. It's easier and sociabler to talk technique than it is to
make art, and the area of "happenings" and their kin is
mainly a way of discussing aesthetics, really; illustrating "dra-
matically" more or less valid and interesting points about the
nature of art and the definition of its terms and genres.

One conspicuous thing, for example, about the "intermedia" arts is their tendency (noted even by *Life* magazine) to
eliminate not only the traditional audience—"those who ap-
prehend the artist's art" (in "happenings" the audience is
often the "cast," as in "environments," and some of the new
music isn't intended to be performed at all)—but also the
most traditional notion of the artist: the Aristotelian conscious agent who achieves with technique and cunning the artistic effect; in other words, one endowed with uncommon
talent, who has moreover developed and disciplined that en-
dowment into virtuosity. It's an aristocratic notion on the
face of it, which the democratic West seems eager to have
done with; not only the "omniscient" author of older fiction
but the very idea of the controlling artist has been condemned as politically reactionary, even fascist.

Now, personally, being of the temper that chooses to
"rebel along traditional lines," I'm inclined to prefer the kind
of art that not many people can *do:* the kind that requires
expertise and artistry as well as bright aesthetic ideas and/or
inspiration. I enjoy the pop art in the famous Albright-Knox
collection, a few blocks from my house in Buffalo, like a
lively conversation for the most part, but was on the whole
more impressed by the jugglers and acrobats at Baltimore's
old Hippodrome, where I used to go every time they changed
shows: genuine *virtuosi* doing things that anyone can dream
up and discuss but almost no one can do.

I suppose the distinction is between things worth remark-
ing—preferably over beer, if one's of my generation—and

things worth doing. "Somebody ought to make a novel with scenes that pop up, like the old children's books," one says, with the implication that one isn't going to bother doing it oneself.

However, art and its forms and techniques live in history and certainly do change. I sympathize with a remark attributed to Saul Bellow, that to be technically up to date is the least important attribute of a writer, though I would have to add that this least important attribute may be nevertheless essential. In any case, to be technically *out* of date is likely to be a genuine defect: Beethoven's Sixth Symphony or the Chartres Cathedral if executed today would be merely embarrassing. A good many current novelists write turn-of-the-century-type novels, only in more or less mid-twentieth-century language and about contemporary people and topics; this makes them considerably less interesting (to me) than excellent writers who are also technically contemporary: Joyce and Kafka, for instance, in their time, and in ours, Samuel Beckett and Jorge Luis Borges. The intermedia arts, I'd say, tend to be intermediary too, between the traditional realms of aesthetics on the one hand and artistic creation on the other; I think the wise artist and civilian will regard them with quite the kind and degree of seriousness with which he regards good shoptalk: he'll listen carefully, if noncommittally, and keep an eye on his intermedia colleagues, if only the corner of his eye. They may very possibly suggest something usable in the making or understanding of genuine works of contemporary art.

The man I want to discuss a little here, Jorge Luis Borges, illustrates well the difference between a technically old-fashioned artist, a technically up-to-date civilian, and a technically up-to-date artist. In the first category I'd locate all those novelists who for better or worse write not as if the twentieth century didn't exist, but as if the great writers of the last sixty years or so hadn't existed (*nota bene* that our century's more than two-thirds done; it's dismaying to see so many of our writers following Dostoevsky or Tolstoy or Flaubert or Balzac, when the real technical question seems to me to be how to succeed not even Joyce and Kafka but those who've *succeeded* Joyce and Kafka and are now in the evenings of their own careers). In the second category are such folk as an artist-neighbor of mine in Buffalo who fashions dead Winnies-the-Pooh in sometimes monumental scale out of oilcloth stuffed with sand and impaled on stakes or hung by the neck. In the third belong the few people whose artistic thinking is as hip as any French new-novelist's, but who manage nonetheless to speak eloquently and memorably to our still-human hearts and conditions, as the great artists have always done. Of these, two of the finest living specimens that I know of are Beckett and Borges, just about the only contemporaries of my reading acquaintance mentionable with the "old masters" of twentieth-century fiction. In the unexciting history of literary awards, the 1961 International Publishers' Prize, shared by Beckett and Borges, is a happy exception indeed.

One of the modern things about these two is that in an age of ultimacies and "final solutions"—at least *felt* ultimacies, in everything from weaponry to theology, the celebrated dehumanization of society, and the history of the novel—their work in separate ways reflects and deals with ultimacy, both technically and thematically, as, for example, *Finnegans Wake* does in its different manner. One notices, by the way, for whatever its symptomatic worth, that Joyce was virtually blind at the end, Borges is literally so, and Beckett has become virtually mute, musewise, having progressed from marvelously constructed English sentences through terser and terser French ones to the unsyntactical, unpunctuated prose of *Comment C'est* and "ultimately" to wordless mimes. One might extrapolate a theoretical course for Beckett: language, after all, consists of silence as well as sound, and the mime is still communication—"that nineteenth-century idea," a Yale student once snarled at me—but by the language of action. But the language of action consists of rest as well as movement, and so in the context of Beckett's progress immobile, silent figures still aren't altogether ultimate. How about an empty, silent stage, then, or blank pages [1]—a "happening" where nothing happens, like Cage's *4′ 33″* performed in an empty hall? But dramatic communication consists of the absence as well as the presence of the actors; "we have our exits and our entrances"; and so even that would be imperfectly ultimate in Beckett's case. Nothing at all, then, I suppose: but Nothingness is necessarily and inextricably the background against which Being et cetera; for Beckett, at this point in his career, to cease to create altogether would be fairly meaning-

[1] An ultimacy already attained in the nineteenth century by that *avant-gardiste* of East Aurora, New York, Elbert Hubbard, in his *Essay on Silence*.

ful: his crowning work, his "last word." What a convenient corner to paint yourself into! "And now I shall finish," the valet Arsene says in *Watt*, "and you will hear my voice no more." Only the silence *Molloy* speaks of, "of which the universe is made."

After which, I add on behalf of the rest of us, it might be conceivable to rediscover validly the artifices of language and literature—such far-out notions as grammar, punctuation . . . even characterization! Even *plot!*—if one goes about it the right way, aware of what one's predecessors have been up to.

Now J. L. Borges is perfectly aware of all these things. Back in the great decades of literary experimentalism he was associated with *Prisma,* a "muralist" magazine that published its pages on walls and billboards; his later *Labyrinths* and *Ficciones* not only anticipate the farthest-out ideas of The Something-Else Press crowd—not a difficult thing to do—but being marvelous works of art as well, illustrate in a simple way the difference between the *fact* of aesthetic ultimacies and their artistic *use*. What it comes to is that an artist doesn't merely exemplify an ultimacy; he employs it.

Consider Borges' story "Pierre Menard, Author of the *Quixote*": the hero, an utterly sophisticated turn-of-the-century French Symbolist, by an astounding effort of imagination, produces—not *copies* or *imitates,* mind, but *composes* —several chapters of Cervantes' novel.

It is a revelation [Borges' narrator tells us] to compare Menard's *Don Quixote* with Cervantes'. The latter, for example, wrote (part one, chapter nine):

. . . truth, whose mother is history, rival of time, depository of deeds, witness of the past, exemplar and adviser to the present, the future's counselor.

Written in the seventeenth century, written by the "lay genius" Cervantes, this enumeration is a mere rhetorical praise of history. Menard, on the other hand, writes:

. . . truth, whose mother is history, rival of time, depository of deeds, witness of the past, exemplar and adviser to the present, the future's counselor.

History, the *mother* of truth: the idea is astounding. Menard, a contemporary of William James, does not define history as an inquiry into reality but as its origin. . . .

Et cetera. Now, this is an interesting idea, of considerable intellectual validity. I mentioned earlier that if Beethoven's Sixth were composed today, it would be an embarrassment; but clearly it wouldn't be, necessarily, if done with iron intent by a composer quite aware of where we've been and where we are. It would have then potentially, for better or worse, the kind of significance of Warhol's Campbell's Soup ads, the difference being that in the former case a work of art is being reproduced instead of a work of nonart, and the ironic comment would therefore be more directly on the genre and history of the art than on the state of the culture. In fact, of course, to make the valid intellectual point one needn't even recompose the Sixth Symphony, any more than Menard really needed to re-create the *Quixote*. It would've been sufficient for Menard to have *attributed* the novel to himself in order to have a new work of art, from the intellectual point of view. Indeed, in several stories Borges plays with this very idea, and I can readily imagine Beckett's next novel, for example, as *Tom Jones*, just as Nabokov's last was that multivolume annotated translation of Pushkin. I myself have always aspired to write Burton's version of *The 1001 Nights*, complete with appendices and the like, in twelve volumes, and for intellectual purposes I needn't even write it. What evenings we might spend (over beer) discussing Saarinen's Parthenon, D. H. Lawrence's *Wuthering Heights,* or the Johnson Administration by Robert Rauschenberg!

The idea, I say, is intellectually serious, as are Borges' other characteristic ideas, most of a metaphysical rather than an aesthetic nature. But the important thing to observe is that Borges *doesn't* attribute the *Quixote* to himself, much less recompose it like Pierre Menard; instead, he writes a remarkable and original work of literature, the implicit theme of which is the difficulty, perhaps the unnecessity, of writing original works of literature. His artistic victory, if you like, is that he confronts an intellectual dead end and employs it against itself to accomplish new human work. If this corresponds to what mystics do—"every moment leaping into the infinite," Kierkegaard says, "and every moment falling surely back into the finite"—it's only one more aspect of that old analogy. In homelier terms, it's a matter of every moment throwing out the bath water without for a moment losing the baby.

Another way of describing Borges' accomplishment is in a pair of his own favorite terms, *algebra and fire*. In his most often anthologized story, "Tlön, Uqbar, Orbis Tertius," he imagines an entirely hypothetical world, the invention of a secret society of scholars who elaborate its every aspect in a surreptitious encyclopedia. This *First Encyclopaedia of Tlön* (what fictionist would not wish to have dreamed up the *Britannica?*) describes a coherent alternative to this world complete in every respect from its algebra to its fire, Borges tells us, and of such imaginative power that, once conceived, it begins to obtrude itself into and eventually to supplant our prior reality. My point is that neither the algebra nor the fire, metaphorically speaking, could achieve this result without the other. Borges' algebra is what I'm considering here—algebra is easier to talk about than fire—but any intellectual giant could equal it. The imaginary authors of the *First Encyclopaedia of Tlön* itself are not artists, though their work is in a manner of speaking fictional and would find a ready publisher in New York nowadays. The author of the story "Tlön, Uqbar, Orbis Tertius," who merely *alludes* to the fascinating *Encyclopaedia, is* an artist; what makes him one of the first rank, like Kafka, is the combination of that intellectually profound vision with great human insight, poetic power, and consummate mastery of his means, a definition which would have gone without saying, I suppose, in any century but ours.

Not long ago, incidentally, in a footnote to a scholarly edition of Sir Thomas Browne (*The Urn Burial,* I believe it was), I came upon a perfect Borges datum, reminiscent of Tlön's self-realization: the actual case of a book called *The Three Impostors,* alluded to in Browne's *Religio Medici* among other places. *The Three Impostors* is a nonexistent blasphemous treatise against Moses, Christ, and Mohammed, which in the seventeenth century was widely held to exist, or to have once existed. Commentators attributed it variously to Boccaccio, Pietro Aretino, Giordano Bruno, and Tommaso Campanella, and though no one, Browne included, had ever seen a copy of it, it was frequently cited, refuted, railed against, and generally discussed as if everyone had read it— until, sure enough, in the *eighteenth* century a spurious work appeared with a forged date of 1598 and the title *De Tribus Impostoribus.* It's a wonder that Borges doesn't mention this work, as he seems to have read absolutely everything, including all the books that don't exist, and Browne is a particular favorite of his. In fact, the narrator of "Tlön, Uqbar, Orbis Tertius" declares at the end:

> . . . English and French and mere Spanish will disappear from the globe. The world will be Tlön. I pay no attention to all this and go on revising, in the still days at the Adrogué hotel, an uncertain Quevedian translation (which I do not intend to publish) of Browne's *Urn Burial*.[2]

This "contamination of reality by dream," as Borges calls it, is one of his pet themes, and commenting upon such contaminations is one of his favorite fictional devices. Like many of the best such devices, it turns the artist's mode or form into a metaphor for his concerns, as does the diary-ending of *Portrait of the Artist As a Young Man* or the cyclical construction of *Finnegans Wake*. In Borges' case, the story "Tlön," etc., for example, is a real piece of imagined reality in our world, analogous to those Tlönian artifacts called *hrönir*, which imagine themselves into existence. In short, it's a paradigm of or metaphor for itself; not just the *form* of the story but the *fact* of the story is symbolic; "the medium is the message."

Moreover, like all of Borges' work, it illustrates in other of its aspects my subject: how an artist may paradoxically turn the felt ultimacies of our time into material and means for his work—*paradoxically* because by doing so he transcends what had appeared to be his refutation, in the same way that the mystic who transcends finitude is said to be enabled to live, spiritually and physically, in the finite world. Suppose you're a writer by vocation—a "print-oriented bastard," as the McLuhanites call us—and you feel, for example, that the novel, if not narrative literature generally, if not the printed word altogether, has by this hour of the world just about shot its bolt, as Leslie Fiedler and others maintain. (I'm inclined to agree, with reservations and hedges. Literary forms certainly have histories and historical contingencies, and it may well be that the novel's time as a major art form is up, as the "times" of classical tragedy, grand opera, or the sonnet se-

[2] Moreover, on rereading "Tlön," etc., I find now a remark I'd swear wasn't in it last year: that the eccentric American millionaire who endows the *Encyclopaedia* does so on condition that "the work will make no pact with the impostor Jesus Christ."

quence came to be. No necessary cause for alarm in this at all, except perhaps to certain novelists, and one way to handle such a feeling might be to write a novel about it. Whether historically the novel expires or persists seems immaterial to me; if enough writers and critics *feel* apocalyptical about it, their feeling becomes a considerable cultural fact, like the *feeling* that Western civilization, or the world, is going to end rather soon. If you took a bunch of people out into the desert and the world didn't end, you'd come home shamefaced, I imagine; but the persistence of an art form doesn't invalidate work created in the comparable apocalyptic ambience. That's one of the fringe benefits of being an artist instead of a prophet. There are others.) If you happened to be Vladimir Nabokov, you might address that felt ultimacy by writing *Pale Fire:* a fine novel by a learned pedant, in the form of a pedantic commentary on a poem invented for the purpose. If you were Borges, you might write *Labyrinths:* fictions by a learned librarian in the form of footnotes, as he describes them, to imaginary or hypothetical books.[3] And I'll add, since I believe Borges' idea is rather more interesting, that if you were the author of this paper, you'd have written something like *The Sot-Weed Factor* or *Giles Goat-Boy:* novels which imitate the form of the Novel, by an author who imitates the role of Author.

If this sort of thing sounds unpleasantly decadent, nevertheless it's about where the genre began, with *Quixote* imitating *Amadis of Gaul,* Cervantes pretending to be the Cid Hamete Benengeli (and Alonso Quijano pretending to be Don Quixote), or Fielding parodying Richardson. "History repeats itself as farce"—meaning, of course, in the form or mode of farce, not that history is farcical. The imitation (like the Dadaist echoes in the work of the "intermedia" types) is something new and *may be* quite serious and passionate despite its farcical aspect. This is the important difference between a proper novel and a deliberate imitation of a novel, or a novel imitative of other sorts of documents. The first attempts (has

[3] Borges was born in Argentina in 1899, educated in Europe, and for some years worked as director of the National Library in Buenos Aires, except for a period when Juan Perón demoted him to the rank of provincial chicken inspector as a political humiliation. Currently he's the *Beowulf*-man at the University in Buenos Aires.

been historically inclined to attempt) to imitate actions more
or less directly, and its conventional devices—cause and
effect, linear anecdote, characterization, authorial selection,
arrangement, and interpretation—can be and have long since
been objected to as obsolete notions, or metaphors for obsolete notions: Robbe-Grillet's essays *For a New Novel* come
to mind. There are replies to these objections, not to the
point here, but one can see that in any case they're obviated
by imitations-of-novels, which attempt to represent not life
directly but a representation of life. In fact such works are no
more removed from "life" than Richardson's or Goethe's epis-
tolary novels are: both imitate "real" documents, and the
subject of both, ultimately, is life, not the documents. A
novel is as much a piece of the real world as a letter, and the
letters in *The Sorrows of Young Werther* are, after all, fictitious.

One might imaginably compound this imitation, and
though Borges doesn't, he's fascinated with the idea: one of
his frequenter literary allusions is to the 602nd night of *The
1001 Nights*, when, owing to a copyist's error, Scheherezade
begins to tell the King the story of the 1001 nights, from the
beginning. Happily, the King interrupts; if he didn't, there'd
be no 603rd night ever, and while this would solve Scheherezade's problem—which is every storyteller's problem: to
publish or perish—it would put the "outside" author in a
bind. (I suspect that Borges dreamed this whole thing up: the
business he mentions isn't in any edition of *The 1001 Nights*
I've been able to consult. Not *yet,* anyhow: after reading
"Tlön, Uqbar," etc., one is inclined to recheck every semester
or so.)

Now Borges (whom someone once vexedly accused *me* of
inventing) is interested in the 602nd Night because it's an instance of the story-within-the-story turned back upon itself,
and his interest in such instances is threefold: first, as he himself declares, they disturb us metaphysically: when the characters in a work of fiction become readers or authors of the
fiction they're in, we're reminded of the fictitious aspect of
our own existence, one of Borges' cardinal themes, as it was
of Shakespeare, Calderón, Unamuno, and other folk. Second,
the 602nd Night is a literary illustration of the *regressus in
infinitum,* as are almost all of Borges' principal images and
motifs. Third, Scheherezade's accidental gambit, like Borges'
other versions of the *regressus in infinitum,* is an image of the
exhaustion, or attempted exhaustion, of possibilities—in this

case literary possibilities—and so we return to our main subject.

What makes Borges' stance, if you like, more interesting to me than, say, Nabokov's or Beckett's, is the premise with which he approaches literature; in the words of his editors: "For [Borges] no one has claim to originality in literature; all writers are more or less faithful amanuenses of the spirit, translators and annotators of preexisting archetypes." Thus his inclination to write brief comments on imaginary books: for one to attempt to add overtly to the sum of "original" literature by even so much as a conventional short story, not to mention a novel, would be too presumptuous, too naive; literature has been done long since. A librarian's point of view! And it would itself be too presumptuous if it weren't part of a lively, passionately relevant metaphysical vision, and slyly employed against itself precisely to make new and original literature. Borges defines the Baroque as "that style which deliberately exhausts (or tries to exhaust) its possibilities and borders upon its own caricature." While his own work is *not* Baroque, except intellectually (the Baroque was never so terse, laconic, economical), it suggests the view that intellectual and literary history has been Baroque, and has pretty well exhausted the possibilities of novelty. His *ficciones* are not only footnotes to imaginary texts, but postscripts to the real corpus of literature.

This premise gives resonance and relation to all his principal images. The facing mirrors that recur in his stories are a dual *régressus*. The doubles that his characters, like Nabokov's, run afoul of suggest dizzying multiples and remind one of Browne's remark that "every man is not only himself . . . men are lived over again." (It would please Borges, and illustrate Browne's point, to call Browne a precursor of Borges. "Every writer," Borges says in his essay on Kafka, "creates his own precursors.") Borges' favorite third-century heretical sect is the Histriones—I think and hope he invented them—who believe that repetition is impossible in history and therefore live viciously in order to purge the future of the vices they commit: in other words, to exhaust the possibilities of the world in order to bring its end nearer.

The writer he most often mentions, after Cervantes, is Shakespeare; in one piece he imagines the playwright on his deathbed asking God to permit him to be one and himself, having been everyone and no one; God replies from the whirlwind that He is no one either; He has dreamed the world like Shakespeare, and including Shakespeare. Homer's story in Book IV of the *Odyssey*, of Menelaus on the beach at Pharos, tackling Proteus, appeals profoundly to Borges: Proteus is he who "exhausts the guises of reality" while Menelaus—who, one recalls, disguised his own identity in order to ambush him—holds fast. Zeno's paradox of Achilles and the Tortoise embodies a *regressus in infinitum* which Borges carries through philosophical history, pointing out that Aristotle uses it to refute Plato's theory of forms, Hume to refute the possibility of cause and effect, Lewis Carroll to refute syllogistic deduction, William James to refute the notion of temporal passage, and Bradley to refute the general possibility of logical relations; Borges himself uses it, citing Schopenhauer, as evidence that the world is our dream, our idea, in which "tenuous and eternal crevices of unreason" can be found to remind us that our creation is false, or at least fictive.

The infinite library of one of his most popular stories is an image particularly pertinent to the literature of exhaustion; the "Library of Babel" houses every possible combination of alphabetical characters and spaces, and thus every possible book and statement, including your and my refutations and vindications, the history of the actual future, the history of every possible future, and, though he doesn't mention it, the encyclopedias not only of Tlön but of every imaginable other world—since, as in Lucretius' universe, the number of elements, and so of combinations, is finite (though very large), and the number of instances of each element and combination of elements is infinite, like the library itself.

That brings us to his favorite image of all, the labyrinth, and to my point. *Labyrinths* is the name of his most substantial translated volume, and the only full-length study of Borges in English, by Ana María Barrenechea, is called *Borges the Labyrinth-Maker*. A labyrinth, after all, is a place in which, ideally, all the possibilities of choice (of direction, in this case) are embodied, and—barring special dispensation like Theseus'—must be exhausted before one reaches the heart. Where, mind, the Minotaur waits with two final possibilities: defeat and death, or victory and freedom. Now, in fact, the legendary Theseus is non-Baroque; thanks to Ariadne's thread he can take a shortcut through the labyrinth at Knossos. But Menelaus on the beach at Pharos, for example, is genuinely Baroque in the Borgesian spirit, and illustrates a positive artistic morality in the literature of exhaustion. He is not there, after all, for kicks (any more than Borges and Beckett are in the fiction racket for their health): Menelaus is *lost*, in the larger labyrinth of the world, and has got to hold fast while the Old Man of the Sea exhausts reality's frightening guises so that he may extort direction from him when Proteus returns to his "true" self. It's a heroic enterprise, with salvation as its object—one recalls that the aim of the Histriones is to get history done with so that Jesus may come again the sooner, and that Shakespeare's heroic metamorphoses culminate not merely in a theophany but in an apotheosis.

Now, not just any old body is equipped for this labor, and Theseus in the Cretan labyrinth becomes in the end the aptest image for Borges after all. Distressing as the fact is to us liberal Democrats, the commonality, alas, will *always* lose their way and their souls: it's the chosen remnant, the virtuoso, the Thesean *hero*, who, confronted with Baroque reality, Baroque history, the Baroque state of his art, need *not* rehearse its possibilities to exhaustion, any more than Borges needs actually to *write* the *Encyclopaedia of Tlön* or the books in the Library of Babel. He need only be aware of their existence or possibility, acknowledge them and with the aid of *very special* gifts—as extraordinary as saint- or hero-hood and not likely to be found in The New York Correspondence School of Literature—go straight through the maze to the accomplishment of his work.

1967

Index

From
Fawcett Crest
and
Fawcett Premier